George Washington Cable

Famous Adventures And Prison Escapes of the Civil War

George Washington Cable

Famous Adventures And Prison Escapes of the Civil War

ISBN/EAN: 9783744752466

Printed in Europe, USA, Canada, Australia, Japan

Cover: Foto ©Andreas Hilbeck / pixelio.de

More available books at **www.hansebooks.com**

QUESTIONING A PRISONER.

FAMOUS ADVENTURES
AND PRISON ESCAPES
OF THE CIVIL WAR

NEW YORK
THE CENTURY CO.
1898

Copyright, 1885, 1888, 1889, 1890, 1891, 1893, by
THE CENTURY CO.

THE DE VINNE PRESS.

CONTENTS

	PAGE
WAR DIARY OF A UNION WOMAN IN THE SOUTH	1
THE LOCOMOTIVE CHASE IN GEORGIA	83
MOSBY'S "PARTIZAN RANGERS"	102
A ROMANCE OF MORGAN'S ROUGH-RIDERS	116
COLONEL ROSE'S TUNNEL AT LIBBY PRISON	184
A HARD ROAD TO TRAVEL OUT OF DIXIE	243
ESCAPE OF GENERAL BRECKINRIDGE	298

ILLUSTRATIONS

	PAGE
QUESTIONING A PRISONER	Frontispiece
THE LOCOMOTIVE CHASE	85
GENERAL JOHN H. MORGAN	117
MAP OF THE MORGAN RAID	118
THE FARMER FROM CALFKILLER CREEK	123
GENERAL DUKE TESTS THE PIES	125
HOSPITALITIES OF THE FARM	131
LOOKING FOR THE FOOTPRINTS OF THE VAN	137
CORRIDOR AND CELLS IN THE OHIO STATE PENITENTIARY — CAPTAIN HINES'S CELL	161
EXTERIOR OF THE PRISON — EXIT FROM TUNNEL	163
WITHIN THE WOODEN GATE	167
OVER THE PRISON WALL	171
"HURRY UP, MAJOR!"	175
CAPTAIN HINES OBJECTS	178
COLONEL THOMAS E. ROSE	185
A CORNER OF LIBBY PRISON	187
LIBBY PRISON IN 1865	189
MAJOR A. G. HAMILTON	191
LIBBY PRISON IN 1884	197
LIBERTY!	223
FIGHTING THE RATS	230
SECTION OF INTERIOR OF LIBBY PRISON AND TUNNEL	233

	PAGE
GROUND-PLAN OF LIBBY PRISON AND SURROUNDINGS	235
LIEUTENANTS E. E. SILL AND A. T. LAMSON	255
WE ARRIVE AT HEADEN'S	263
THE ESCAPE OF HEADEN	271
GREENVILLE JAIL	277
PINK BISHOP AT THE STILL	283
ARRIVAL HOME OF THE BAPTIST MINISTER	285
SURPRISED AT MRS. KITCHEN'S	291
THE MEETING WITH THE SECOND OHIO HEAVY ARTILLERY	295
SAND AS A DEFENSE AGAINST MOSQUITOS	307
SEARCHING FOR TURTLES' EGGS	310
THROUGH A SHALLOW LAGOON	313
EXCHANGING THE BOAT FOR THE SLOOP	315
OVER A CORAL-REEF	325
A ROUGH NIGHT IN THE GULF STREAM	331

FAMOUS ADVENTURES AND PRISON ESCAPES OF THE CIVIL WAR

✢

WAR DIARY OF A UNION WOMAN IN THE SOUTH

EDITED BY G. W. CABLE

THE following diary was originally written in lead-pencil and in a book the leaves of which were too soft to take ink legibly. I have it direct from the hands of its writer, a lady whom I have had the honor to know for nearly thirty years. For good reasons the author's name is omitted, and the initials of people and the names of places are sometimes fictitiously given. Many of the persons mentioned were my own acquaintances and friends. When, some twenty years afterward, she first resolved to publish it, she brought me a clear, complete copy in ink. It had cost much trouble, she said; for much of the pencil writing had been made under such disadvantages and was so faint that at times she could decipher it only under direct sunlight. She had succeeded, however, in making a copy, *verbatim* except for occasional improvement in the grammatical form of a sentence, or now and then the omission, for brevity's sake, of something unessential. The narrative has since been severely abridged to bring it within magazine limits.

In reading this diary one is much charmed with its constant understatement of romantic and perilous incidents and conditions. But the original penciled pages show that, even in copying, the strong bent of the writer to be brief has often led to the exclusion of facts that enhance the interest of exciting situations, and sometimes the omission robs her own heroism of due emphasis. I have restored one example of this in a foot-note following the perilous voyage down the Mississippi.   G. W. CABLE.

I

SECESSION

New Orleans, Dec. 1, 1860.—I understand it now. Keeping journals is for those who cannot, or dare not, speak out. So I shall set up a journal, being only a rather lonely young girl in a very small and hated minority. On my return here in November, after a foreign voyage and absence of many months, I found myself behind in knowledge of the political conflict, but heard the dread sounds of disunion and war muttered in threatening tones. Surely no native-born woman loves her country better than I love America. The blood of one of its Revolutionary patriots flows in my veins, and it is the Union for which he pledged his "life, fortune, and sacred honor" that I love, not any divided or special section of it. So I have been reading attentively and seeking light from foreigners and natives on all questions at issue. Living from birth in slave countries, both foreign and American, and passing through one slave insurrection in early childhood, the saddest and also the pleasantest features of slavery have been familiar. If the South goes to war for slavery, slavery is doomed in this country. To say so is like opposing one drop to a roaring torrent.

Sunday, Dec. —, 1860.—In this season for peace I had hoped for a lull in the excitement, yet this day has been full of bitterness. "Come, G.," said Mrs. —— at breakfast, "leave *your* church for to-day and come with us to hear Dr. —— on the situation. He will convince you." "It is good to be convinced," I said; "I will go." The church was crowded to suffocation with the élite of New Orleans. The preacher's text was, "Shall we have fellowship with the stool of iniquity which frameth mischief as a law?" . . . The sermon was over at last, and then followed a prayer. . . . Forever blessed be the fathers of the Episcopal Church for giving us a fixed liturgy! When we met at dinner Mrs. F. exclaimed, "Now, G., you heard him prove from the Bible that slavery is right and that therefore secession is. Were you not convinced?" I said, "I was so busy thinking how completely it proved too that Brigham Young is right about polygamy that it quite weakened the force of the argument for me." This raised a laugh, and covered my retreat.

Jan. 26, 1861.—The solemn boom of cannon to-day announced that the convention have passed the ordinance of secession. We must take a reef in our patriotism and narrow it down to State limits. Mine still sticks out all around the borders of the State. It will be bad if New Orleans should secede from Louisiana and set up for herself. Then indeed I would be "cabined, cribbed, confined." The faces in the house are jubilant to-day. Why is it so easy for them and not for me to "ring out the old, ring in the new"? I am out of place.

Jan. 28, Monday.—Sunday has now got to be a day of special excitement. The gentlemen save all the sensational papers to regale us with at the late Sunday breakfast. Rob opened the battle yesterday morning by saying to me in his most aggressive manner, "G., I believe these are your sentiments"; and then he read aloud an article from the "Journal des Debats" expressing in rather contemptuous terms the fact that France will follow the policy of non-intervention. When I answered, "Well, what do you expect? This is not their quarrel," he raved at me, ending by a declaration that he would willingly pay my passage to foreign parts if I would like to go. "Rob," said his father, "keep cool; don't let that threat excite you. Cotton is king. Just wait till they feel the pinch a little; their tone will change." I went to Trinity Church. Some Union people who are not Episcopalians go there now because the pastor has not so much chance to rail at the Lord when things are not going to suit. But yesterday was a marked Sunday. The usual prayer for the President and Congress was changed to the "governor and people of this commonwealth and their representatives in convention assembled."

The city was very lively and noisy this evening with

rockets and lights in honor of secession. Mrs. F., in common with the neighbors, illuminated. We walked out to see the houses of others gleaming amid the dark shrubbery like a fairy scene. The perfect stillness added to the effect, while the moon rose slowly with calm splendor. We hastened home to dress for a soirée, but on the stairs Edith said, "G., first come and help me dress Phœbe and Chloe [the negro servants]. There is a ball to-night in aristocratic colored society. This is Chloe's first introduction to New Orleans circles, and Henry Judson, Phœbe's husband, gave five dollars for a ticket for her." Chloe is a recent purchase from Georgia. We superintended their very stylish toilets, and Edith said, "G., run into your room, please, and write a pass for Henry. Put Mr. D.'s name to it." "Why, Henry is free," I said. "That makes no difference; all colored people must have a pass if out late. They choose a master for protection, and always carry his pass. Henry chose Mr. D., but he's lost the pass he had."

II

THE VOLUNTEERS—FORT SUMTER

Feb. 24, 1861.—The toil of the week is ended. Nearly a month has passed since I wrote here. Events have crowded upon one another. On the 4th the cannon boomed in honor of Jefferson Davis's election, and day before yesterday Washington's birthday was made the occasion of another grand display and illumination, in honor of the birth of a new nation and the breaking of that Union which he labored to cement. We drove to the race-course to see the review of troops. A flag was presented to the Washington Artillery by ladies. Senator Judah Benjamin made an impassioned speech. The banner was orange satin on one side, crimson silk on the other, the pelican and brood embroidered in pale green and gold. Silver crossed cannon surmounted it. orange-colored fringe surrounded it, and crimson tassels drooped from it. It was a brilliant, unreal scene; with military bands clashing triumphant music, elegant vehicles, high-stepping horses, and lovely women richly appareled.

Wedding-cards have been pouring in till the contagion has reached us; Edith will be married next Thursday. The wedding-dress is being fashioned, and the bridesmaids and groomsmen have arrived. Edith has requested me to be special mistress of ceremonies on Thursday evening, and I have told this terrible little rebel, who talks nothing but blood and thunder, yet faints at the sight of a worm, that if I fill that office no one shall mention war or politics during the whole evening, on pain of expulsion.

March 10, 1861.—The excitement in this house has risen to fever-heat during the past week. The four gentlemen have each a different plan for saving the country, and now that the bridal bouquets have faded, the three ladies have again turned to public affairs; Lincoln's inauguration and the story of the disguise in which he traveled to Washington is a never-ending source of gossip. The family board being the common forum, each gentleman as he appears first unloads his pockets of papers from all the Southern States, and then his overflowing heart to his eager female listeners, who in turn relate, inquire, sympathize, or cheer. If I dare express a doubt that the path to victory will be a flowery one, eyes flash, cheeks burn, and tongues clatter, till all are checked up suddenly by a warning rap for "Order, order!" from the amiable lady presiding. Thus we swallow politics with every meal. We take a mouthful and read a telegram, one eye on table, the other on the paper. One must be made of cool stuff to keep calm and collected, but I say but little. This war fever has banished small talk. Through all the black servants move about quietly, never seeming to notice that this is all about them.

"How can you speak so plainly before them?" I say.

"Why, what matter? They know that we shall keep the whip-handle."

April 13, 1861.—More than a month has passed since the last date here. This afternoon I was seated on the floor covered with loveliest flowers, arranging a floral offering for the fair, when the gentlemen arrived and with papers bearing news of the fall of Fort Sumter, which, at her request, I read to Mrs. F.

April 20.—The last few days have glided away in a halo of beauty. But nobody has time or will to enjoy it. War, war! is the one idea. The children play only with toy cannons and soldiers; the oldest inhabitant goes by every day with his rifle to practice; the public squares are full of companies drilling, and are now the fashionable resorts. We have been told that it is best for women to learn how to shoot too, so as to protect themselves when the men have all gone to battle. Every evening after dinner we adjourn to the back lot and fire at a target with pistols. Yesterday I dined at Uncle Ralph's. Some members of the bar were present, and were jubilant about their brand-new Confederacy. It would soon be the grandest government ever known. Uncle Ralph said solemnly, "No, gentlemen; the day we seceded the star of our glory set." The words sunk into my mind like a knell, and made me wonder at the mind that could recognize that and yet adhere to the doctrine of secession.

In the evening I attended a farewell gathering at a friend's whose brothers are to leave this week for Richmond. There was music. No minor chord was permitted.

III

TRIBULATION

April 25.—Yesterday I went with Cousin E. to have her picture taken. The picture-galleries are doing a thriving business. Many companies are ordered off to take possession of Fort Pickens (Florida), and all seem to be leaving sweethearts behind them. The crowd was in high spirits; they don't dream that any destinies will be spoiled. When I got home Edith was reading from the daily paper of the dismissal of Miss G. from her place as teacher for expressing abolition sentiments, and that she would be ordered to leave the city. Soon a lady came with a paper setting forth that she has established a "company"—we are nothing if not military—for making lint and getting stores of linen to supply the hospitals.

My name went down. If it had n't, my spirit would have been wounded as with sharp spears before night. Next came a little girl with a subscription paper to get a flag for a certain company. The little girls, especially the pretty ones, are kept busy trotting around with subscription lists. Latest of all came little Guy, Mr. F.'s youngest clerk, the pet of the firm as well as of his home, a mere boy of sixteen. Such senseless sacrifices seem a sin. He chattered brightly, but lingered about, saying good-by. He got through it bravely until Edith's husband incautiously said, "You did n't kiss your little sweetheart," as he always called Ellie, who had been allowed to sit up. He turned and suddenly broke into agonizing sobs and then ran down the steps.

May 10.—I am tired and ashamed of myself. Last week I attended a meeting of the lint society to hand in the small contribution of linen I had been able to gather. We scraped lint till it was dark. A paper was shown, entitled the "Volunteer's Friend," started by the girls of the high school, and I was asked to help the girls with it. I positively declined. To-day I was pressed into service to make red flannel cartridge-bags for ten-inch columbiads. I basted while Mrs. S. sewed, and I felt ashamed to think that I had not the moral courage to say, "I don't approve of your war and won't help you, particularly in the murderous part of it."

May 27.—This has been a scenic Sabbath. Various companies about to depart for Virginia occupied the prominent churches to have their flags consecrated. The streets were resonant with the clangor of drums and trumpets. E. and myself went to Christ Church because the Washington Artillery were to be there.

June 13.—To-day has been appointed a Fast Day. I spent the morning writing a letter on which I put my first Confederate postage-stamp. It is of a brown color and has a large 5 in the center. To-morrow must be devoted to all my foreign correspondents before the expected blockade cuts us off.

June 29.—I attended a fine luncheon yesterday at one of the public schools. A lady remarked to a school official that the cost of provisions in the Confederacy was getting very high, butter, especially, being scarce and costly. "Never fear, my dear madam," he replied. "Texas alone can furnish butter enough to supply the whole Confederacy; we'll soon be getting it from there." It's just as well to have this sublime confidence.

July 15.—The quiet of midsummer reigns, but ripples of excitement break around us as the papers tell of skirmishes and attacks here and there in Virginia. "Rich Mountain" and "Carrick's Ford" were the last. "You see," said Mrs. D. at breakfast to-day, "my prophecy is coming true that Virginia will be the seat of war." "Indeed," I burst out, forgetting my resolution not to argue, "you may think yourselves lucky if this war turns out to have any seat in particular."

So far, no one especially connected with me has gone to fight. How glad I am for his mother's sake that Rob's lameness will keep him at home. Mr. F., Mr. S., and Uncle Ralph are beyond the age for active service, and Edith says Mr. D. can't go now. She is very enthusiastic about other people's husbands being enrolled, and regrets that her Alex is not strong enough to defend his country and his rights.

July 22.—What a day! I feel like one who has been out in a high wind, and cannot get my breath. The newsboys are still shouting with their extras, "Battle of Bull's Run! List of the killed! Battle of Manassas! List of the wounded!" Tender-hearted Mrs. F. was sobbing so she could not serve the tea; but nobody cared for tea. "O G.!" she said, "three thousand of our own, dear Southern boys are lying out there." "My dear Fannie," spoke Mr. F., "they are heroes now. They died in a glorious cause, and it is not in vain. This will end it. The sacrifice had to be made, but those killed have gained immortal names." Then Rob rushed in with a new extra, reading of the spoils captured, and grief was forgotten. Words cannot paint the excitement. Rob capered about and cheered; Edith danced around ringing the dinner-bell and shouting, "Victory!" Mrs. F. waved a small Confederate flag, while she wiped her eyes, and Mr. D. hastened to the piano and in his most brilliant style struck up "Dixie," followed by "My Maryland" and the "Bonnie Blue Flag."

"Do not look so gloomy, G.," whispered Mr. S. "You should be happy to-night; for, as Mr. F. says, now we shall have peace."

"And is that the way you think of the men of your own blood and race?" I replied. But an utter scorn came over me and choked me, and I walked out of the room. What proof is there in this dark hour that they are not right? Only the emphatic answer of my own soul. To-morrow I will pack my trunk and accept the invitation to visit at Uncle Ralph's country house.

Sept. 25.—When I opened the door of Mrs. F.'s room

on my return, the rattle of two sewing-machines and a blaze of color met me.

"Ah, G., you are just in time to help us; these are coats for Jeff Thompson's men. All the cloth in the city is exhausted; these flannel-lined oil-cloth table-covers are all we could obtain to make overcoats for Thompson's poor boys. They will be very warm and serviceable."

"Serviceable— yes! The Federal army will fly when they see those coats! I only wish I could be with the regiment when these are shared around." Yet I helped make them.

Seriously, I wonder if any soldiers will ever wear these remarkable coats—the most bewildering combination of brilliant, intense reds, greens, yellows, and blues in big flowers meandering over as vivid grounds; and as no table-cover was large enough to make a coat, the sleeves of each were of a different color and pattern. However, the coats were duly finished. Then we set to work on gray pantaloons, and I have just carried a bundle to an ardent young lady who wishes to assist. A slight gloom is settling down, and the inmates here are not quite so cheerfully confident as in July.

IV

A BELEAGUERED CITY

Oct. 22.—When I came to breakfast this morning Rob was capering over another victory—Ball's Bluff. He would read me, "We pitched the Yankees over the bluff," and ask me in the next breath to go to the theater this evening. I turned on the poor fellow. "Don't tell me about your victories. You vowed by all your idols that the blockade would be raised by October 1, and I notice the ships are still serenely anchored below the city."

"G., you are just as pertinacious yourself in championing your opinions. What sustains you when nobody agrees with you?"

Oct. 28.—When I dropped in at Uncle Ralph's last evening to welcome them back, the whole family were busy at a great center-table copying sequestration acts for the Confederate Government. The property of all Northerners and Unionists is to be sequestrated, and Uncle Ralph can hardly get the work done fast enough. My aunt apologized for the rooms looking chilly; she feared to put the carpets down, as the city might be taken and burned by the Federals. "We are living as much packed up as possible. A signal has been agreed upon, and the instant the army approaches we shall be off to the country again."

Great preparations are being made for defense. At several other places where I called the women were almost hysterical. They seemed to look forward to being blown up with shot and shell, finished with cold steel, or whisked off to some Northern prison. When I got home Edith and Mr. D. had just returned also.

"Alex," said Edith, "I was up at your orange-lots to-day, and the sour oranges are dropping to the ground, while they cannot get lemons for our sick soldiers."

"That's my kind, considerate wife," replied Mr. D.

"Why did n't I think of that before? Jim shall fill some barrels to-morrow and take them to the hospitals as a present from you."

Nov. 10.—Surely this year will ever be memorable to me for its perfection of natural beauty. Never was sunshine such pure gold, or moonlight such transparent silver. The beautiful custom prevalent here of decking the graves with flowers on All Saints' day was well fulfilled, so profuse and rich were the blossoms. On All-hallow eve Mrs. S. and myself visited a large cemetery. The chrysanthemums lay like great masses of snow and flame and gold in every garden we passed, and were piled on every costly tomb and lowly grave. The battle of Manassas robed many of our women in mourning, and some of those who had no graves to deck were weeping silently as they walked through the scented avenues.

A few days ago Mrs. E. arrived here. She is a widow, of Natchez, a friend of Mrs. F.'s, and is traveling home with the dead body of her eldest son, killed at Manassas. She stopped two days waiting for a boat, and begged me to share her room and read her to sleep, saying she could n't be alone since he was killed; she feared her mind would give way. So I read all the comforting chapters to be found till she dropped into forgetfulness, but the recollection of those weeping mothers in the cemetery banished sleep for me.

Nov. 26.—The lingering summer is passing into those misty autumn days I love so well, when there is gold and fire above and around us. But the glory of the natural and the gloom of the moral world agree not well together. This morning Mrs. F. came to my room in dire distress. "You see," she said, "cold weather is coming on fast, and our poor fellows are lying out at night with nothing to cover them. There is a wail for blankets, but there is not a blanket in town. I have gathered up all the spare bed-clothing, and now want every available rug or table-cover in the house. Can't I have yours, G.? We must make these small sacrifices of comfort and elegance, you know, to secure independence and freedom."

"Very well," I said, denuding the table. "This may do for a drummer boy."

Dec. 26, 1861.—The foul weather cleared off bright and cool in time for Christmas. There is a midwinter lull in the movement of troops. In the evening we went to the grand bazaar in the St. Louis Hotel, got up to clothe the soldiers. This bazaar has furnished the gayest, most fashionable war-work yet, and has kept social circles in a flutter of pleasant, heroic excitement all through December. Everything beautiful or rare garnered in the homes of the rich was given for exhibition, and in some cases for raffle and sale. There were many fine paintings, statues, bronzes, engravings, gems, laces—in fact, heirlooms and bric-à-brac of all sorts. There were many lovely creole girls present, in exquisite toilets, passing to and fro through the decorated rooms, listening to the band clash out the Anvil Chorus.

Jan. 2, 1862.—I am glad enough to bid '61 good-by. Most miserable year of my life! What ages of thought and experience have I not lived in it!

The city authorities have been searching houses for firearms. It is a good way to get more guns, and the homes of those men suspected of being Unionists were searched first. Of course they went to Dr. B.'s. He met them with his own delightful courtesy. "Wish to search for arms? Certainly, gentlemen." He conducted them all through the house with smiling readiness, and after what seemed a very thorough search bowed them politely out. His gun was all the time safely reposing between the canvas folds of a cot-bed which leaned folded up together against the wall, in the very room where they had ransacked the closets. Queerly, the rebel families have been the ones most anxious to conceal all weapons. They have dug graves quietly at night in the back yards, and carefully wrapping the weapons, buried them out of sight. Every man seems to think he will have some private fighting to do to protect his family.

V

MARRIED

Friday, Jan. 24, 1862. (On Steamboat W., Mississippi River.)—With a changed name I open you once more, my journal. It was a sad time to wed, when one knew not how long the expected conscription would spare the bridegroom. The women-folk knew how to sympathize with a girl expected to prepare for her wedding in three days, in a blockaded city, and about to go far from any base of supplies. They all rallied round me with tokens of love and consideration, and sewed, shopped, mended, and packed, as if sewing soldier clothes. And they decked the whole house and the church with flowers. Music breathed, wine sparkled, friends came and went. It seemed a dream, and comes up now again out of the afternoon sunshine where I sit on deck. The steamboat slowly plows its way through lumps of floating ice,—a novel sight to me,—and I look forward wondering whether the new people I shall meet will be as fierce about the war as those in New Orleans. That past is to be all forgotten and forgiven; I understood thus the kindly acts that sought to brighten the threshold of a new life.

Feb. 15. (*Village of* X.)—We reached Arkansas Landing at nightfall. Mr. Y., the planter who owns the landing, took us right up to his residence. He ushered me into a large room where a couple of candles gave a dim light, and close to them, and sewing as if on a race with Time, sat Mrs. Y. and a little negro girl, who was so black and sat so stiff and straight she looked like an ebony image. This was a large plantation; the Y.'s knew H. very well, and were very kind and cordial in their welcome and congratulations. Mrs. Y. apologized for continuing her work; the war had pushed them this year in getting the negroes clothed, and she had to sew by dim candles, as they could obtain no more oil. She asked if there were any new fashions in New Orleans.

Next morning we drove over to our home in this village. It is the county-seat, and was, till now, a good place for the practice of H.'s profession. It lies on the edge of a lovely lake. The adjacent planters count their slaves by the hundreds. Some of them live with a good deal of magnificence, using service of plate, having smoking-rooms for the gentlemen built off the house, and entertaining with great hospitality. The Baptists, Episcopalians, and Methodists hold services on alternate Sundays in the court-house. All the planters and many others near the lake shore keep a boat at their landing, and a raft for crossing vehicles and horses. It seemed very piquant at first, this taking our boat to go visiting, and on moonlight nights it was charming. The woods around are lovelier than those in Louisiana, though one misses the moaning of the pines. There is fine fishing and hunting, but these cotton estates are not so pleasant to visit as sugar plantations.

But nothing else has been so delightful as, one morning, my first sight of snow and a wonderful new, white world.

Feb. 27.—The people here have hardly felt the war yet. There are but two classes. The planters and the professional men form one; the very poor villagers the other. There is no middle class. Ducks and partridges, squirrels and fish, are to be had. H. has bought me a nice pony, and cantering along the shore of the lake in the sunset is a panacea for mental worry.

VI

HOW IT WAS IN ARKANSAS

March 11, 1862.—The serpent has entered our Eden. The rancor and excitement of New Orleans have invaded this place. If an incautious word betrays any want of sympathy with popular plans, one is "traitorous," "ungrateful," "crazy." If one remains silent and controlled, then one is "phlegmatic," "cool-blooded," "unpatriotic." Cool-blooded! Heavens! if they only knew. It is very painful to see lovable and intelligent women rave till the blood mounts to face and brain. The immediate cause of this access of war fever has been the battle of Pea Ridge. They scout the idea that Price and Van Dorn have been completely worsted. Those who brought the news were speedily told what they ought to say. "No, it is only a serious check; they must have more men sent forward at once. This country must do its duty." So the women say another company *must* be raised.

We were guests at a dinner-party yesterday. Mrs. A. was very talkative. "Now, ladies, you must all join in with a vim and help equip another company."

"Mrs. L.," she said, turning to me, "are you not going to send your husband? Now use a young bride's influence and persuade him; he would be elected one of the officers." "Mrs. A.," I replied, longing to spring up and throttle her, "the Bible says, 'When a man hath married a new wife, he shall not go to war for one year, but remain at home and cheer up his wife.'"

"Well, H.," I questioned, as we walked home after crossing the lake, "can you stand the pressure, or shall you be forced into volunteering?" "Indeed," he replied, "I will not be bullied into enlisting by women, or by men. I will sooner take my chance of conscription and feel honest about it. You know my attachments, my interests are here; these are my people. I could never fight against them; but my judgment disapproves their course, and the result will inevitably be against us."

This morning the only Irishman left in the village presented himself to H. He has been our wood-sawyer, gardener, and factotum, but having joined the new company, his time recently has been taken up with drilling. H. and Mr. R. feel that an extensive vegetable garden must be prepared while he is here to assist, or we shall be short of food, and they sent for him yesterday.

"So, Mike, you are really going to be a soldier?"

"Yes, sor; but faith, Mr. L., I don't see the use of me going to shtop a bullet when sure an' I 'm willin' for it to go where it plazes."

March 18, 1862.—There has been unusual gaiety in this little village the past few days. The ladies from the surrounding plantations went to work to get up a festival to equip the new company. As Annie and myself are both brides recently from the city, requisition was made upon us for engravings, costumes, music, garlands, and so forth. Annie's heart was in the work; not so with me. Nevertheless, my pretty things were captured, and shone with just as good a grace last evening as if willingly lent. The ball was a merry one. One of the songs sung was "Nellie Gray," in which the most distressing feature of slavery is bewailed so pitifully. To sing this at a festival for raising money to clothe soldiers fighting to perpetuate that very thing was strange.

March 20, 1862.—A man professing to act by General Hindman's orders is going through the country impressing horses and mules. The overseer of a certain estate came to inquire of H. if he had not a legal right to protect the property from seizure. Mr. L. said yes, unless the agent could show some better credentials than his bare word. This answer soon spread about, and the overseer returned to report that it excited great indignation, especially among the company of new volunteers. H. was pronounced a traitor, and they declared that no one so untrue to the Confederacy should live there. When H. related the circumstance at dinner, his partner, Mr. R., became very angry, being ignorant of H.'s real opinions. He jumped up in a rage and marched away to the village thoroughfare. There he met a batch of the volunteers, and said, "We know what you have said of us, and I have come to tell you that you are liars, and you know where to find us."

Of course I expected a difficulty; but the evening passed, and we retired undisturbed. Not long afterward a series of indescribable sounds broke the stillness of the night, and the tramp of feet was heard outside the house. Mr. R. called out, "It's a serenade, H. Get up and bring out all the wine you have." Annie and I peeped through the parlor window, and lo! it was the company of volunteers and a diabolical band composed of bones and broken-winded brass instruments. They piped and clattered and whined for some time, and then swarmed in, while we ladies retreated and listened to the clink of glasses.

March 22.—H., Mr. R., and Mike have been very busy the last few days getting the acre of kitchen-garden plowed and planted. The stay-law has stopped all legal business, and they have welcomed this work. But to-day a thunderbolt fell in our household. Mr.

R. came in and announced that he had agreed to join the company of volunteers. Annie's Confederate principles would not permit her to make much resistance, and she has been sewing and mending as fast as possible to get his clothes ready, stopping now and then to wipe her eyes. Poor Annie! She and Max have been married only a few months longer than we have; but a noble sense of duty animates and sustains her.

VII

THE FIGHT FOR FOOD AND CLOTHING

April 1.—The last ten days have brought changes in the house. Max R. left with the company to be mustered in, leaving with us his weeping Annie. Hardly were her spirits somewhat composed when her brother arrived from Natchez to take her home. This morning he, Annie, and Reeney, the black handmaiden, posted off. Out of seven of us only H., myself, and Aunt Judy are left. The absence of Reeney will be not the least noted. She was as precious an imp as any Topsy ever was. Her tricks were endless and her innocence of them amazing. When sent out to bring in eggs she would take them from nests where hens were hatching, and embryo chickens would be served up at breakfast, while Reeney stood by grinning to see them opened; but when accused she was imperturbable. "Laws, Mis' L., I nebber done bin nigh dem hens. Mis' Annie, you can go count dem dere eggs." That when counted they were found minus the number she had brought had no effect on her stolid denial. H. has plenty to do finishing the garden all by himself, but the time rather drags for me.

April 13, 1862.—This morning I was sewing up a rent in H.'s garden coat, when Aunt Judy rushed in.

"Laws! Mis' L., here's Mr. Max and Mis' Annie done come back!" A buggy was coming up with Max, Annie, and Reeney.

"Well, is the war over?" I asked.

"Oh, I got sick!" replied our returned soldier, getting slowly out of the buggy.

He was very thin and pale, and explained that he took a severe cold almost at once, had a mild attack of pneumonia, and the surgeon got him his discharge as unfit for service. He succeeded in reaching Annie, and a few days of good care made him strong enough to travel back home.

"I suppose, H., you've heard that Island No. 10 is gone?"

Yes, we had heard that much, but Max had the particulars, and an exciting talk followed. At night H. said to me, "G., New Orleans will be the next to go, you'll see, and I want to get there first; this stagnation here will kill me."

April 28.—This evening has been very lovely, but full of a sad disappointment. H. invited me to drive. As we turned homeward he said:

"Well, my arrangements are completed. You can begin to pack your trunks to-morrow, and I shall have a talk with Max."

Mr. R. and Annie were sitting on the gallery as I ran up the steps.

"Heard the news?" they cried.

"No. What news?"

"New Orleans is taken! All the boats have been run up the river to save them. No more mails."

How little they knew what plans of ours this dashed away. But our disappointment is truly an infinitesimal drop in the great waves of triumph and despair surging to-night in thousands of hearts.

April 30.—The last two weeks have glided quietly away without incident except the arrival of new neighbors—Dr. Y., his wife, two children, and servants. That a professional man prospering in Vicksburg should come now to settle in this retired place looks queer. Max said:

"H., that man has come here to hide from the conscript officers. He has brought no end of provisions, and is here for the war. He has chosen well, for this county is so cleaned of men it won't pay to send the conscript officers here."

Our stores are diminishing and cannot be replenished from without; ingenuity and labor must evoke them. We have a fine garden in growth, plenty of chickens, and hives of bees to furnish honey in lieu of sugar. A good deal of salt meat has been stored in the smokehouse, and, with fish from the lake, we expect to keep the wolf from the door. The season for game is about over, but an occasional squirrel or duck comes to the larder, though the question of ammunition has to be considered. What we have may be all we can have, if the war lasts five years longer; and they say they are prepared to hold out till the crack of doom. Food, however, is not the only want. I never realized before the varied needs of civilization. Every day something is *out*. Last week but two bars of soap remained, so we began to save bones and ashes. Annie said: "Now, if we only had some china-berry trees here, we should n't need any other grease. They are making splendid soap at Vicksburg with china-balls. They just put the berries into the lye and it eats them right up and makes a fine soap." I did long for some china-berries to make this experiment. H. had laid in what seemed a good supply of kerosene, but it is nearly gone, and we are down to two candles kept for an emergency. Annie brought a receipt from Natchez for making candles of rosin and wax, and with great forethought brought also the wick and rosin. So yesterday we tried making candles. We had no molds, but Annie said the latest style in Natchez was to make a waxen rope by dipping, then wrap it round a corn-cob. But H. cut smooth blocks of wood about four inches square, into which he set a polished cylinder about four inches high. The waxen ropes were coiled round the cylinder like a serpent, with the head raised about two inches; as the light burned down to the cylinder, more of the rope was unwound. To-day the vinegar was found to be all gone, and we have started to make some. For tyros we succeed pretty well.

VIII

DROWNED OUT AND STARVED OUT

May 9.—A great misfortune has come upon us all. For several days every one has been uneasy about the unusual rise of the Mississippi and about a rumor that the Federal forces had cut levees above to swamp the country. There is a slight levee back of the village, and H. went yesterday to examine it. It looked strong, and we hoped for the best. About dawn this morning a strange gurgle woke me. It had a pleasing, lulling effect. I could not fully rouse at first, but curiosity conquered at last, and I called H.

"Listen to that running water. What is it?"

He sprung up, listened a second, and shouted: "Max, get up! The water is on us!" They both rushed off to the lake for the skiff. The levee had not broken. The water was running clean over it and through the garden fence so rapidly that by the time I dressed and got outside Max was paddling the pirogue they had brought in among the pea-vines, gathering all the ripe peas left above the water. We had enjoyed one mess, and he vowed we should have another.

H. was busy nailing a raft together while he had a dry place to stand on. Annie and I, with Reeney, had to secure the chickens, and the back piazza was given up to them. By the time a hasty breakfast was eaten the water was in the kitchen. The stove and everything there had to be put up in the dining-room. Aunt Judy and Reeney had likewise to move into the house, their floor also being covered with water. The raft had to be floated to the storehouse and a platform built, on which everything was elevated. At evening we looked around and counted the cost. The garden was utterly gone. Last evening we had walked round the strawberry-beds that fringed the whole acre and tasted a few just ripe. The hives were swamped. Many of the chickens were drowned. Sancho had been sent to high ground, where he could get grass. In the village everything green was swept away. Yet we were better off than many others; for this house, being raised, we have escaped the water indoors. It just laves the edge of the galleries.

May 26.—During the past week we have lived somewhat like Venetians, with a boat at the front steps and a raft at the back. Sunday H. and I took skiff to church. The clergyman, who is also tutor at a planter's across the lake, preached to the few who had arrived in skiffs. We shall not try it again, it is so troublesome getting in and out at the court-house steps. The imprisonment is hard to endure. It threatened to make me really ill, so every evening H. lays a thick wrap in the pirogue, I sit on it, and we row off to the ridge of dry land running along the lake-shore and branching off to a strip of wood also out of water. Here we disembark and march up and down till dusk. A great deal of the wood got wet and had to be laid out to dry on the galleries, with clothing, and everything that must be dried. One's own trials are intensified by the worse suffering around that we can do nothing to relieve.

Max has a puppy named after General Price. The gentlemen had both gone up-town yesterday in the skiff when Annie and I heard little Price's despairing cries from under the house, and we got on the raft to find and save him. We wore light morning dresses and slippers, for shoes are becoming precious. Annie donned a Shaker and I a broad hat. We got the raft pushed out to the center of the grounds opposite the house, and could see Price clinging to a post; the next move must be to navigate the raft up to the side of the house and reach for Price. It sounds easy; but poke around with our poles as wildly or as scientifically as we might, the raft would not budge. The noonday sun was blazing right overhead, and the muddy water running all over slippered feet and dainty dresses. How long we stayed praying for rescue, yet wincing already at the laugh that would come with it, I shall never know. It seemed like a day before the welcome boat and the "Ha, ha!" of H. and Max were heard. The confinement tells severely on all the animal life about us. Half the chickens are dead and the other half sick.

The days drag slowly. We have to depend mainly on books to relieve the tedium, for we have no piano; none of us like cards; we are very poor chess-players, and the chess-set is incomplete. When we gather round the one lamp—we dare not light any more— each one exchanges the gems of thought or mirthful ideas he finds. Frequently the gnats and the mosquitos are so bad we cannot read at all. This evening, till a strong breeze blew them away, they were intolerable. Aunt Judy goes about in a dignified silence, too full for words, only asking two or three times, "W'at I done tole you fum de fust?" The food is a trial. This evening the snaky candles lighted the glass and silver on the supper-table with a pale gleam, and disclosed a frugal supper indeed—tea without milk (for all the cows are gone), honey, and bread. A faint ray twinkled on the water swishing against the house and stretching away into the dark woods. It looked like civilization and barbarism met together. Just as we sat down to it, some one passing in a boat shouted that Confederates and Federals were fighting at Vicksburg.

Monday, June 2.—On last Friday morning, just three weeks from the day the water rose, signs of its falling began. Yesterday the ground appeared, and a hard rain coming down at the same time washed off much of the unwholesome debris. To-day is fine, and we went out without a boat for a long walk.

June 13.—Since the water ran off, we have, of course, been attacked by swamp fever. H. succumbed first, then Annie, Max next, and then I. Luckily, the new Dr. Y. had brought quinine with him, and we took heroic doses. Such fever never burned in my veins before or sapped strength so rapidly, though probably the want of good food was a factor. The two or three other professional men have left. Dr. Y. alone remains. The roads now being dry enough, H. and Max started on horseback, in different directions, to make an exhaustive search for food supplies. H. got back this evening with no supplies.

June 15.—Max got back to-day. He started right off again to cross the lake and interview the planters on that side, for they had not suffered from overflow.

June 16.—Max got back this morning. H. and he were in the parlor talking and examining maps together till dinner-time. When that was over they laid the matter before us. To buy provisions had proved impossible. The planters across the lake had decided to issue rations of corn-meal and pease to the villagers whose men had all gone to war, but they utterly refused to sell anything. "They told me," said Max, "'We will not see your family starve, Mr. R.; but with such numbers of slaves and the village poor to feed, we can spare nothing for sale.'" "Well, of course," said H., "we do not purpose to stay here and live on charity rations. We must leave the place at all hazards. We have studied out every route and made inquiries everywhere we went. We shall have to go down the Mississippi in an open boat as far as Fetler's Landing (on the eastern bank). There we can cross by land and put the boat into Steele's Bayou, pass thence to the Yazoo River, from there to Chickasaw Bayou, into McNutt's Lake, and land near my uncle's in Warren County."

June 20.—As soon as our intended departure was announced, we were besieged by requests for all sorts of things wanted in every family—pins, matches, gunpowder, and ink. One of the last cases H. and Max had before the stay-law stopped legal business was the settlement of an estate that included a country store. The heirs had paid in chattels of the store. These had remained packed in the office. The main contents of the cases were hardware; but we found treasure indeed—a keg of powder, a case of matches, a paper of pins, a bottle of ink. Red ink is now made out of pokeberries. Pins are made by capping thorns with sealing-wax, or using them, as nature made them. These were articles money could not get for us. We would give our friends a few matches to save for the hour of tribulation. The paper of pins we divided evenly, and filled a bank-box each with the matches. H. filled a tight tin case apiece with powder for Max and himself and sold the rest, as we could not carry any more on such a trip. Those who did not hear of this in time offered fabulous prices afterward for a single pound. But money has not its old attractions. Our preparations were delayed by Aunt Judy falling sick of swamp fever.

Friday, June 27.—As soon as the cook was up again, we resumed preparations. We put all the clothing in order, and had it nicely done up with the last of the soap and starch. "I wonder," said Annie, "when I shall ever have nicely starched clothes after these? They had no starch in Natchez or Vicksburg when I was there." We are now furbishing up dresses suitable for such rough summer travel. While we sat at work yesterday, the quiet of the clear, calm noon was broken by a low, continuous roar like distant thunder. To-day we are told it was probably cannon at Vicksburg. This is a great distance, I think, to have heard it—over a hundred miles.

H. and Max have bought a large yawl and are busy on the lake-bank repairing it and fitting it with lockers. Aunt Judy's master has been notified when to send for her; a home for the cat Jeff has been engaged; Price is dead, and Sancho sold. Nearly all the furniture is disposed of, except things valued from association, which will be packed in H.'s office and left with some one likely to stay through the war. It is hardest to leave the books.

Tuesday, July 8.—We start to-morrow. Packing the trunks was a problem. Annie and I are allowed one large trunk apiece, the gentlemen a smaller one each, and we a light carpet-sack apiece for toilet articles. I arrived with six trunks and leave with one! We went over everything carefully twice, rejecting, trying to shake off the bonds of custom and get down to primitive needs. At last we made a judicious selection. Everything old or worn was left; everything merely ornamental, except good lace, which was light. Gossamer evening dresses were all left. I calculated on taking two or three books that would bear the most reading if we were again shut up where none could be had, and so, of course, took Shakspere first. Here I was interrupted to go and pay a farewell visit, and when we returned Max had packed and nailed the cases of books to be left. Chance thus limited my choice to those that happened to be in my room — "Paradise Lost," the "Arabian Nights," a volume of Macaulay's History I was reading, and my prayer-book. To-day the provisions for the trip were cooked: the last of the flour was made into large loaves of bread; a ham and several dozen eggs were boiled; the few chickens that have survived the overflow were fried; the last of the coffee was parched and ground; and the modicum of the tea was well corked up. Our friends across the lake added a jar of butter and two of preserves. H. rode off to X. after dinner to conclude some business there, and I sat down before a table to tie bundles of things to be left. The sunset glowed and faded, and the quiet evening came on calm and starry. I sat by the window till evening deepened into night, and as the moon rose I still looked a reluctant farewell to the lovely lake and the grand woods, till the sound of H.'s horse at the gate broke the spell.

IX

HOMELESS AND SHELTERLESS

Thursday, July 10. (—— *Plantation.*)—Yesterday about four o'clock we walked to the lake and embarked. Provisions and utensils were packed in the lockers, and a large trunk was stowed at each end. The blankets and cushions were placed against one of them, and Annie and I sat on them Turkish fashion. Near the center the two smaller trunks made a place for Reeney. Max and H. were to take turns at the rudder and oars. The last word was a fervent God-speed from Mr. E., who is left in charge of all our affairs. We believe him to be a Union man, but have never spoken of it to him. We were gloomy enough crossing the lake, for it was evident the heavily laden boat would be difficult to manage. Last night we stayed at this plantation, and from the window of my room I see the men unloading the boat to place it on the cart, which a team of oxen will haul to the river. These hospitable people are kindness itself, till you mention the war.

Saturday, July 12. (*Under a cotton-shed on the bank of the Mississippi River.*)—Thursday was a lovely day, and the sight of the broad river exhilarating. The negroes launched and reloaded the boat, and when we had paid them and spoken good-by to them we felt we were really off. Every one had said that if we kept in the current the boat would almost go of itself, but in fact the current seemed to throw it about, and hard pulling was necessary. The heat of the sun was very severe, and it proved impossible to use an umbrella or any kind of shade, as it made steering more difficult. Snags and floating timbers were very troublesome. Twice we hurried up to the bank out of the way of passing gunboats, but they took no notice of us. When we got thirsty, it was found that Max had set the jug of water in the shade of a tree and left it there. We must dip up the river water or go without. When it got too dark to travel safely we disembarked. Reeney gathered wood, made a fire and some tea, and we had a good supper. We then divided, H. and I remaining to watch the boat, Max and Annie on shore. She hung up a mosquito-bar to the trees and went to bed comfortably. In the boat the mosquitos were horrible, but I fell asleep and slept till voices on the bank woke me. Annie was wandering disconsolate round her bed, and when I asked the trouble, said, "Oh, I can't sleep there! I found a toad and a lizard in the bed." When dropping off again, H. woke me to say he was very sick; he thought it was from drinking the river water. With difficulty I got a trunk opened to find some medicine. While doing so a gunboat loomed up vast and gloomy, and we gave each other a good fright. Our voices doubtless reached her, for instantly every one of her lights disappeared and she ran for a few minutes along the opposite bank. We momently expected a shell as a feeler.

At dawn next morning we made coffee and a hasty breakfast, fixed up as well as we could in our sylvan dressing-rooms, and pushed on; for it is settled that traveling between eleven and two will have to be given up unless we want to be roasted alive. H. grew worse. He suffered terribly, and the rest of us as much to see him pulling in such a state of exhaustion. Max would not trust either of us to steer. About eleven we reached the landing of a plantation. Max walked up to the house and returned with the owner, an old gentleman living alone with his slaves. The housekeeper, a young colored girl, could not be surpassed in her graceful efforts to make us comfortable and anticipate every want. I was so anxious about H. that I remember nothing except that the cold drinking-water taken from a cistern beneath the building, into which only the winter rains were allowed to fall, was like an elixir. They offered luscious peaches that, with such water, were nectar and ambrosia to our parched lips. At night the housekeeper said she was sorry they had no mosquito-bars ready, and hoped the mosquitos would not be thick, but they came out in legions. I knew that on sleep that night depended recovery or illness for H., and all possibility of proceeding next day. So I sat up fanning away mosquitos that he might sleep, toppling over now and then on the pillows till roused by his stirring. I contrived to keep this up till, as the chill before dawn came, they abated and I got a short sleep. Then, with the aid of cold water, a fresh toilet, and a good breakfast, I braced up for another day's baking in the boat.

If I had been well and strong as usual, the discomforts of such a journey would not have seemed so much to me; but I was still weak from the effects of the fever, and annoyed by a worrying toothache which there had been no dentist to rid me of in our village.

Having paid and dismissed the boat's watchman, we started and traveled till eleven to-day, when we stopped at this cotton-shed. When our dais was spread and lunch laid out in the cool breeze, it seemed a blessed spot. A good many negroes came offering chickens and milk in exchange for tobacco, which we had not. We bought some milk with money.

A United States transport just now steamed by, and the men on the guards cheered and waved to us. We all replied but Annie. Even Max was surprised into an answering cheer, and I waved my handkerchief with a very full heart as the dear old flag we had not seen for so long floated by; but Annie turned her back.

Sunday, July 13. (Under a tree on the east bank of the Mississippi.)—Late on Saturday evening we reached a plantation whose owner invited us to spend the night at his house. What a delightful thing is courtesy! The first tone of our host's welcome indicated the true gentleman. We never leave the oars with the watchman; Max takes these, Annie and I each take a bandbox, H. takes my carpet-sack, and Reeney brings up the rear with Annie's. It is a funny procession. Mr. B.'s family were absent, and as we sat on the gallery talking, it needed only a few minutes to show this was a "Union man." His home was elegant and tasteful, but even here there was neither tea nor coffee.

About eleven we stopped here in this shady place. While eating lunch the negroes again came imploring for tobacco. Soon an invitation came from the house for us to come and rest. We gratefully accepted, but found their idea of rest for warm, tired travelers was to sit in the parlor on stiff chairs while the whole family trooped in, cool and clean in fresh toilets, to stare and question. We soon returned to the trees;

however, they kindly offered corn-meal pound-cake and beer, which were excellent.

Eight gunboats and one transport have passed us. Getting out of their way has been troublesome. Our gentlemen's hands are badly blistered.

Tuesday, July 15.—Sunday night about ten we reached the place where, according to our map, Steele's Bayou comes nearest to the Mississippi, and where the landing should be; but when we climbed the steep bank there was no sign of habitation. Max walked off into the woods on a search, and was gone so long we feared he had lost his way. He could find no road. H. suggested shouting, and both began. At last a distant halloo replied, and by cries the answerer was guided to us. A negro came forward and said that was the right place, his master kept the landing, and he would watch the boat for five dollars. He showed the road, and said his master's house was one mile off and another house two miles. We mistook, and went to the one two miles off. At one o'clock we reached Mr. Fetler's, who was pleasant, and said we should have the best he had. The bed into whose grateful softness I sank was piled with mattresses to within two or three feet of the ceiling; and, with no step-ladder, getting in and out was a problem. This morning we noticed the high-water mark, four feet above the lower floor. Mrs. Fetler said they had lived up-stairs several weeks.

X

FRIGHTS AND PERILS IN STEELE'S BAYOU

Wednesday, July 16. (Under a tree on the bank of Steele's Bayou.)—Early this morning our boat was taken out of the Mississippi and put on Mr. Fetler's ox-cart. After breakfast we followed on foot. The walk in the woods was so delightful that all were disappointed when a silvery gleam through the trees showed the bayou sweeping along, full to the banks, with dense forest trees almost meeting over it. The boat was launched, calked, and reloaded, and we were off again. Toward noon the sound of distant cannon began to echo around, probably from Vicksburg again. About the same time we began to encounter rafts. To get around them required us to push through brush so thick that we had to lie down in the boat. The banks were steep and the land on each side a bog. About one o'clock we reached this clear space with dry shelving banks, and disembarked to eat lunch. To our surprise a neatly dressed woman came tripping down the declivity, bringing a basket. She said she lived above and had seen our boat. Her husband was in the army, and we were the first white people she had talked to for a long while. She offered some corn-meal pound-cake and beer, and as she climbed back told us to "look out for the rapids." H. is putting the boat in order for our start, and says she is waving good-by from the bluff above.

Thursday, July 17. (On a raft in Steele's Bayou.)— Yesterday we went on nicely awhile, and at afternoon came to a strange region of rafts, extending about three miles, on which persons were living. Many saluted us, saying they had run away from Vicksburg at the first attempt of the fleet to shell it. On one of these rafts, about twelve feet square,[1] bagging had been hung up to form three sides of a tent. A bed was in one corner, and on a low chair, with her provisions in jars and boxes grouped round her, sat an old woman feeding a lot of chickens.

Having moonlight, we had intended to travel till late. But about ten o'clock, the boat beginning to go with great speed, H., who was steering, called to Max:

"Don't row so fast; we may run against something."

"I'm hardly pulling at all."

"Then we're in what she called the rapids!"

The stream seemed indeed to slope downward, and in a minute a dark line was visible ahead. Max tried to turn, but could not, and in a second more we dashed against this immense raft, only saved from breaking up by the men's quickness. We got out upon it and ate supper. Then, as the boat was leaking and the current swinging it against the raft, H. and Max thought it safer to watch all night, but told us to go to sleep. It was a strange spot to sleep in—a raft in the middle of a boiling stream, with a wilderness stretching on either side. The moon made ghostly shadows, and showed H., sitting still as a ghost, in the stern of the boat, while mingled with the gurgle of the water round the raft beneath was the boom of cannon in the air, solemnly breaking the silence of night. It drizzled now and then, and the mosquitos swarmed over us. My fan and umbrella had been knocked overboard, so I had no

[1] More likely twelve yards.—G. W. C.

weapon against them. Fatigue, however, overcomes everything, and I contrived to sleep.

H. roused us at dawn. Reeney found lightwood enough on the raft to make a good fire for coffee, which never tasted better. Then all hands assisted in unloading; a rope was fastened to the boat, Max got in, H. held the rope on the raft, and, by much pulling and pushing, it was forced through a narrow passage to the farther side. Here it had to be calked, and while that was being done we improvised a dressing-room in the shadow of our big trunks. During the trip I had to keep the time, therefore properly to secure belt and watch was always an anxious part of my toilet. The boat is now repacked, and while Annie and Reeney are washing cups I have scribbled, wishing much that mine were the hand of an artist.

Friday morn, July 18. (*House of Colonel K., on Yazoo River.*)—After leaving the raft yesterday all went well till noon, when we came to a narrow place where an immense tree lay clear across the stream. It seemed the insurmountable obstacle at last. We sat despairing what to do, when a man appeared beside us in a pirogue. So sudden, so silent was his arrival that we were thrilled with surprise. He said if we had a hatchet he could help us. His fairy bark floated in among the branches like a bubble, and he soon chopped a path for us, and was delighted to get some matches in return. He said the cannon we heard yesterday were in an engagement with the ram *Arkansas*, which ran out of the Yazoo that morning. We did not stop for dinner to-day, but ate a hasty lunch in the boat, after which nothing but a small piece of bread was left. About two we reached the forks, one of which ran to the Yazoo, the other to the Old River. Max said the right fork was our road; H. said the left, that there was an error in Max's map; but Max steered into the right fork. After pulling about three miles he admitted his mistake and turned back; but I shall never forget Old River. It was the vision of a drowned world, an illimitable waste of dead waters, stretching into a great, silent, desolate forest.

Just as we turned into the right way, down came the rain so hard and fast we had to stop on the bank. It defied trees or umbrellas, and nearly took away the breath. The boat began to fill, and all five of us had to bail as fast as possible for the half-hour the sheet of water was pouring down. As it abated a cold breeze sprang up that, striking our clothes, chilled us to the bone. All were shivering and blue—no, I was green. Before leaving Mr. Fetler's Wednesday morning I had donned a dark-green calico. I wiped my face with a handkerchief out of my pocket, and face and hands were all dyed a deep green. When Annie turned round and looked at me she screamed, and I realized how I looked; but she was not much better, for of all dejected things wet feathers are the worst, and the plumes in her hat were painful.

About five we reached Colonel K.'s house, right where Steele's Bayou empties into the Yazoo. We had both to be fairly dragged out of the boat, so cramped and weighted were we by wet skirts. The family were absent, and the house was headquarters for a squad of Confederate cavalry, which was also absent. The old colored housekeeper received us kindly, and lighted fires in our rooms to dry the clothing. My trunk had got cracked on top, and all the clothing to be got at was wet. H. had dropped his in the river while lifting it out, and his clothes were wet. A spoonful of brandy apiece was left in the little flask, and I felt that mine saved me from being ill. Warm blankets and the brandy revived us, and by supper-time we got into some dry clothes.

Just then the squad of cavalry returned; they were only a dozen, but they made much uproar, being in great excitement. Some of them were known to Max and H., who learned from them that a gunboat was coming to shell them out of this house. Then ensued a clatter such as twelve men surely never made before — rattling about the halls and galleries in heavy boots and spurs, feeding horses, calling for supper, clanking swords, buckling and unbuckling belts and pistols. At last supper was despatched, and they mounted and were gone like the wind. We had a quiet supper and a good night's rest in spite of the expected shells, and did not wake till ten to-day to realize we were not killed. About eleven breakfast was furnished. Now we are waiting till the rest of our things are dried to start on our last day of travel by water.

Sunday, July 20.— A little way down the Yazoo on Friday we ran into McNutt's Lake, thence into Chickasaw Bayou, and at dark landed at Mrs. C.'s farm, the nearest neighbors of H.'s uncle. The house was full of Confederate sick, friends from Vicksburg, and while we ate supper all present poured out the story of the shelling and all that was to be done at Vicksburg. Then our stuff was taken from the boat, and we finally abandoned the stanch little craft that had carried us for over one hundred and twenty-five miles in a trip occupying nine days. The luggage in a wagon, and ourselves packed in a buggy, were driven for four or five miles, over the roughest road I ever traveled, to the farm of Mr. B., H.'s uncle, where we arrived at midnight and hastened to hide in bed the utter exhaustion of mind and body. Yesterday we were too tired to think, or to do anything but eat peaches.

XI

WILD TIMES IN MISSISSIPPI

This morning there was a most painful scene. Annie's father came into Vicksburg, ten miles from here, and learned of our arrival from Mrs. C.'s messenger. He sent out a carriage to bring Annie and Max to town that they might go home with him, and with it came a letter for me from friends on the Jackson Railroad, written many weeks before. They had heard that our village home was under water, and invited us to visit them. The letter had been sent to Annie's people to forward, and thus had reached us. This decided H., as the place was near New Orleans, to go there and wait the chance of getting into that city. Max, when he heard this from H., lost all self-control and cried like a baby. He stalked about the garden in the most tragic manner, exclaiming:

"Oh! my soul's brother from youth up is a traitor! A traitor to his country!"

Then H. got angry and said, "Max, don't be a fool."

"Who has done this?" bawled Max. "You felt with the South at first; who has changed you?"

"Of course I feel *for* the South now, and nobody has changed me but the logic of events, though the twenty-negro law has intensified my opinions. I can't see why I, who have no slaves, must go to fight for them, while every man who has twenty may stay at home."

I also tried to reason with Max and pour oil on his wound. "Max, what interest has a man like you, without slaves, in a war for slavery? Even if you had them, they would not be your best property. That lies in your country and its resources. Nearly all the world has given up slavery; why can't the South do the same and end the struggle. It has shown you what the South needs, and if all went to work with united hands the South would soon be the greatest country on earth. You have no right to call H. a traitor; it is we who are the true patriots and lovers of the South."

This had to come, but it has upset us both. H. is deeply attached to Max, and I can't bear to see a cloud between them. Max, with Annie and Reeney, drove off an hour ago, Annie so glad at the prospect of again seeing her mother that nothing could cloud her day. And so the close companionship of six months, and of dangers, trials, and pleasures shared together, is over.

Oak Ridge, July 26, Saturday.—It was not till Wednesday that H. could get into Vicksburg, ten miles distant, for a passport, without which we could not go on the cars. We started Thursday morning. I had to ride seven miles on a hard-trotting horse to the nearest station. The day was burning at white heat. When the station was reached my hair was down, my hat on my neck, and my feelings were indescribable.

On the train one seemed to be right in the stream of war, among officers, soldiers, sick men and cripples, adieus, tears, laughter, constant chatter, and, strangest of all, sentinels posted at the locked car doors demanding passports. There was no train south from Jackson that day, so we put up at the Bowman House. The excitement was indescribable. All the world appeared to be traveling through Jackson. People were besieging the two hotels, offering enormous prices for the privilege of sleeping anywhere under a roof. There were many refugees from New Orleans, among them some acquaintances of mine. The peculiar styles of [women's] dress necessitated by the exigencies of war gave the crowd a very striking appearance. In single suits I saw sleeves of one color, the waist of another, the skirt of another; scarlet jackets and gray skirts; black waists and blue skirts; black skirts and gray waists; the trimming chiefly gold braid and buttons, to give a military air. The gray and gold uniforms of the officers, glittering between, made up a carnival of color. Every moment we saw strange meetings and partings of people from all over the South. Conditions of time, space, locality, and estate were all loosened; everybody seemed floating he knew not whither, but determined to be jolly, and keep up an excitement. At supper we had tough steak, heavy, dirty-looking bread, Confederate coffee. The coffee was made of either parched rye or corn-meal, or of sweet potatoes cut in small cubes and roasted. This was the favorite. When flavored with "coffee essence," sweetened with sorghum, and tinctured with chalky milk, it made a curious beverage which, after tasting, I preferred not to drink. Every one else was drinking it, and an acquaintance said, "Oh, you'll get bravely over that. I used to be a Jewess about pork, but now we just kill a hog and eat it, and kill another and do the same. It's all we have."

Friday morning we took the down train for the station near my friend's house. At every station we had to go through the examination of passes, as if in a foreign country.

The conscript camp was at Brookhaven, and every man had been ordered to report there or to be treated as a deserter. At every station I shivered mentally, expecting H. to be dragged off. Brookhaven was also the station for dinner. I choked mine down, feeling the sword hanging over me by a single hair. At sunset we reached our station. The landlady was pouring tea when we took our seats, and I expected a treat, but when I tasted it was sassafras tea, the very odor of which sickens me. There was a general surprise when I asked to exchange it for a glass of water; every one was drinking it as if it were nectar. This morning we drove out here.

My friend's little nest is calm in contrast to the tumult not far off. Yet the trials of war are here too. Having no matches, they keep fire, carefully covering it at night, for Mr. G. has no powder, and cannot flash the gun into combustibles as some do. One day they had to go with the children to the village, and the servant let the fire go out. When they returned at nightfall, wet and hungry, there was neither fire nor food. Mr. G. had to saddle the tired mule and ride three miles for a pan of coals, and blow them, all the way back, to keep them alight. Crockery has gradually been broken and tin cups rusted out, and a visitor told me they had made tumblers out of clear glass bottles by cutting them smooth with a heated wire, and that they had nothing else to drink from.

Aug. 11.—We cannot get to New Orleans. A special passport must be shown, and we are told that to apply for it would render H. very likely to be conscripted. I begged him not to try; and as we hear that active hostilities have ceased at Vicksburg, he left me this morning to return to his uncle's and see what the prospects are there. I shall be in misery about conscription till he returns.

Sunday, Sept. 7. (*Vicksburg, Washington Hotel.*)—H. did not return for three weeks. An epidemic disease broke out in his uncle's family and two children died. He stayed to assist them in their trouble. Tuesday evening he returned for me, and we reached Vicksburg yesterday. It was my first sight of the "Gibraltar of the South." Looking at it from a slight elevation suggests the idea that the fragments left from world-building had tumbled into a confused mass of hills, hollows, hillocks, banks, ditches, and ravines, and that the houses had rained down afterward. Over all there was dust impossible to conceive. The bombardment has done little injury. People have returned and resumed business. A gentleman asked H. if he knew of a nice girl for sale. I asked if he did not think it impolitic to buy slaves now.

"Oh, not young ones. Old ones might run off when

the enemy's lines approach ours, but with young ones there is no danger."

We had not been many hours in town before a position was offered to H. which seemed providential. The chief of a certain department was in ill health and wanted a deputy. It secures him from conscription, requires no oath, and pays a good salary. A mountain seemed lifted off my heart.

Thursday, Sept. 18. (*Thanksgiving Day.*)—We stayed three days at the Washington Hotel; then a friend of H.'s called and told him to come to his house till he could find a home. Boarding-houses have all been broken up, and the army has occupied the few houses that were for rent. To-day H. secured a vacant room for two weeks in the only boarding-house.

Oak Haven, Oct. 3.—To get a house in V. proved impossible, so we agreed to part for a time till H. could find one. A friend recommended this quiet farm, six miles from —— [a station on the Jackson Railroad]. On last Saturday H. came with me as far as Jackson and put me on the other train for the station.

On my way hither a lady, whom I judged to be a Confederate "blockade-runner," told me of the tricks resorted to to get things out of New Orleans, including this: A very large doll was emptied of its bran, filled with quinine, and elaborately dressed. When the owner's trunk was opened, she declared with tears that the doll was for a poor crippled girl, and it was passed.

This farm of Mr. W.'s[1] is kept with about forty ne-

---

[1] On this plantation, and in this domestic circle, I myself afterward sojourned, and from them enlisted in the army. The initials are fictitious, but the description is perfect. — G. W. C.

groes. Mr. W., nearly sixty, is the only white man on it. He seems to have been wiser in the beginning than most others, and curtailed his cotton to make room for rye, rice, and corn. There is a large vegetable-garden and orchard; he has bought plenty of stock for beef and mutton, and laid in a large supply of sugar. He must also have plenty of ammunition, for a man is kept hunting and supplies the table with delicious wild turkeys and other game. There is abundance of milk and butter, hives for honey, and no end of pigs. Chickens seem to be kept like game in parks, for I never see any, but the hunter shoots them, and eggs are plentiful. We have chicken for breakfast, dinner, and supper, fried, stewed, broiled, and in soup, and there is a family of ten. Luckily I never tire of it. They make starch out of corn-meal by washing the meal repeatedly, pouring off the water, and drying the sediment. Truly the uses of corn in the Confederacy are varied. It makes coffee, beer, whisky, starch, cake, bread. The only privations here are the lack of coffee, tea, salt, matches, and good candles. Mr. W. is now having the dirt floor of his smoke-house dug up and boiling from it the salt that has dripped into it for years. To-day Mrs. W. made tea out of dried blackberry leaves, but no one liked it. The beds, made out of equal parts of cotton and corn-shucks, are the most elastic I ever slept in. The servants are dressed in gray homespun. Hester, the chambermaid, has a gray gown so pretty that I covet one like it. Mrs. W. is now arranging dyes for the thread to be woven into dresses for herself and the girls. Sometimes her hands are a curiosity.

The school at the nearest town is broken up, and

Mrs. W. says the children are growing up heathens. Mr. W. has offered me a liberal price to give the children lessons in English and French, and I have accepted transiently.

Oct. 28.—It is a month to-day since I came here. I only wish H. could share these benefits—the nourishing food, the pure aromatic air, the sound sleep away from the fevered life of Vicksburg. He sends me all the papers he can get hold of, and we both watch carefully the movements reported lest an army should get between us. The days are full of useful work, and in the lovely afternoons I take long walks with a big dog for company. The girls do not care for walking. In the evening Mr. W. begs me to read aloud all the war news. He is fond of the "Memphis Appeal," which has moved from town to town so much that they call it the "Moving Appeal." I sit in a low chair by the fire, as we have no other light to read by. Sometimes traveling soldiers stop here, but that is rare.

Oct. 31.—Mr. W. said last night the farmers felt uneasy about the "Emancipation Proclamation" to take effect in December. The slaves have found it out, though it had been carefully kept from them.

"Do yours know it?" I asked.

"Oh, yes. Finding it to be known elsewhere, I told it to mine with fair warning what to expect if they tried to run away. The hounds are not far off."

The need of clothing for their armies is worrying them too. I never saw Mrs. W. so excited as on last evening. She said the provost-marshal at the next town had ordered the women to knit so many pairs of socks.

"Just let him try to enforce it and they will cowhide him. He'll get none from me. I'll take care of my own friends without an order from him."

"Well," said Mr. W., "if the South is defeated and the slaves set free, the Southern people will all become atheists; for the Bible justifies slavery and says it shall be perpetual."

"You mean, if the Lord does not agree with you, you'll repudiate him."

"Well, we'll feel it's no use to believe in anything."

At night the large sitting-room makes a striking picture. Mr. W., spare, erect, gray-headed, patriarchal, sits in his big chair by the odorous fire of pine logs and knots roaring up the vast fireplace. His driver brings to him the report of the day's picking and a basket of snowy cotton for the spinning. The hunter brings in the game. I sit on the other side to read. The great spinning-wheels stand at the other end of the room, and Mrs. W. and her black satellites, the elderly women with their heads in bright bandanas, are hard at work. Slender and auburn-haired, she steps back and forth out of shadow into shine following the thread with graceful movements. Some card the cotton, some reel it into hanks. Over all the firelight glances, now touching the golden curls of little John toddling about, now the brown heads of the girls stooping over their books, now the shadowy figure of little Jule, the girl whose duty it is to supply the fire with rich pine to keep up the vivid light. If they would only let the child sit down! But that is not allowed, and she gets sleepy and stumbles and knocks her head against the wall and then straightens up again. When that happens often it drives me off. Sometimes while I read the bright room fades and a vision rises of figures clad in gray and blue lying pale and stiff on the blood-sprinkled ground.

Nov. 15.—Yesterday a letter was handed me from H. Grant's army was moving, he wrote, steadily down the Mississippi Central, and might cut the road at Jackson. He has a house and will meet me in Jackson to-morrow.

Nov. 20. (*Vicksburg.*)—A fair morning for my journey back to Vicksburg. On the train was the gentleman who in New Orleans had told us we should have all the butter we wanted from Texas. On the cars, as elsewhere, the question of food alternated with news of the war.

When we ran into the Jackson station, H. was on the platform, and I gladly learned that we could go right on. A runaway negro, an old man, ashy-colored from fright and exhaustion, with his hands chained, was being dragged along by a common-looking man. Just as we started out of Jackson the conductor led in a young woman sobbing in a heartbroken manner. Her grief seemed so overpowering, and she was so young and helpless, that every one was interested. Her husband went into the army in the opening of the war, just after their marriage, and she had never heard from him since. After months of weary searching she learned he had been heard of at Jackson, and came full of hope, but found no clue. The sudden breaking down of her hope was terrible. The conductor placed her in care of a gentleman going her way and left her sobbing. At the next station the conductor came to ask her about her baggage. She raised her head to try and answer. "Don't cry so; you'll find him yet." She gave a start, jumped from her seat with arms flung out and eyes staring. "There he is now!" she cried. Her husband stood before her.

The gentleman beside her yielded his seat, and as hand grasped hand a hysterical gurgle gave place to a look like Heaven's peace. The low murmur of their talk began, and when I looked around at the next station they had bought pies and were eating them together like happy children.

Midway between Jackson and Vicksburg we reached the station near where Annie's parents were staying. I looked out, and there stood Annie with a little sister on each side of her, brightly smiling at us. Max had written to H., but we had not seen them since our parting. There was only time for a word and the train flashed away.

XII

VICKSBURG

WE reached Vicksburg that night and went to H.'s room. Next morning the cook he had engaged arrived, and we moved into this house. Martha's ignorance keeps me busy, and H. is kept close at his office.

January 7, 1863.—I have had little to record here recently, for we have lived to ourselves, not visiting or visited. Every one H. knows is absent, and I know no one but the family we stayed with at first, and they are now absent. H. tells me of the added triumph since the repulse of Sherman in December, and the one paper published here shouts victory as much as its gradually diminishing size will allow. Paper is a serious want. There is a great demand for envelops in the office where H. is. He found and bought a lot of thick and smooth colored paper, cut a tin pattern, and we have whiled away some long evenings cutting envelops and making them up. I have put away a package of the best to look at when we are old. The books I brought from Arkansas have proved a treasure, but we can get no more. I went to the only book-store open; there were none but Mrs. Stowe's "Sunny Memories of Foreign Lands." The clerk said I could have that cheap, because he couldn't sell her books, so I got it and am reading it now. The monotony has only been broken by letters from friends here and there in the Confederacy. One of these letters tells of a Federal raid to their place, and says: "But the worst thing was, they would take every toothbrush in the house, because we can't buy any more; and one cavalryman put my sister's new bonnet on his horse, and said, 'Get up, Jack,' and her bonnet was gone."

February 25.—A long gap in my journal, because H. has been ill unto death with typhoid fever, and I nearly broke down from loss of sleep, there being no one to relieve me. I never understood before how terrible it was to be alone at night with a patient in delirium, and no one within call. To wake Martha was simply impossible. I got the best doctor here, but when convalescence began the question of food was a trial. I got with great difficulty two chickens.

The doctor made the drug-store sell two of their six bottles of port; he said his patient's life depended on it. An egg is a rare and precious thing. Meanwhile the Federal fleet has been gathering, has anchored at the bend, and shells are thrown in at intervals.

March 20.—The slow shelling of Vicksburg goes on all the time, and we have grown indifferent. It does not at present interrupt or interfere with daily avocations, but I suspect they are only getting the range of different points; and when they have them all complete, showers of shot will rain on us all at once. Non-combatants have been ordered to leave or prepare accordingly. Those who are to stay are having caves built. Cave-digging has become a regular business; prices range from twenty to fifty dollars, according to size of cave. Two diggers worked at ours a week and charged thirty dollars. It is well made in the hill that slopes just in the rear of the house, and well propped with thick posts, as they all are. It has a shelf also, for holding a light or water. When we went in this evening and sat down, the earthy, suffocating feeling, as of a living tomb, was dreadful to me. I fear I shall risk death outside rather than melt in that dark furnace. The hills are so honeycombed with caves that the streets look like avenues in a cemetery. The hill called the Sky-parlor has become quite a fashionable resort for the few upper-circle families left here. Some officers are quartered there, and there is a band and a field-glass. Last evening we also climbed the hill to watch the shelling, but found the view not so good as on a quiet hill nearer home. Soon a lady began to talk to one of the officers: "It is such folly for them to waste their ammunition like that. How can they ever take a town that has such advantages for defense and protection as this? We'll just burrow into these hills and let them batter away as hard as they please."

"You are right, madam; and besides, when our women are so willing to brave death and endure discomfort, how can we ever be conquered?"

Soon she looked over with significant glances to where we stood, and began to talk at H.

"The only drawback," she said, "are the contemptible men who are staying at home in comfort, when they ought to be in the army if they had a spark of honor."

I cannot repeat all, but it was the usual tirade. It is strange I have met no one yet who seems to comprehend an honest difference of opinion, and stranger yet that the ordinary rules of good breeding are now so entirely ignored. As the spring comes one has the craving for fresh, green food that a monotonous diet produces. There was a bed of radishes and onions in the garden that were a real blessing. An onion salad, dressed only with salt, vinegar, and pepper, seemed a dish fit for a king; but last night the soldiers quartered near made a raid on the garden and took them all.

April 2.—We have had to move, and thus lost our cave. The owner of the house suddenly returned and notified us that he intended to bring his family back; did n't think there'd be any siege. The cost of the cave could go for the rent. That means he has got tired of the Confederacy and means to stay here and thus get out of it. This house was the only one to be had. It was built by ex-Senator G., and is so large our tiny household is lost in it. We use only the lower floor. The bell is often rung by persons who take it for a hotel and come beseeching food at any price. To-day one came who would not be denied. "We do not keep a hotel, but would willingly feed hungry soldiers if we had the food." "I have been traveling all night, and am starving; will pay any price for just bread." I went to the dining-room and found some biscuits, and set out two, with a large piece of corn-bread, a small piece of bacon, some nice syrup, and a pitcher of water. I locked the door of the safe and left him to enjoy his lunch. After he left I found he had broken open the safe and taken the remaining biscuits.

April 28.— I never understood before the full force of those questions—What shall we eat? what shall we drink? and wherewithal shall we be clothed? We have no prophet of the Lord at whose prayer the meal and oil will not waste. Such minute attention must be given the wardrobe to preserve it that I have learned to darn like an artist. Making shoes is now another accomplishment. Mine were in tatters. H. came across a moth-eaten pair that he bought me, giving ten dollars, I think, and they fell into rags when I tried to wear them; but the soles were good, and that has helped me to shoes. A pair of old coat-sleeves saved— nothing is thrown away now—was in my trunk. I cut an exact pattern from my old shoes, laid it on the sleeves, and cut out thus good uppers and sewed them carefully; then soaked the soles and sewed the cloth to them. I am so proud of these home-made shoes, think I 'll put them in a glass case when the war is over, as an heirloom. H. says he has come to have an abiding faith that everything he needs to wear will come out of that trunk while the war lasts. It is like a fairy casket. I have but a dozen pins remaining, so many I gave away. Every time these are used they are straightened and kept from rust. All these curious labors are performed while the shells are leisurely screaming through the air; but as long as we are out of range we don't worry. For many nights we have had but little sleep, because the Federal gunboats have been running past the batteries. The uproar when this is happening is phenomenal. The first night the thundering artillery burst the bars of sleep, we thought it an attack by the river. To get into garments and rush up-stairs was the work of a moment. From the upper gallery we have a fine view of the river, and soon a red glare lit up the scene and showed a small boat, towing two large barges, gliding by. The Confederates had set fire to a house near the bank. Another night, eight boats ran by, throwing a shower of shot, and two burning houses made the river clear as day. One of the batteries has a remarkable gun they call "Whistling Dick," because of the screeching, whistling sound it gives, and certainly it does sound like a tortured thing. Added to all this is the indescribable Confederate yell, which is a soul-harrowing sound to hear. I have gained respect for the mechanism of the human ear, which stands it all without injury. The streets are seldom quiet at night; even the dragging about of cannon makes a din in these echoing gullies. The other night we were on the gallery till the last of the eight boats got by. Next day a friend said to H., "It was a wonder you did n't have your heads taken off last night. I passed and saw them stretched over the gallery, and grape-shot were whizzing up the street just on a level with you." The double roar of batteries and boats was so great, we never noticed the whizzing. Yesterday the *Cincinnati* attempted to go by in daylight, but was disabled and sunk. It was a pitiful sight; we could not see the finale, though we saw her rendered helpless.

XIII

PREPARATIONS FOR THE SIEGE

Vicksburg, May 1, 1863.—It is settled at last that we shall spend the time of siege in Vicksburg. Ever since we were deprived of our cave, I had been dreading that H. would suggest sending me to the country, where his relatives lived. As he could not leave his position and go also without being conscripted, and as I felt certain an army would get between us, it was no part of my plan to be obedient. A shell from one of the practising mortars brought the point to an issue yesterday and settled it. Sitting at work as usual, listening to the distant sound of bursting shells, apparently aimed at the court-house, there suddenly came a nearer explosion; the house shook, and a tearing sound was followed by terrified screams from the kitchen. I rushed thither, but met in the hall the cook's little girl America, bleeding from a wound in the forehead, and fairly dancing with fright and pain, while she uttered fearful yells. I stopped to examine the wound, and her mother bounded in, her black face ashy from terror. "Oh! Miss V., my child is killed and the kitchen tore up." Seeing America was too lively to be a killed subject, I consoled Martha and hastened to the kitchen. Evidently a shell had exploded just outside, sending three or four pieces through. When order was restored I endeavored to impress on Martha's mind the necessity for calmness and the uselessness of such excitement. Looking round at the close of the lecture, there stood a group of Confederate soldiers laughing heartily at my sermon and the promising audience I had. They chimed in with a parting chorus:

"Yes, it 's no use hollerin', old lady."

"Oh! H.," I exclaimed, as he entered soon after, "America is wounded."

"That is no news; she has been wounded by traitors long ago."

"Oh, this is real, living, little black America. I am not talking in symbols. Here are the pieces of shell, the first bolt of the coming siege."

"Now you see," he replied, "that this house will be but paper to mortar-shells. You must go in the country."

The argument was long, but when a woman is obstinate and eloquent, she generally conquers. I came off victorious, and we finished preparations for the siege to-day. Hiring a man to assist, we descended to the wine-cellar, where the accumulated bottles told of the "banquet-hall deserted," the spirit and glow of the festive hours whose lights and garlands were dead, and the last guest long since departed. To empty this cellar was the work of many hours. Then in the safest corner a platform was laid for our bed, and in another portion one arranged for Martha. The dungeon, as I call it, is lighted only by a trap-door, and is so damp it will be necessary to remove the bedding and mosquito-bars every day. The next question was of supplies. I had nothing left but a sack of rice-flour, and no manner of cooking I had heard or invented contrived to make it eatable. A column of recipes for making delicious preparations of it had been going the rounds of Confederate papers. I tried them all; they resulted only in brick-bats or sticky paste. H. sallied out on a hunt for provisions, and when he returned the disproportionate quantity of the different articles obtained provoked a smile. There was a *hogshead* of sugar, a barrel of syrup, ten pounds of bacon and peas, four pounds of wheat-flour, and a small sack of corn-meal, a little vinegar, and actually some spice! The wheat-flour he purchased for ten dollars as a special favor from the sole remaining barrel for sale. We decided that must be left for sickness. The sack of meal, he said, was a case of corruption, through a special providence to us. There is no more for sale at any price; but, said he, "a soldier who was hauling some of the Government sacks to the hospital offered me this for five dollars, if I could keep a secret. When the meal is exhausted, perhaps we can keep alive on sugar. Here are some wax candles; hoard them like gold." He handed me a parcel containing about two pounds of candles, and left me to arrange my treasures. It would be hard for me to picture the memories those candles called up. The long years melted away, and I

Trod again my childhood's track,
And felt its very gladness.

In those childish days, whenever came dreams of household splendor or festal rooms or gay illuminations, the lights in my vision were always wax candles burning with a soft radiance that enchanted every scene. . . . And, lo! here on this spring day of '63, with war raging through the land, I was in a fine house, and had my wax candles sure enough; but, alas! they were neither cerulean blue nor rose-tinted, but dirty brown; and when I lighted one, it spluttered and wasted like any vulgar tallow thing, and lighted only a desolate scene in the vast handsome room. They were not so good as the waxen rope we had made in Arkansas. So, with a long sigh for the dreams of youth, I return to the stern present in this besieged town—my only consolation to remember the old axiom, "A city besieged is a city taken,"—so if we live through it we shall be out of the Confederacy. H. is very tired of having to carry a pass around in his pocket and go every now and then to have it renewed. We have been so very free in America, these restrictions are irksome.

May 9.—This morning the door-bell rang a startling peal. Martha being busy, I answered it. An orderly in gray stood with an official envelop in his hand.

" Who lives here ? "

" Mr. L."

Very imperiously—" Which Mr. L. ? "

" Mr. H. L."

" Is he here ? "

" No."

" Where can he be found ? "

" At the office of Deputy ——."

"I'm not going there. This is an order from General Pemberton for you to move out of this house in two hours. He has selected it for headquarters. He will furnish you with wagons."

"Will he furnish another house also?"

"Of course not."

"Has the owner been consulted?"

"He has not; that is of no consequence; it has been taken. Take this order."

"I shall not take it, and I shall not move, as there is no place to move to but the street."

"Then I'll take it to Mr. L."

"Very well; do so."

As soon as Mr. Impertine walked off, I locked, bolted, and barred every door and window. In ten minutes H. came home.

"Hold the fort till I've seen the owner and the general," he said, as I locked him out.

Then Dr. B.'s remark in New Orleans about the effect of Dr. C.'s fine presence on the Confederate officials there came to mind. They are just the people to be influenced in that way, I thought. I look rather shabby now; I will dress. I made an elaborate toilet, put on the best and most becoming dress I had, the richest lace, the handsomest ornaments, taking care that all should be appropriate to a morning visit; dressed my hair in the stateliest braids, and took a seat in the parlor ready for the fray. H. came to the window and said:

"Landlord says, 'Keep them out. Wouldn't let them have his house at any price.' He is just riding off to the country and can't help us now. Now I'm going to see Major C., who sent the order."

Next came an officer, banged at the door till tired, and walked away. Then the orderly came again and beat the door—same result. Next, four officers with bundles and lunch-baskets, followed by a wagon-load of furniture. They went round the house, tried every door, peeped in the windows, pounded and rapped, while I watched them through the blind-slats. Presently the fattest one, a real Falstaffian man, came back to the front door and rang a thundering peal. I saw the chance for fun and for putting on their own grandiloquent style. Stealing on tiptoe to the door, I turned the key and bolt noiselessly, and suddenly threw wide back the door and appeared behind it. He had been leaning on it, and nearly pitched forward with an "Oh! what's this!" Then seeing me as he straightened up, "Ah, madam!" almost stuttering from surprise and anger, "are you aware I had the right to break down this door if you had n't opened it?"

"That would make no difference to me. I 'm not the owner. You or the landlord would pay the bill for the repairs."

"Why did n't you open the door?"

"Have I not done so as soon as you rung? A lady does not open the door to men who beat on it. Gentlemen usually ring; I thought it might be stragglers pounding."

"Well," growing much blander, "we are going to send you some wagons to move; you must get ready."

"With pleasure, if you have selected a house for me. This is too large; it does not suit me."

"No, I did n't find a house for you."

"You surely don't expect me to run about in the dust and shelling to look for it, and Mr. L. is too busy."

"Well, madam, then we must share the house. We will take the lower floor."

"I prefer to keep the lower floor myself; you surely don't expect me to go up and down stairs when you are so light and more able to do it."

He walked through the hall, trying the doors. "What room is that?" "The parlor." "And this?" "My bedroom." "And this?" "The dining-room."

"Well, madam, we'll find you a house and then come and take this."

"Thank you, colonel; I shall be ready when you find the house. Good-morning, sir."

I heard him say as he ran down the steps, "We must go back, captain; you see I did n't know they were this kind of people."

Of course the orderly had lied in the beginning to scare me, for General P. is too far away from Vicksburg to send an order. He is looking about for General Grant. We are told he has gone out to meet Johnston; and together they expect to annihilate Grant's army and free Vicksburg forever. There is now a general hospital opposite this house, and a smallpox hospital next door. War, famine, pestilence, and fire surround us. Every day the band plays in front of the smallpox hospital. I wonder if it is to keep up their spirits? One would suppose quiet would be more cheering.

May 17.—Hardly was our scanty breakfast over this morning when a hurried ring drew us both to the door.

Mr. J., one of H.'s assistants, stood there in high excitement.

"Well, Mr. L., they are upon us; the Yankees will be here by this evening."

"What do you mean?"

"That Pemberton has been whipped at Baker's Creek and Big Black, and his army are running back here as fast as they can come, and the Yanks after them, in such numbers nothing can stop them. Has n't Pemberton acted like a fool?"

"He may not be the only one to blame," replied H.

"They 're coming along the Big B. road, and my folks went down there to be safe, you know; now they 're right in it. I hear you can't see the armies for the dust; never was anything else known like it. But I must go and try to bring my folks back here."

What struck us both was the absence of that concern to be expected, and a sort of relief or suppressed pleasure. After twelve some worn-out-looking men sat down under the window.

"What is the news?" I inquired.

"Ritreat, ritreat!" they said, in broken English — they were Louisiana Acadians.

About three o'clock the rush began. I shall never forget that woeful sight of a beaten, demoralized army that came rushing back, — humanity in the last throes of endurance. Wan, hollow-eyed, ragged, foot-sore, bloody, the men limped along unarmed, but followed by siege-guns, ambulances, gun-carriages, and wagons in aimless confusion. At twilight two or three bands on the court-house hill and other points began playing "Dixie," "Bonnie Blue Flag," and so on, and drums began to beat all about; I suppose they were rallying the scattered army.

May 28.—Since that day the regular siege has continued. We are utterly cut off from the world, surrounded by a circle of fire. Would it be wise like the scorpion to sting ourselves to death? The fiery shower of shells goes on day and night. H.'s occupation, of course, is gone; his office closed. Every man has to carry a pass in his pocket. People do nothing but eat what they can get, sleep when they can, and dodge the shells. There are three intervals when the shelling stops, either for the guns to cool or for the gunners' meals, I suppose,—about eight in the morning, the same in the evening, and at noon. In that time we have both to prepare and eat ours. Clothing cannot be washed or anything else done. On the 19th and 22d, when the assaults were made on the lines, I watched the soldiers cooking on the green opposite. The half-spent balls coming all the way from those lines were flying so thick that they were obliged to dodge at every turn. At all the caves I could see from my high perch, people were sitting, eating their poor suppers at the cave doors, ready to plunge in again. As the first shell again flew they dived, and not a human being was visible. The sharp crackle of the musketry-firing was a strong contrast to the scream of the bombs. I think all the dogs and cats must be killed or starved: we don't see any more pitiful animals prowling around. . . . The cellar is so damp and musty the bedding has to be carried out and laid in the sun every day, with the forecast that it may be demolished at any moment. The confinement is dreadful. To sit and listen as if waiting for death in a horrible manner would drive me insane. I don't know what others do, but we read when I am not scribbling in this. H. borrowed somewhere a lot of Dickens's novels, and we reread them by the dim light in the cellar. When the shelling abates, H. goes to walk about a little or get the "Daily Citizen," which is still issuing a tiny sheet at twenty-five and fifty cents a copy. It is, of course, but a rehash of speculations which amuses a half hour. To-day he heard while out that expert swimmers are crossing the Mississippi on logs at night to bring and carry news to Johnston. I am so tired of corn-bread, which I never liked, that I eat it with tears in my eyes. We are lucky to get a quart of milk daily from a family near who have a cow they hourly expect to be killed. I send five dollars to market each morning, and it buys a small piece of mule-meat. Rice and milk is my main food; I can't eat the mule-meat. We boil the rice and eat it cold with milk for supper. Martha runs the gauntlet to buy the meat and milk once a day in a perfect terror. The shells seem to have many different names: I hear the soldiers say, "That's a mortar-shell. There goes a Parrott. That's a rifle-shell." They are all equally terrible. A pair of chimney-swallows have built in the parlor chimney. The concussion of the house often sends down parts of their nest, which they patiently pick up and reascend with.

Friday, June 5. In the cellar.—Wednesday evening H. said he must take a little walk, and went while the shelling had stopped. He never leaves me alone for long, and when an hour had passed without his return

I grew anxious; and when two hours, and the shelling had grown terrific, I momentarily expected to see his mangled body. All sorts of horrors fill the mind now, and I am so desolate here; not a friend. When he came he said that, passing a cave where there were no others near, he heard groans, and found a shell had struck above and caused the cave to fall in on the man within. He could not extricate him alone, and had to get help and dig him out. He was badly hurt, but not mortally, and I felt fairly sick from the suspense.

Yesterday morning a note was brought H. from a bachelor uncle out in the trenches, saying he had been taken ill with fever, and could we receive him if he came? H. sent to tell him to come, and I arranged one of the parlors as a dressing-room for him, and laid a pallet that he could move back and forth to the cellar. He did not arrive, however. It is our custom in the evening to sit in the front room a little while in the dark, with matches and candle held ready in hand, and watch the shells, whose course at night is shown by the fuse. H. was at the window and suddenly sprang up, crying, "Run!"—"Where?"—"*Back!*"

I started through the back room, H. after me. I was just within the door when the crash came that threw me to the floor. It was the most appalling sensation I'd ever known — worse than an earthquake, which I've also experienced. Shaken and deafened, I picked myself up; H. had struck a light to find me. I lighted mine, and the smoke guided us to the parlor I had fixed for Uncle J. The candles were useless in the dense smoke, and it was many minutes before we could see. Then we found the entire side of the room torn out. The soldiers who had rushed in said, "This is an eighty-pound Parrott." It had entered through the front, burst on the pallet-bed, which was in tatters; the toilet service and everything else in the room smashed. The soldiers assisted H. to board up the break with planks to keep out prowlers, and we went to bed in the cellar as usual. This morning the yard is partially plowed by a couple that fell there in the night. I think this house, so large and prominent from the river, is perhaps taken for headquarters and specially shelled. As we descend at night to the lower regions, I think of the evening hymn that grandmother taught me when a child:

> Lord, keep us safe this night,
> Secure from all our fears;
> May angels guard us while we sleep,
> Till morning light appears.

Surely, if there are heavenly guardians, we need them now.

June 7. (In the cellar.)—There is one thing I feel especially grateful for, that amid these horrors we have been spared that of suffering for water. The weather has been dry a long time, and we hear of others dipping up the water from ditches and mudholes. This place has two large underground cisterns of good cool water, and every night in my subterranean dressing-room a tub of cold water is the nerve-calmer that sends me to sleep in spite of the roar. One cistern I had to give up to the soldiers, who swarm about like hungry animals seeking something to devour. Poor fellows! my heart bleeds for them. They have nothing but spoiled, greasy bacon, and bread made of musty pea-flour, and but little of that. The sick ones can't bolt it. They come into the kitchen when Martha puts the pan of corn-bread in the stove, and beg for the bowl she mixed it in. They shake up the scrapings with water, put in their bacon, and boil the mixture into a kind of soup, which is easier to swallow than pea-bread. When I happen in, they look so ashamed of their poor clothes. I know we saved the lives of two by giving a few meals. To-day one crawled on the gallery to lie in the breeze. He looked as if shells had lost their terrors for his dumb and famished misery. I've taught Martha to make first-rate corn-meal gruel, because I can eat meal easier that way than in hoe-cake, and I fixed him a saucerful, put milk and sugar and nutmeg—I've actually got a nutmeg! When he ate it the tears ran from his eyes. "Oh, madam, there was never anything so good! I shall get better."

June 9.—The churches are a great resort for those who have no caves. People fancy they are not shelled so much, and they are substantial and the pews good to sleep in. We had to leave this house last night, they were shelling our quarter so heavily. The night before, Martha forsook the cellar for a church. We went to H.'s office, which was comparatively quiet last night. H. carried the bank-box; I the case of matches; Martha the blankets and pillows, keeping an eye on the shells. We slept on piles of old newspapers. In the streets the roar seems so much more confusing, I feel sure I shall run right in the way of a shell. They seem to have five different sounds from the second of throwing them to the hollow echo wandering among the hills, and that sounds the most blood-curdling of all.

June 13.— Shell burst just over the roof this morning. Pieces tore through both floors down into the dining-room. The entire ceiling of that room fell in a mass. We had just left it. Every piece of crockery on the table was smashed up. The "Daily Citizen" to-day is a foot and a half long and six inches wide. It has a long letter from a Federal officer, P. P. Hill, who was on the gunboat *Cincinnati*, that was sunk May 27. Says it was found in his floating trunk. The editorial says, "The utmost confidence is felt that we can maintain our position until succor comes from outside. The undaunted Johnston is at hand."

June 18.— To-day the "Citizen" is printed on wall-paper; therefore has grown a little in size. It says, " But a few days more and Johnston will be here"; also that " Kirby Smith has driven Banks from Port Hudson," and that "the enemy are throwing incendiary shells in."

June 20.— The gentleman who took our cave came yesterday to invite us to come to it, because, he said, "it's going to be very bad to-day." I don't know why he thought so. We went, and found his own and another family in it; sat outside and watched the shells till we concluded the cellar was as good a place as that hillside. I fear the want of good food is breaking down H. I know from my own feelings of weakness, but mine is not an American constitution and has a recuperative power that his has not.

June 21.— I had gone up-stairs to-day during the interregnum to enjoy a rest on my bed, and read the reliable items in the "Citizen," when a shell burst right outside the window in front of me. Pieces flew in, striking all around me, tearing down masses of plaster that came tumbling over me. When H. rushed in I was crawling out of the plaster, digging it out of my eyes and hair. When he picked up a piece as large as a saucer beside my pillow, I realized my narrow escape. The window-frame began to smoke, and we saw the house was on fire. H. ran for a hatchet and I for water, and we put it out. Another [shell] came crashing near, and I snatched up my comb and brush and ran down here. It has taken all the afternoon to get the plaster out of my hair, for my hands were rather shaky.

June 25.—A horrible day. The most horrible yet to me, because I've lost my nerve. We were all in the cellar, when a shell came tearing through the roof, burst up-stairs, tore up that room, and the pieces coming through both floors down into the cellar, one of them tore open the leg of H.'s pantaloons. This was tangible proof the cellar was no place of protection from them. On the heels of this came Mr. J. to tell us that young Mrs. P. had had her thigh-bone crushed. When Martha went for the milk she came back horror-stricken to tell us the black girl there had her arm taken off by a shell. For the first time I quailed. I do not think people who are physically brave deserve much credit for it; it is a matter of nerves. In this way I am constitutionally brave, and seldom think of danger till it is over; and death has not the terrors for me it has for some others. Every night I had lain down expecting death, and every morning rose to the same prospect, without being unnerved. It was for H. I trembled. But now I first seemed to realize that something worse than death might come: I might be crippled, and not killed. Life, without all one's powers and limbs, was a thought that broke down my courage. I said to H., "You must get me out of this horrible place; I cannot stay; I know I shall be crippled." Now the regret comes that I lost control, because H. is worried, and has lost his composure, because my coolness has broken down.

July 1.—Some months ago, thinking it might be useful, I obtained from the consul of my birthplace, by sending to another town, a passport for foreign parts. H. said if we went out to the lines we might be permitted to get through on that. So we packed the trunks, got a carriage, and on the 30th drove out there. General V. offered us seats in his tent. The rifle-bullets were whizzing so *zip*, *zip* from the sharp-shooters on the Federal lines that involuntarily I moved on my chair. He said, "Don't be alarmed; you are out of range. They are firing at our mules yonder." His horse, tied by the tent door, was quivering all over, the most intense exhibition of fear I 'd ever seen in an animal. General V. sent out a flag of truce to the Federal headquarters, and while we waited wrote on a piece of silk paper a few words. Then he said, "My wife is in Tennessee. If you get through the lines, send her this. They will search you, so I will put it in this toothpick." He crammed the silk paper into a quill toothpick, and handed it to H. It was completely concealed. The flag-of-truce officer came back flushed and angry. "General Grant says no human being shall pass out of Vicksburg; but the lady may feel sure danger will soon be over. Vicksburg will surrender on the 4th."

"Is that so, general?" inquired H. "Are arrangements for surrender made?"

"We know nothing of the kind. Vicksburg will not surrender."

"Those were General Grant's exact words, sir," said the flag-officer. "Of course it is nothing but their brag."

We went back sadly enough, but to-day H. says he will cross the river to General Porter's lines and try there; I shall not be disappointed.

July 3.—H. was going to headquarters for the requisite pass, and he saw General Pemberton crawling out of a cave, for the shelling had been as hot as ever. He got the pass, but did not act with his usual caution, for the boat he secured was a miserable, leaky one—a mere trough. Leaving Martha in charge, we went to the river, had our trunks put in the boat, and embarked; but the boat became utterly unmanageable, and began to fill with water rapidly. H. saw that we could not cross in it, and turned to come back; yet in spite of that the pickets at the battery fired on us. H. raised the white flag he had, yet they fired again, and I gave a cry of horror that none of these dreadful things had wrung from me. I thought H. was struck. When we landed H. showed the pass, and said that the officer had told him the battery would be notified we were to cross. The officer apologized and said they were not notified. He furnished a cart to get home, and to-day we are down in the cellar again, shells flying as thick as ever; provisions so nearly gone, except the hogshead of sugar, that a few more days will bring us to starvation indeed. Martha says rats are hanging dressed in the market for sale with mule-meat: there is nothing else. The officer at the battery told me he had eaten one yesterday. We have tried to leave this Tophet and failed, and if the siege continues I must summon that higher kind of courage—moral bravery—to subdue my fears of possible mutilation.

July 4.—It is evening. All is still. Silence and night are once more united. I can sit at the table in the parlor and write. Two candles are lighted. I would like a dozen. We have had wheat supper and wheat bread once more. H. is leaning back in the rocking-chair; he says:

"G., it seems to me I can hear the silence, and feel it, too. It wraps me like a soft garment; how else can I express this peace?"

But I must write the history of the last twenty-four hours. About five yesterday afternoon, Mr. J., H.'s assistant, who, having no wife to keep him in, dodges about at every change and brings us the news, came to H. and said:

"Mr. L., you must both come to our cave to-night. I hear that to-night the shelling is to surpass everything yet. An assault will be made in front and rear. You know we have a double cave; there is room for you in mine, and mother and sister will make a place for Mrs. L. Come right up; the ball will open about seven."

We got ready, shut up the house, told Martha to go to the church again if she preferred it to the cellar, and walked up to Mr. J.'s. When supper was eaten, all secure, and ladies in their cave night toilet, it was just six, and we crossed the street to the cave opposite. As I crossed a mighty shell flew screaming right over my head. It was the last thrown into Vicksburg. We lay on our pallets waiting for the expected roar, but no sound came except the chatter from neighboring caves, and at last we dropped asleep. I woke at dawn stiff. A draft from the funnel-shaped opening had been blowing on me all night. Every one was expressing surprise at the quiet. We started for home and met the editor of the "Daily Citizen." H. said:

"This is strangely quiet, Mr. L."

"Ah, sir," shaking his head gloomily, "I 'm afraid (?) the last shell has been thrown into Vicksburg."

"Why do you fear so?"

"It is surrender. At six last evening a man went down to the river and blew a truce signal; the shelling stopped at once."

When I entered the kitchen a soldier was there waiting for the bowl of scrapings (they took turns for it).

"Good morning, madam," he said; "we won't bother you much longer. We can't thank you enough for letting us come, for getting this soup boiled has helped some of us to keep alive; but now all this is over."

"Is it true about the surrender?"

"Yes; we have had no official notice, but they are paroling out at the lines now, and the men in Vicksburg will never forgive Pemberton. An old granny! A child would have known better than to shut men up in this cursed trap to starve to death like useless vermin." His eyes flashed with an insane fire as he spoke. "Have n't I seen my friends carried out three or four in a box, that had died of starvation! Nothing else, madam! Starved to death because we had a fool for a general."

"Don't you think you're rather hard on Pemberton? He thought it his duty to wait for Johnston."

"Some people may excuse him, ma'am; but we'll curse him to our dying day. Anyhow, you'll see the blue-coats directly."

Breakfast despatched, we went on the upper gallery. What I expected to see was files of soldiers marching in, but it was very different. The street was deserted, save by a few people carrying home bedding from their caves. Among these was a group taking home a little creature born in a cave a few days previous, and its wan-looking mother. About eleven o'clock a soldier in blue came sauntering along, who looked about curiously. Then two more followed him, and then another.

"H., do you think these can be the Federal soldiers?"

"Why, yes; here come more up the street."

Soon a group appeared on the court-house hill, and the flag began slowly to rise to the top of the staff. As the breeze caught it, and it sprang out like a live thing exultant, H. drew a long breath of contentment.

"Now I feel once more at home in mine own country."

In an hour more a grand rush of people setting toward the river began,—foremost among them the gentleman who took our cave; all were flying as if for life.

"What can this mean, H.? Are the populace turning out to greet the despised conquerors?"

"Oh," said H., springing up, "look! It is the boats coming around the bend."

Truly, it was a fine spectacle to see that fleet of transports sweep around the curve and anchor in the teeth of the battery so lately vomiting fire. Presently Mr. J. passed and called:

"Are n't you coming, Mr. L.? There's provisions on those boats: coffee and flour. 'First come, first served,' you know."

"Yes, I'll be there pretty soon," replied H.

But now the newcomers began to swarm into our yard, asking H. if he had coin to sell for greenbacks. He had some, and a little bartering went on with the new greenbacks. H. went out to get provisions. When he returned a Confederate officer came with him. H. went to the box of Confederate money and took out four hundred dollars, and the officer took off his watch, a plain gold one, and laid it on the table, saying, "We have not been paid, and I must get home to my family." H. added a five-dollar greenback to the pile, and wished him a happy meeting. The townsfolk continued to dash through the streets with their arms full, canned goods predominating. Toward five, Mr. J. passed again. "Keep on the lookout," he said; "the army of occupation is coming along," and in a few minutes the head of the column appeared. What a contrast to the suffering creatures we had seen so long were these stalwart, well-fed men, so splendidly set up and accoutred! Sleek horses, polished arms, bright plumes,— this was the pride and panoply of war! Civilization, discipline, and order seemed to enter with the measured tramp of those marching columns; and the heart turned with throbs of added pity to the worn men in gray, who were being blindly dashed against this embodiment of modern power. And now this "silence that is golden" indeed is over all, and my limbs are unhurt, and I suppose if I were a Catholic, in my fervent gratitude I would hie me with a rich offering to the shrine of "our Lady of Mercy."

July 7.—I did not enjoy quiet long. First came Martha, who announced her intention of going to search for her sons, as she was free now. I was hardly able to stand since the severe cold taken in the cave that night; but she would not wait a day. A colored woman came in and said she had asked her mistress for wages and she had turned her out (wanting a place). I was in no condition to stand upon ceremony then, and engaged her at once, but hear to-day that I am thoroughly pulled to pieces in Vicksburg circles; there is no more salvation for me. Next came two Federal officers and wanted rooms and board. To have some protection was a necessity; both armies were still in town, and for the past three days every Confederate soldier I see has a cracker in his hand. There is hardly any water in town, no prospect of rain, and the soldiers have emptied one cistern in the yard already and begun on the other. The colonel put a guard at the gate to limit the water given. Next came the owner of the house and said we must move; he wanted the house, but it was so big he'd just bring his family in; we could stay till we got one. They brought boarders with them too, and children. Men are at work all over the house shoveling up the plaster before repairing. Up-stairs they are pouring it by bucketfuls through the windows. Colonel D. brought work for H. to help with from headquarters. Making out the paroles and copying them has taken so long they wanted help. I am surprised and mortified to find that two thirds of all the men who have signed made their mark; they cannot write. I never thought there was so much ignorance in the South. One of the men at headquarters took a fancy to H., and presented him with a portfolio that he said he had captured when the Confederates evacuated their headquarters at Jackson. It contained mostly family letters written in French, and a few official papers. Among them was the following note, which I will copy here, and file away the original as a curiosity when the war is over.

HEADQUARTERS DEPT. OF TENN.
TUPELO, Aug. 6, 1862.

CAPT: The Major-General Commanding directs me to say that he submits it altogether to your own discretion whether you make the attempt to capture General Grant or not. While the exploit would be very brilliant if successful, you must remember that failure would be disastrous to you and your men. The General commends your activity and energy, and expects you to continue to show these qualities.

I am, very respectfully, yr. obt. svt.
THOMAS L. SNEAD, A. A. G.

CAPT. GEO. L. BAXTER,
  Commanding Beauregard Scouts.

I would like to know if he tried it and came to grief or abandoned the project. As letters can now get through to New Orleans, I wrote there.

July 14.— Moved yesterday into a house I call "Fair Rosamond's bower" because it would take a clue of thread to go through it without getting lost. One room has five doors opening into the house, and no windows. The stairs are like ladders, and the colonel's contraband valet won't risk his neck taking down water, but pours it through the windows on people's heads. We sha'n't stay in it. Men are at work closing up the caves; they had become hiding-places for trash. Vicksburg is now like one vast hospital—every one is getting sick or is sick. My cook was taken to-day with bilious fever, and nothing but will keeps me up.

July 23.—We moved again two days ago.

Aug. 20.—Sitting in my easy-chair to-day, looking out upon a grassy slope of the hill in the rear of this house, I have looked over this journal as if in a dream; for since the last date sickness and sorrow have been with me. I feel as if an angry wave had passed over me, bearing away strength and treasure. For on one day there came to me from New Orleans the news of Mrs. B.'s death, a friend whom no tie of blood could have made nearer. The next day my beautiful boy ended his brief life of ten days, and died in my arms. My own illness caused him to perish; the fatal cold in the cave was the last straw that broke down strength. The colonel's sweet wife has come, and I do not lack now for womanly companionship. She says that with such a prenatal experience perhaps death was the best for him. I try to think so, and to be glad that H. has not been ill, though I see the effects. This book is exhausted, and I wonder whether there will be more adventures by flood and field to cause me to begin another.

THE LOCOMOTIVE CHASE IN GEORGIA

BY WILLIAM PITTENGER

THE railroad raid to Georgia, in the spring of 1862, has always been considered to rank high among the striking and novel incidents of the civil war. At that time General O. M. Mitchel, under whose authority it was organized, commanded Union forces in middle Tennessee, consisting of a division of Buell's army. The Confederates were concentrating at Corinth, Mississippi, and Grant and Buell were advancing by different routes toward that point. Mitchel's orders required him to protect Nashville and the country around, but allowed him great latitude in the disposition of his division, which, with detachments and garrisons, numbered nearly seventeen thousand men. His attention had long been strongly turned toward the liberation of east Tennessee, which he knew that President Lincoln also earnestly desired, and which would, if achieved, strike a most damaging blow at the resources of the rebellion. A Union army once in possession of east Tennessee would have the inestimable advantage, found nowhere else in the South, of operating in the midst of a friendly population, and having at hand abundant supplies of all kinds. Mitchel had no reason to believe that Corinth would detain the Union armies much longer than Fort Donelson had done, and was satisfied that as soon as that position had been captured the next movement would be eastward toward Chattanooga, thus throwing his own division in advance. He determined, therefore, to press into the heart of the enemy's country as far as possible, occupying strategical points before they were adequately defended and assured of speedy and powerful reinforcement. To this end his measures were vigorous and well chosen.

On the 8th of April, 1862,— the day after the battle of Pittsburg Landing, of which, however, Mitchel had received no intelligence,— he marched swiftly southward from Shelbyville, and seized Huntsville in Alabama on the 11th of April, and then sent a detachment westward over the Memphis and Charleston Railroad to open railway communication with the Union army at Pittsburg Landing. Another detachment, commanded by Mitchel in person, advanced on the same day seventy miles by rail directly into the enemy's territory, arriving unchecked with two thousand men within thirty miles of Chattanooga,— in two hours' time he could now reach that point,— the most important position in the West. Why did he not go on? The story of the railroad raid is the answer. The night before breaking camp at Shelbyville, Mitchel sent an expedition secretly into the heart of Georgia to cut the railroad communications of Chattanooga to the south and east. The fortune of this attempt had a most important bearing upon his movements, and will now be narrated.

In the employ of General Buell was a spy named

James J. Andrews, who had rendered valuable services in the first year of the war, and had secured the full confidence of the Union commanders. In March, 1862, Buell had sent him secretly with eight men to burn the bridges west of Chattanooga; but the failure of expected coöperation defeated the plan, and Andrews, after visiting Atlanta, and inspecting the whole of the

enemy's lines in that vicinity and northward, had returned, ambitious to make another attempt. His plans for the second raid were submitted to Mitchel, and on the eve of the movement from Shelbyville to Huntsville Mitchel authorized him to take twenty-four men, secretly enter the enemy's territory, and, by means of capturing a train, burn the bridges on the northern part of the Georgia State Railroad, and also one on on the East Tennessee Railroad where it approaches the Georgia State line, thus completely isolating Chattanooga, which was virtually ungarrisoned.

The soldiers for this expedition, of whom the writer was one, were selected from the three Ohio regiments belonging to General J. W. Sill's brigade, being simply told that they were wanted for secret and very dangerous service. So far as known, not a man chosen declined the perilous honor. Our uniforms were exchanged for ordinary Southern dress, and all arms except revolvers were left in camp. On the 7th of April, by the roadside about a mile east of Shelbyville, in the late evening twilight, we met our leader. Taking us a little way from the road, he quietly placed before us the outlines of the romantic and adventurous plan, which was: to break into small detachments of three or four, journey eastward into the Cumberland Mountains, then work southward, traveling by rail after we were well within the Confederate lines, and finally, the evening of the third day after the start, meet Andrews at Marietta, Georgia, more than two hundred miles away. When questioned, we were to profess ourselves Kentuckians going to join the Southern army.

On the journey we were a good deal annoyed by the swollen streams and the muddy roads consequent on three days of almost ceaseless rain. Andrews was led to believe that Mitchel's column would be inevitably delayed; and as we were expected to destroy the bridges the very day that Huntsville was entered, he took the responsibility of sending word to our different groups that our attempt would be postponed one day—from Friday to Saturday, April 12. This was a natural but a most lamentable error of judgment.

One of the men detailed was belated, and did not join us at all. Two others were very soon captured by the enemy; and though their true character was not detected, they were forced into the Southern army, and two reached Marietta, but failed to report at the rendezvous. Thus, when we assembled very early in the morning in Andrews's room at the Marietta Hotel for final consultation before the blow was struck we were but twenty, including our leader. All preliminary difficulties had been easily overcome, and we were in good spirits. But some serious obstacles had been revealed on our ride from Chattanooga to Marietta the previous evening.[1] The railroad was found to be crowded with trains, and many soldiers were among the passengers. Then the station—Big Shanty—at which the capture was to be effected had recently been made a Confederate camp. To succeed in our enterprise it would be necessary first to capture the engine in a guarded camp with soldiers standing around as spectators, and then to run it from one to two hundred miles through the enemy's country, and to deceive or overpower all trains that should be met—a large contract for twenty men. Some of our party thought the chances of success so slight, under existing circumstances, that they urged the abandonment of the whole enterprise. But Andrews declared his purpose to succeed or die, offering to each man, however, the privilege of withdrawing from the attempt—an offer no one was in the least disposed to accept. Final instructions were then given, and we hurried to the ticket-office in time for the northward-bound mail-train, and purchased tickets for different stations along the line in the direction of Chattanooga.

Our ride, as passengers, was but eight miles. We

---

[1] The different detachments reached the Georgia State Railroad at Chattanooga, and traveled as ordinary passengers on trains running southward.—EDITOR.

swept swiftly around the base of Kenesaw Mountain, and soon saw the tents of the Confederate forces camped at Big Shanty gleam white in the morning mist. Here we were to stop for breakfast, and attempt the seizure of the train. The morning was raw and gloomy, and a rain, which fell all day, had already begun. It was a painfully thrilling moment. We were but twenty, with an army about us, and a long and difficult road before us, crowded with enemies. In an instant we were to throw off the disguise which had been our only protection, and trust to our leader's genius and our own efforts for safety and success. Fortunately we had no time for giving way to reflections and conjectures which could only unfit us for the stern task ahead.

When we stopped, the conductor, the engineer, and many of the passengers hurried to breakfast, leaving the train unguarded. Now was the moment of action. Ascertaining that there was nothing to prevent a rapid start, Andrews, our two engineers, Brown and Knight, and the firemen hurried forward, uncoupling a section of the train consisting of three empty baggage or box-cars, the locomotive, and the tender. The engineers and the firemen sprang into the cab of the engine, while Andrews, with hand on the rail and foot on the step, waited to see that the remainder of the party had gained entrance into the rear box-car. This seemed difficult and slow, though it really consumed but a few seconds, for the car stood on a considerable bank, and the first who came were pitched in by their comrades, while these in turn dragged in the others, and the door was instantly closed. A sentinel, with musket in hand, stood not a dozen feet from the engine, watching the whole proceeding; but before he or any of the soldiers or guards around could make up their minds to interfere all was done, and Andrews, with a nod to his engineer, stepped on board. The valve was pulled wide open, and for a moment the wheels slipped round in rapid, ineffective revolutions; then, with a bound that jerked the soldiers in the box-car from their feet, the little train darted away, leaving the camp and the station in the wildest uproar and confusion. The first step of the enterprise was triumphantly accomplished.

According to the time-table, of which Andrews had secured a copy, there were two trains to be met. These presented no serious hindrance to our attaining high speed, for we could tell just where to expect them. There was also a local freight not down on the time-table, but which could not be far distant. Any danger of collision with it could be avoided by running according to the schedule of the captured train until it was passed; then at the highest possible speed we could run to the Oostenaula and Chickamauga bridges, lay them in ashes, and pass on through Chattanooga to Mitchel at Huntsville, or wherever eastward of that point he might be found, arriving long before the close of the day. It was a brilliant prospect, and so far as human estimates can determine it would have been realized had the day been Friday instead of Saturday. On Friday every train had been on time, the day dry, and the road in perfect order. Now the road was in disorder, every train far behind time, and two "extras" were approaching us. But of these unfavorable conditions we knew nothing, and pressed confidently forward.

We stopped frequently, and at one point tore up the track, cut telegraph wires, and loaded on cross-ties to be used in bridge-burning. Wood and water were taken without difficulty, Andrews very coolly telling the story to which he adhered throughout the run — namely, that he was one of General Beauregard's officers, running an impressed powder-train through to that commander at Corinth. We had no good instruments for track-raising, as we had intended rather to depend upon fire; but the amount of time spent in taking up a rail was not material at this stage of our journey, as we easily kept on the time of our captured train. There was a wonderful exhilaration in passing swiftly by towns and stations through the heart of an enemy's country in this manner. It possessed just enough of the spice of danger, in this part of the run, to render it thoroughly enjoyable. The slightest accident to our engine, however, or a miscarriage in any part of our program, would have completely changed the conditions.

At Etowah we found the "Yonah," an old locomotive owned by an iron company, standing with steam up; but not wishing to alarm the enemy till the local freight had been safely met, we left it unharmed. Kingston, thirty miles from the starting-point, was safely reached. A train from Rome, Georgia, on a branch road, had just arrived and was waiting for the morning mail — our train. We learned that the local freight would soon come also, and, taking the side-track, waited for it. When it arrived, however,

Andrews saw, to his surprise and chagrin, that it bore a red flag, indicating another train not far behind. Stepping over to the conductor, he boldly asked: "What does it mean that the road is blocked in this manner when I have orders to take this powder to Beauregard without a minute's delay?" The answer was interesting, but not reassuring: "Mitchel has captured Huntsville, and is said to be coming to Chattanooga, and we are getting everything out of there." He was asked by Andrews to pull his train a long way down the track out of the way, and promptly obeyed.

It seemed an exceedingly long time before the expected "extra" arrived, and when it did come it bore another red flag. The reason given was that the "local," being too great for one engine, had been made up in two sections, and the second section would doubtless be along in a short time. This was terribly vexatious; yet there seemed nothing to do but to wait. To start out between the sections of an extra train would be to court destruction. There were already three trains around us, and their many passengers and others were all growing very curious about the mysterious train, manned by strangers, which had arrived on the time of the morning mail. For an hour and five minutes from the time of arrival at Kingston we remained in this most critical position. The sixteen of us who were shut up tightly in a box-car,—personating Beauregard's ammunition,—hearing sounds outside, but unable to distinguish words, had perhaps the most trying position. Andrews sent us, by one of the engineers, a cautious warning to be ready to fight in case the uneasiness of the crowd around led them to make any investigation, while he himself kept near the station to prevent the sending off of any alarming telegram. So intolerable was our suspense, that the order for a deadly conflict would have been felt as a relief. But the assurance of Andrews quieted the crowd until the whistle of the expected train from the north was heard; then as it glided up to the depot, past the end of our side-track, we were off without more words.

But unexpected danger had arisen behind us. Out of the panic at Big Shanty two men emerged, determined, if possible, to foil the unknown captors of their train. There was no telegraph station, and no locomotive at hand with which to follow; but the conductor of the train, W. A. Fuller, and Anthony Murphy, foreman of the Atlanta railway machine-shops, who happened to be on board of Fuller's train, started on foot after us as hard as they could run. Finding a hand-car they mounted it and pushed forward till they neared Etowah, where they ran on the break we had made in the road, and were precipitated down the embankment into the ditch. Continuing with more caution, they reached Etowah and found the "Yonah," which was at once pressed into service, loaded with soldiers who were at hand, and hurried with flying wheels toward Kingston. Fuller prepared to fight at that point, for he knew of the tangle of extra trains, and of the lateness of the regular trains, and did not think we should be able to pass. We had been gone only four minutes when he arrived and found himself stopped by three long, heavy trains of cars, headed in the wrong direction. To move them out of the way so as to pass would cause a delay he was little inclined to afford—would, indeed, have almost certainly given us the victory. So, abandoning his engine, he with Murphy ran across to the Rome train, and, uncoupling the engine and one car, pushed forward with about forty armed men. As the Rome branch connected with the main road above the depot, he encountered no hindrance, and it was now a fair race. We were not many minutes ahead.

Four miles from Kingston we again stopped and cut the telegraph. While trying to take up a rail at this point we were greatly startled. One end of the rail was loosened, and eight of us were pulling at it, when in the distance we distinctly heard the whistle of a pursuing engine. With a frantic effort we broke the rail, and all tumbled over the embankment with the effort. We moved on, and at Adairsville we found a mixed train (freight and passenger) waiting, but there was an express on the road that had not yet arrived. We could afford no more delay, and set out for the next station, Calhoun, at terrible speed, hoping to reach that point before the express, which was behind time, should arrive. The nine miles which we had to travel were left behind in less than the same number of minutes. The express was just pulling out, but, hearing our whistle, backed before us until we were able to take the side-track. It stopped, however, in such a manner as completely to close up the other end of the switch. The two trains, side by side, almost touched each other, and our precipitate arrival caused natural suspicion. Many searching questions were asked, which had to be answered before we could get the opportunity of proceeding. We in the box-car could hear the altercation, and were almost sure that a fight would be necessary before the conductor would consent to "pull up" in order to let us out. Here again our position was most critical, for the pursuers were rapidly approaching.

Fuller and Murphy saw the obstruction of the broken rail in time, by reversing their engine, to prevent wreck, but the hindrance was for the present insuperable. Leaving all their men behind, they started for a second foot-race. Before they had gone far they met the train we had passed at Adairsville, and turned it back after us. At Adairsville they dropped the cars, and with locomotive and tender loaded with armed men, they drove forward at the highest speed possible. They knew that we were not many minutes ahead, and trusted to overhaul us before the express train could be safely passed.

But Andrews had told the powder story again with all his skill, and added a direct request in peremptory form to have the way opened before him, which the Confederate conductor did not see fit to resist; and just before the pursuers arrived at Calhoun we were again under way. Stopping once more to cut wires and tear up the track, we felt a thrill of exhilaration to which we had long been strangers. The track was now clear before us to Chattanooga; and even west of that city we had good reason to believe that we should find no other train in the way till we had reached Mitchel's lines. If one rail could now be lifted we would be in a few minutes at the Oostenaula bridge; and that burned, the rest of the task would be little more than simple manual labor, with the enemy absolutely powerless. We worked with a will.

But in a moment the tables were turned. Not far behind we heard the scream of a locomotive bearing down upon us at lightning speed. The men on board were in plain sight and well armed. Two minutes— perhaps one—would have removed the rail at which we were toiling; then the game would have been in our own hands, for there was no other locomotive beyond that could be turned back after us. But the most desperate efforts were in vain. The rail was simply bent, and we hurried to our engine and darted away, while remorselessly after us thundered the enemy.

Now the contestants were in clear view, and a race followed unparalleled in the annals of war. Wishing to gain a little time for the burning of the Oostenaula bridge, we dropped one car, and, shortly after, another; but they were "picked up" and pushed ahead to Resaca. We were obliged to run over the high trestles and covered bridge at that point without a pause. This was the first failure in the work assigned us.

The Confederates could not overtake and stop us on the road; but their aim was to keep close behind, so that we might not be able to damage the road or take in wood or water. In the former they succeeded, but not in the latter. Both engines were put at the highest rate of speed. We were obliged to cut the wire after every station passed, in order that an alarm might not be sent ahead; and we constantly strove to throw our pursuers off the track, or to obstruct the road permanently in some way, so that we might be able to burn the Chickamauga bridges, still ahead. The chances seemed good that Fuller and Murphy would be wrecked. We broke out the end of our last box-car and dropped cross-ties on the track as we ran, thus checking their progress and getting far enough ahead to take in wood and water at two separate stations. Several times we almost lifted a rail, but each time the coming of the Confederates within rifle-range compelled us to desist and speed on. Our worst hindrance was the rain. The previous day (Friday) had been clear, with a high wind, and on such a day fire would have been easily and tremendously effective. But to-day a bridge could be burned only with abundance of fuel and careful nursing.

Thus we sped on, mile after mile, in this fearful chase, round curves and past stations in seemingly endless perspective. Whenever we lost sight of the enemy beyond a curve, we hoped that some of our obstructions had been effective in throwing him from the track, and that we should see him no more; but at each long reach backward the smoke was again seen, and the shrill whistle was like the scream of a bird of prey. The time could not have been so very long, for the terrible speed was rapidly devouring the distance; but with our nerves strained to the highest tension each minute seemed an hour. On several occasions the escape of the enemy from wreck was little less than miraculous. At one point a rail was placed across the track on a curve so skilfully that it was not seen till the train ran upon it at full speed. Fuller says that they were terribly jolted, and seemed to bounce altogether from the track, but lighted on the rails in safety. Some of the Confederates wished to leave a train which was driven at such a reckless rate, but their wishes were not gratified.

Before reaching Dalton we urged Andrews to turn and attack the enemy, laying an ambush so as to get into close quarters, that our revolvers might be on equal terms with their guns. I have little doubt that if this had been carried out it would have succeeded. But either because he thought the chance of wrecking or obstructing the enemy still good, or feared that the country ahead had been alarmed by a telegram around the Confederacy by the way of Richmond, Andrews merely gave the plan his sanction without making any attempt to carry it into execution.

Dalton was passed without difficulty, and beyond we stopped again to cut wires and to obstruct the track. It happened that a regiment was encamped not a hundred yards away, but they did not molest us. Fuller had written a despatch to Chattanooga, and dropped a man with orders to have it forwarded instantly, while he pushed on to save the bridges. Part of the message got through and created a wild panic in Chattanooga, although it did not materially influence our fortunes. Our supply of fuel was now very short, and without getting rid of our pursuers long enough to take in more, it was evident that we could not run as far as Chattanooga.

While cutting the wire we made an attempt to get up another rail; but the enemy, as usual, were too quick for us. We had no tool for this purpose except a wedge-pointed iron bar. Two or three bent iron claws for pulling out spikes would have given us such incontestable superiority that, down to almost the last of our run, we should have been able to escape and even to burn all the Chickamauga bridges. But it had not been our intention to rely on this mode of obstruction—an emergency only rendered necessary by our unexpected delay and the pouring rain.

We made no attempt to damage the long tunnel north of Dalton, as our enemies had greatly dreaded. The last hope of the raid was now staked upon an effort of a kind different from any that we had yet made, but which, if successful, would still enable us to destroy the bridges nearest Chattanooga. But, on the other hand, its failure would terminate the chase. Life and success were put upon one throw.

A few more obstructions were dropped on the track, and our own speed increased so that we soon forged a considerable distance ahead. The side and end boards of the last car were torn into shreds, all available fuel was piled upon it, and blazing brands were brought back from the engine. By the time we approached a long, covered bridge a fire in the car was fairly started. We uncoupled it in the middle of the bridge, and with painful suspense waited the issue. Oh for a few minutes till the work of conflagration was fairly begun! There was still steam pressure enough in our boiler to carry us to the next wood-yard, where we could have replenished our fuel by force, if necessary, so as to run as near to Chattanooga as was deemed prudent. We did not know of the telegraph message which the pursuers had sent ahead. But, alas! the minutes were not given. Before the bridge was extensively fired the enemy was upon us, and we moved slowly onward, looking back to see what they would do next. We had not long to conjecture. The Confederates pushed right into the smoke, and drove the burning car before them to the next side-track.

With no car left, and no fuel, the last scrap having been thrown into the engine or upon the burning car, and with no obstruction to drop on the track, our situation was indeed desperate. A few minutes only remained until our steed of iron which had so well served us would be powerless.

But it might still be possible to save ourselves. If we left the train in a body, and, taking a direct course toward the Union lines, hurried over the mountains at right angles with their course, we could not, from the nature of the country, be followed by cavalry, and could easily travel—athletic young men as we were, and fleeing for life—as rapidly as any pursuers. There was no telegraph in the mountainous districts west and northwest of us, and the prospect of reaching the Union lines seemed to me then, and has always since seemed, very fair. Confederate pursuers with whom I have since conversed freely have agreed on two points —that we could have escaped in the manner here pointed out, and that an attack on the pursuing train would likely have been successful. But Andrews thought otherwise, at least in relation to the former plan, and ordered us to jump from the locomotive one by one, and, dispersing in the woods, each endeavor to save himself. Thus ended the Andrews railroad raid.

It is easy now to understand why Mitchel paused thirty miles west of Chattanooga. The Andrews raiders had been forced to stop eighteen miles south of the same town, and no flying train met him with the expected tidings that all railroad communications of Chattanooga were destroyed, and that the town was in a panic and undefended. He dared advance no farther without heavy reinforcements from Pittsburg Landing or the north; and he probably believed to the day of his death, six months later, that the whole Andrews party had perished without accomplishing anything.

A few words will give the sequel to this remarkable enterprise. There was great excitement in Chattanooga and in the whole of the surrounding Confederate territory for scores of miles. The hunt for the fugitive raiders was prompt, energetic, and completely successful. Ignorant of the country, disorganized, and far from the Union lines, they strove in vain to escape. Several were captured the same day on which they left the cars, and all but two within a week. Even these two were overtaken and brought back when they supposed that they were virtually out of danger. Two of those who had failed to be on the train were identified and added to the band of prisoners.

Now follows the saddest part of the story. Being in citizens' dress within an enemy's lines, the whole party were held as spies, and closely and vigorously guarded. A court-martial was convened, and the leader and seven others out of the twenty-two were condemned and executed. The remainder were never brought to trial, probably because of the advance of Union forces, and the consequent confusion into which the affairs of the departments of east Tennessee and Georgia were thrown. Of the remaining fourteen, eight succeeded by a bold effort — attacking their guard in broad daylight—in making their escape from Atlanta, Georgia, and ultimately in reaching the North. The other six who shared in this effort, but were recaptured, remained prisoners until the latter part of March, 1863, when they were exchanged through a special arrangement made with Secretary Stanton. All the survivors of this expedition received medals and promotion.[1] The pursuers also received expressions of gratitude from their fellow-Confederates, notably from the governor and the legislature of Georgia.

[1] Below is a list of the participants in the raid:

James J. Andrews,* leader; William Campbell,* a civilian who volunteered to accompany the raiders; George D. Wilson,* Company B, 2d Ohio Volunteers; Marion A. Ross,* Company A, 2d Ohio Volunteers; Perry G. Shadrack,* Company K, 2d Ohio Volunteers; Samuel Slavens,* 33d Ohio Volunteers; Samuel Robinson,* Company G, 33d Ohio Volunteers; John Scott,* Company K, 21st Ohio Volunteers; Wilson W. Brown,† Company F, 21st Ohio Volunteers; William Knight,† Company E, 21st Ohio Volunteers; Mark Wood,† Company C, 21st Ohio Volunteers; James A. Wilson,† Company C, 21st Ohio Volunteers; John Wollam,† Company C, 33d Ohio Volunteers; D. A. Dorsey,† Company H, 33d Ohio Volunteers; Jacob Parrott,‡ Company K, 33d Ohio Volunteers; Robert Buffum,‡ Company H, 21st Ohio Volunteers; William Benzinger,‡ Company G, 21st Ohio Volunteers; William Reddick,‡ Company B, 33d Ohio Volunteers; E. H. Mason,‡ Company K, 21st Ohio Volunteers; William Pittenger,‡ Company G, 2d Ohio Volunteers.

J. R. Porter, Company C, 21st Ohio, and Martin J. Hawkins, Company A, 33d Ohio, reached Marietta, but did not get on board of the train. They were captured and imprisoned with their comrades.

* Executed. † Escaped. ‡ Exchanged.

MOSBY'S "PARTIZAN RANGERS"

BY A. E. RICHARDS

DURING the early stages of the war between the States, the Confederate Congress enacted a statute known as the Partizan Ranger Act, which provided for independent bodies of cavalry to be organized as other government troops. The officers were to be regularly commissioned and the men to be paid like other soldiers. The distinctive features were, that the rangers should operate independently of the regular army and be entitled to the legitimate spoil captured from the enemy.

While John S. Mosby was employed as a scout by General J. E. B. Stuart, he had concluded that a command organized and operated as contemplated by this act could do great damage to the enemy guarding that portion of Northern Virginia abandoned by the Confederate armies. But the partizan branch of the service having been brought into disrepute by the worse than futile efforts of others, his superior officers at first refused him permission to engage in so questionable an enterprise. Finally, however, General Stuart gave Mosby a detail of nine men from the regular cavalry with which to experiment.

At that time the two main armies operating in Virginia were confronting each other near Fredericksburg. To protect their lines of communication with Washington, the Federals had stationed a considerable force across the Potomac, with headquarters at Fairfax Court-house. They also established a complete cordon of pickets from a point on the river above Washington to a point below, thus encompassing many square miles of Virginia territory. Upon these outposts Mosby commenced his operations. The size of his command compelled him to confine his attacks to the small details made nightly for picket duty. But he was so uniformly successful that when the time came for him to report back to General Stuart, that officer was so pleased with the experiment that he allowed Mosby to select fifteen men from his old regiment and return, for an indefinite period, to his chosen field of operations.

His first exploits had been so noised abroad that the young men from the neighboring counties and the soldiers at home on furloughs would request permission to join in his raids. He could easily muster fifty of these, known as "Mosby's Conglomerates," for any expedition. The opportunity for developing his ideas of border warfare was thus presented. With great vigor he renewed his attacks upon the Federal outposts. As a recognition of one of his successful exploits, the Confederate government sent him a captain's commission with authority to raise a company of partizan rangers. The material for this was already at hand, and on June 10, 1862, he organized his first company. This was the nucleus around which he subsequently shaped his ideal command. The fame of his achievements had already spread throughout Virginia and Maryland, and attracted to his standard many kindred spirits from both States. No conscripting was necessary. Those for whom this mode of warfare possessed a charm would brave hardship and danger for the privilege of enlisting under his banner. His recruits from Maryland, and many of those from Virginia, were compelled to pass through the Federal pickets in order to join his command. Yet great care had to be exercised in the selection of his men, and not every applicant was received. If an unworthy soldier procured admission, so soon as the mistake was discovered he was sent under guard as a conscript to the regular service.

Mosby reserved the right to select all of his officers, who were invariably chosen from those who had already demonstrated their fitness for this particular service. It has been said of a great military hero that the surest proof of his genius was his skill in finding out genius in others, and his promptness in calling it into action. Mosby, in his limited sphere, displayed a similar talent, and to this faculty, almost as much as any one thing, may be attributed his success with his enlarged command. When a sufficient number of men had enlisted to form a new company, he would have them drawn up in line and his adjutant would read to them the names of those selected for officers, with the announcement that all who were not in favor of their election could step out of the ranks and go to the regular service. Of course no one ever left. In order to comply with the law, the form of an election was then gone through with, and their commander's choice ratified. In no other body of troops were all the officers thus *unanimously* elected.

Mosby's command, as finally organized, consisted of eight companies of cavalry and one of mounted artillery, officered by a colonel, a lieutenant-colonel, and a major, with the usual complement of company officers. But the entire force was seldom combined. Instead of this, they would be divided into two or more detachments operating in different places. So it was not at all unusual for an attack to be made the same night upon Sheridan's line of transportation in the valley, upon the pickets guarding the Baltimore and Ohio Railroad, upon the outposts in Fairfax County, and upon the rear of the army manœuvering against Lee. This explains—what at the time seemed to many of the readers of the Northern newspapers a mystery—how Mosby's men could be in so many different places at the same time. The safety and success of the Rangers were enhanced by these subdivisions, the Federals having become so alert as to make it extremely difficult for a large command either to evade their pickets or manœuver within their lines. From fifty to one hundred men were all that were usually marched together, and many of their most brilliant successes were achieved with even a smaller force. Mosby had only twenty men with him when he captured Brigadier-General Edwin H. Stoughton. With these he penetrated the heart of the Federal camp, and carried off its commander. General Stoughton was in charge of an army of cavalry, infantry, and artillery, with headquarters at Fairfax Court-house. One dark night in March, 1863, Mosby, with this small detachment, evaded the Federal pickets, passed through the sleeping army, and with their camp-fires gleaming all around him, and their sentinels on duty, aroused their general from his slumbers, and took him captive with thirty-seven of his comrades.

But the novelty of Mosby's mode of warfare consisted chiefly in the manner of subsisting, quartering, and protecting his men. The upper portion of Loudoun and Fauquier counties, embracing a circuit of about thirty miles in diameter, was then known as "Mosby's Confederacy." By a glance at the map it will be observed that it bordered upon the Blue Ridge Mountains on the west, and the Bull Run Mountains on the east. The valley between is one of the richest, most beautiful, and highly cultivated in the State of Virginia. It was thickly inhabited with old Virginia families, who were loyal and true to the Southern cause. These people received Mosby's men into their houses as their guests, and neither danger nor want could tempt their betrayal. Robin Hood's band sought safety in the solitudes of Sherwood Forest, Marion's men secreted themselves "in the pleasant wilds of Snow's Island" and other South Carolina swamps, but the Partizan Rangers of Virginia protected themselves by dispersing in an open country among a sympathizing people. They never established a camp; to have done so would have invited capture. Each soldier had his boarding-house, where he lived when off duty, as a member of the family. From these they would come, singly or in groups, bringing their rations with them to some designated rendezvous, march rapidly to and from the point of attack, send their prisoners under guard to the nearest Confederate post, divide the spoil, and disperse. If they were pursued by an overwhelming force, as was frequently the case, the evening found them scattered to the four winds, where each man, mounted upon his own fleet steed, could protect himself from capture. If the Federals attempted to follow the chase in small parties, the Rangers, from behind every hill and grove, would concentrate and dash upon them. If they marched in solid column, the Rangers would hang upon their flanks, firing upon them from behind trees, fences, and hilltops. In this way, General Julius Stahel, who had invaded Mosby's Confederacy with two brigades of cavalry and four pieces of artillery for the avowed purpose of utterly demolishing the Rangers, was so annoyed that he retired, thoroughly disgusted with an enemy "who only fought when they got their foe at a disadvantage."

As there were no civil officers commissioned by either party in all that section of Virginia, the people naturally turned to Mosby as their only representative of law and order. It was not unusual for them to submit their property controversies to him for decision. In this way he acquired a civil jurisdiction in connection with his military dictatorship. Being a lawyer by profession, educated at the University of Virginia, his civil administration became as remarkable for its prudence and justice as his military leadership was for magnanimity and dash. I heard an old citizen remark, "For two years Mosby was our ruler, and the country never was better governed." He protected the people from stragglers and deserters, who pillaged friend and foe alike. Every captured horse-thief was promptly executed. He required his own men to treat the citizens with fairness and courtesy, and any violation of this rule was punished by sending the offender to the regular service. Its observance was more easily enforced than would appear possible at first glance. The men were scarcely ever off duty, except for necessary rest. The officers were then distributed among them, and by their example and authority controlled, when necessary, the deportment of their men. The citizens with whom they lived also exercised a healthy influence over them. These relations engendered many attachments that ran like golden threads through the soldier's life and outlived the rough usages of war.

It thus became no easy matter to drive the Rangers from a territory so dear to them, and in which they were befriended by all. On two occasions the entire Federal army operating against General Lee passed through Mosby's Confederacy, and yet his men did not abandon it. They hid themselves in the mountains during the day, and descended upon the enemy at night. They thus observed every movement of the Federal army, and all valuable information was promptly sent to the Confederate general. On one of these occasions, June 17, 1863, Mosby found himself at ten o'clock at night between the infantry and cavalry commands of General Hooker's army. Observing three horses hitched near a house, with an orderly standing by, he left his command with the prisoners already captured, and taking with him three men, rode up to the orderly and was informed by him that the horses belonged to Major William R. Sterling and another officer. In a whisper he said to the orderly:

"My name is Mosby. Keep quiet!"

The man understood him to say that he (the orderly) was "Mosby," and very indignantly replied:

"No, sir, I am as good a Union man as ever walked the earth."

"Those are just the sort I am after," said Mosby.

Just then the two officers emerged from the house. As they approached, one of the Rangers stretched out his hand to disarm the major. Supposing him to be an acquaintance, Major Sterling offered his hand in return, but was overwhelmed with surprise when informed that he was a prisoner. Upon examination he was found to be the bearer of important despatches from General Hooker to his chief of cavalry, General Pleasonton. These despatches, which developed the contemplated movements of the army and directed the coöperation of the cavalry, were placed in General Stuart's hands by dawn of day. On this and many similar occasions information furnished by the Rangers proved invaluable to the Confederate generals.

But furnishing information was not the most important service they rendered. It has been fairly estimated that they detained on guard duty thirty thousand Federal soldiers, who otherwise might have been employed at the front. Even then the Federal lines of transportation were constantly being attacked, with more or less success. It was impossible to protect them against such reckless activity as the Rangers were constantly displaying. No matter how vigilant the Federals were, Mosby was sure to find an opportunity for attacking. Sometimes his success would lie in the very boldness of the attempt. This was never more strikingly illustrated than in one of his attacks upon

Sheridan's line of transportation. The Federal army which had driven General Early up the valley beyond Winchester was drawing its supplies over the turnpike from Harper's Ferry. Mosby, taking a command of five companies of cavalry and two mountain howitzers,—numbering two hundred and fifty men,— passed at night across the Blue Ridge, and fording the Shenandoah, halted a few miles below Berryville. Riding out to the turnpike, he discovered in his immediate front two large trains parked for the night — one going toward the army loaded, the other returning empty. He determined to capture the former, composed of one hundred and fifty wagons. At daybreak it commenced to move, guarded by a brigade of infantry and two hundred and fifty cavalry. The train and its guard were soon strung along the turnpike. The cavalry rode on the flank near the center, a company of infantry marched in front of each tenth wagon, and the remaining force was distributed between the rear- and advance-guards. It was a bright summer morning, and just as the sun was rising the Rangers marched across the open fields and halted about four hundred yards from the road, and within full view of the moving train. Observing the Federal cavalry dismounted across the road a quarter of a mile to his left, Mosby sent two companies of his cavalry and one howitzer, with orders to take a position immediately opposite them and there await the signal of attack, which was to be three shots fired from the howitzer left behind. This detachment did not halt until it was within seventy-five yards of the moving train. Of course the Federals observed all these manœuvers, but were misled by their very boldness; they never imagined but what this new force was a part of their own army. So when the first shot, which fell short, was fired from the howitzer, several of their officers rode to the eminence not more than thirty steps in front of the detached Confederate squadron, and lifting their glasses to their eyes, prepared to witness what they supposed to be artillery practice. Just then the second shell from the howitzer burst in the midst of their cavalry, who, supposing it had been fired in that direction through mistake, hastily prepared to move beyond range. Immediately the rebel yell was raised, and the squadron dashed at the Federals, scattering them in every direction, and capturing the officers with their glasses still in their hands. Turning abruptly to the left, the Rangers charged along the road, riding over company after company of infantry until checked by a volley from the advance-guard. At the same time another squadron had struck the turnpike immediately in front of their first position, and turning to the right, had ridden down everything between them and the rear-guard. Then, with one howitzer playing upon the advance- and the other upon the rear-guard, the Rangers rapidly collected their prisoners, unhitched the teams, and burned the wagons. When reinforcements reached the Federals they deployed their skirmishers and advanced in line of battle, only to see the Rangers riding over the hills in the distance, taking with them three hundred prisoners, seven hundred mules and horses, and two hundred and thirty beef-cattle. But the rejoicing of the Rangers was almost turned into chagrin when they learned from the

Northern papers that one of the wagons from which they had taken the mules was loaded with an iron safe containing one million dollars to pay off the army. Upon reading it, Mosby dropped the paper with a sigh, exclaiming, "There's a cool million gone after it was fairly earned! What other man could sustain such losses with so little embarrassment?"

But this failure of the Rangers to secure their "earnings" did not always attend them. Shortly after that they collected a sufficient amount of "dues" to enable them to determine upon greenbacks as the future currency of their Confederacy. It happened in this wise. Taking with him seventy-five men, Mosby crossed, at an early hour of the night, in rear of Sheridan's army, and struck the Baltimore and Ohio Railroad above Harper's Ferry, near Duffield Station. Here they prized up one side of the track to a height of four feet, placing a secure foundation under it. Soon the night express came rushing along. The engine upset, and the train came to a stand without serious injury to the passengers. Immediately the cars were boarded, and every one in Federal uniform captured. Among the prisoners were two paymasters, Majors Moore and Ruggles, who had in a satchel and tin box $168,000, in greenbacks, to pay off the troops stationed along the road. Securing this rich booty, the Rangers burned the cars and repassed Sheridan's pickets before the day had dawned. The money was divided upon reaching their Confederacy, each man receiving something over two thousand dollars, Mosby taking nothing.

Only the men who participated in a particular raid

were allowed to share in its spoil. The officer who commanded the expedition always controlled the distribution. It was seldom there was anything to divide except horses and their equipments. Those who had distinguished themselves in the fight were allowed the first choice as a reward for their gallantry, the shares of the others being divided by lot. This system, by rewarding individual merit, encouraged a healthy rivalry among the men, and at the same time removed all inducement to leave the fight for plunder. Often when a charge was ordered, a genuine horse-race followed, the swiftest steeds leading the way.

In this manner the men were mounted and equipped without expense to themselves or the Confederate Government. On the contrary, the army quartermaster kept an agent in Mosby's Confederacy, to purchase from the Rangers their surplus stock and arms. His standing price for a horse was forty dollars in gold. But each Ranger retained two or more of the best for his own use. In this way they were always splendidly mounted. I once heard a Federal officer say he was not surprised that Mosby's men rode such fine horses, as they had both armies to pick from. The cavalry was armed with pistols alone, of which each man carried at least two. Their superiority over all other arms for this branch of the service was frequently demonstrated. It is a weapon that can be used with one hand, leaving the other to guide the horse. Cavalry is never really efficient unless trained to rush into close contact with the enemy. To see the whites of their eyes is not sufficient; they must ride over the foe. In the rapid charge the carbine is not only useless, but a positive incumbrance. The saber is comparatively harmless; it serves to frighten the timid, but rarely ever deals a death-wound. Let two men encounter each other in the charge, one relying upon his pistol, the other upon his saber, and the former, though an ordinary marksman, will almost invariably get the better of his antagonist. The Rangers realized their advantage in this respect. It encouraged them to rush into close quarters, where the rapid discharge of their pistols soon told upon the enemy, no matter how bravely they had withstood the onset. I have seen the victory decided alone by the superiority of the pistol over the saber, where the opposing columns had crossed each other in the charge and, wheeling, had mingled in the fight.

But the Rangers were compelled to discard the carbine and the saber for other reasons than their inferiority in the hand-to-hand conflict. It was always their policy to take the enemy by surprise if possible. Their favorite plan was to wind their way through the Federal pickets during the night, and make the attack at break of day. The rattling of the carbine and saber would have made it impossible to execute these movements with the silence necessary to success. To the uninitiated it would be surprising to see with what noiseless secrecy these manœuvers could be accomplished. Only whispered commands were necessary from the officers, and the presence of danger insured silence in the ranks. This silence, which was observed so long as silence was proper, served to make the charge, with its shout and its cheer, the more terrible to the foe.

But it must not be imagined the Rangers were always successful. They were themselves sometimes surprised, sometimes repulsed. Nothing else could be expected from almost daily encounters in a country abandoned to the enemy. There were occasions when they were saved from total ruin only by their knowledge of the country and the swiftness of their steeds.

A ROMANCE OF MORGAN'S ROUGH-RIDERS

THE RAID, THE CAPTURE, AND THE ESCAPE

I. THE RAID

BY BASIL W. DUKE

IN the summer of 1863, when, at Tullahoma, Tennessee, General Bragg's army was menaced by superior numbers in flank and rear, he determined to send a body of cavalry into Kentucky, which should operate upon Rosecrans's communications between Nashville and Louisville, break the railroads, capture or threaten all the minor depots of supplies, intercept and defeat all detachments not too strong to be engaged, and keep the enemy so on the alert in his own rear that he would lose or neglect his opportunity to embarrass or endanger the march of the army when its retrograde movement began. He even hoped that a part of the hostile forces before him might be thus detained long enough to prevent their participation in the battle which he expected to fight when he had crossed the Tennessee.

The officer whom he selected to accomplish this diversion was General John H. Morgan, whose division of mounted riflemen was well fitted for the work in hand. Equal in courage, dash, and discipline to the other fine cavalry commands which General Bragg had at his disposal, it had passed a longer apprenticeship in expeditionary service than had any other. Its rank and file was of that mettle which finds its natural element in active and audacious enterprise, and was yet thrilled with the fire of youth; for there were few men in the division over twenty-five years of age. It was imbued with the spirit of its commander, and confided in his skill and fortune; no endeavor was deemed impossible or even hazardous when he led. It was inured to constant,

GENERAL JOHN H. MORGAN.

almost daily, combat with the enemy, of all arms and under every possible contingency. During its four years of service the 2d Kentucky Cavalry, of which General Morgan was the first colonel, lost sixty-three commissioned officers killed and wounded; Company A of that regiment, of which Morgan was the first captain, losing during the war seventy-five men killed. It had on its muster-roll, from first to last, nearly two hundred and fifty men. The history of this company and regiment was scarcely exceptional in the command.

Morgan was beyond all men adapted to independent command of this nature. His energy never flagged, and his invention was always equal to the emergency. Boldness and caution were united in all that he undertook. He had a most remarkable aptitude for promptly acquiring a knowledge of any country in which he was operating; and as he kept it, so to speak, "in his head," he was enabled easily to extricate himself from difficulties. The celerity with which he marched, the promptness with which he attacked or eluded a foe, intensified the confidence of his followers, and kept his antagonists always in doubt and apprehension.

In his conference with General Bragg, Morgan differed with his chief regarding the full effect of a raid that should not be extended beyond the Ohio. General Bragg desired it to be confined to Kentucky. He gave Morgan *carte blanche* to go where he pleased in that State and stay as long as he pleased; suggesting, among other things, that he capture Louisville. Morgan urged that while by such a raid he might so divert to himself the attention of General Henry M. Judah and the cavalry of Rosecrans that they would not molest General Bragg's retreat, he could do nothing, in this way, in behalf of the other equally important feature of the plan — the detention of troops that would otherwise strengthen Rosecrans in the decisive battle to be fought south of

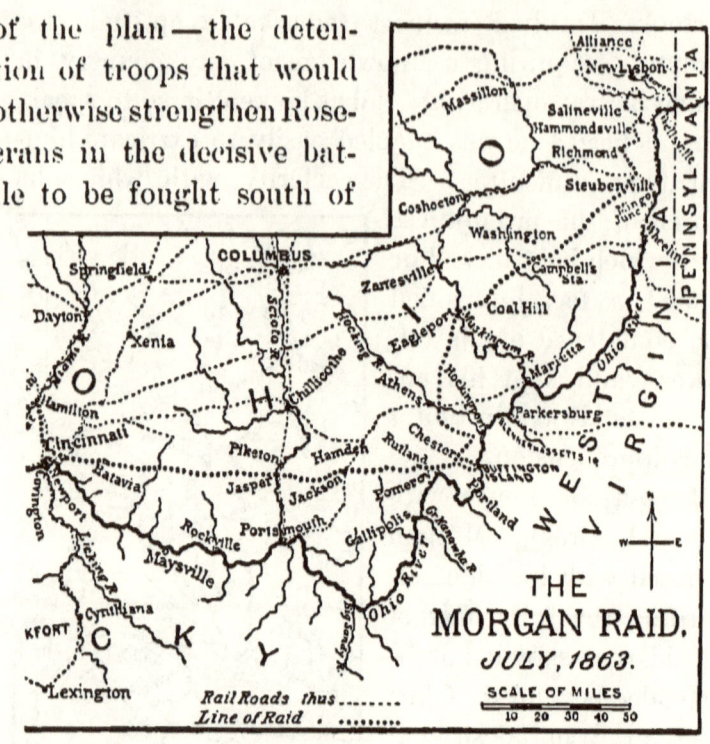

the Tennessee. He contended, moreover, that a raid into Indiana and Ohio, the more especially as important political elections were pending there, would cause troops to be withdrawn from Rosecrans and Burnside for the protection of those States. But General Bragg refused permission to cross the Ohio, and instructed Morgan to make the raid as originally designed.

Some weeks previous to this conference, by Morgan's direction I had sent competent men to examine the fords of the upper Ohio. He had even then contemplated such an expedition. It had long been his conviction that the Confederacy could maintain the struggle only by transferring hostilities and waging war, whenever opportunity offered, on Northern soil. Upon his return from this interview he told me what had been discussed, and what were General Bragg's instructions. He said that he meant to disobey them; that the emergency, he believed, justified disobedience. He was resolved to cross the Ohio River and invade Indiana and Ohio. His command would probably be captured, he said; but in no other way could he give substantial aid to the army. General Bragg had directed Morgan to detail two thousand men for the expedition. From the two brigades commanded respectively by myself and Colonel Adam R. Johnson, Morgan selected twenty-four hundred and sixty of the best-mounted and most effective. He took with him four pieces of artillery—two 3-inch Parrotts, attached to the First Brigade, and two 12-pounder howitzers, attached to the Second.

I should state that Morgan had thoroughly planned the raid before he marched from Tennessee. He meant to cross the Cumberland in the vicinity of Burkesville, and to march directly across Kentucky to the nearest point at which he could reach the Ohio west of Louisville, so closely approaching Louisville as to compel belief that he meant to attempt its capture. Turning to the right after entering Indiana, and marching as nearly due east as possible, he would reduce to a minimum the distance necessary to be covered, and yet threaten and alarm the population of the two States as completely as by penetrating deeply into them; more so, indeed, for pursuing this line he would reach the immediate vicinity of Cincinnati and excite fears for the safety of that city. While he intended to prolong the raid to the uttermost, he proposed to be at no time far from the Ohio, so that he might avail himself of an opportunity to recross. On reaching the borders of Pennsylvania, he intended, if General Lee should be in that State, to make every effort to join him; failing in that, to make his escape through West Virginia. Information he had gotten about the fords of the upper Ohio had induced him to indicate Buffington's Island as the point where he would attempt to recross that stream. He deemed the passage of the Cumberland one of the four chief difficulties of the expedition that might prove really dangerous and insuperable; the other three were the passage of the Ohio, the circuit around Cincinnati, and the recrossing of the Ohio.

Before noon on the 2d of July my brigade began to cross the Cumberland at Burkesville and at Scott's Ferry, two miles higher up the stream. The river, swollen by heavy and long-continued rains, was pouring down a volume of water which overspread its banks and rushed with a velocity that seemed to defy any attempt to stem it. Two or three canoes lashed together and two small flats served to transport the men and the field-pieces, while the horses were made to swim. Many of them were swept far down by the boiling flood. This process was necessarily slow, as well as precarious. Colonel Johnson, whose brigade was crossing at Turkey Neck Bend, several miles below Burkesville, was scarcely so well provided with the means of ferriage as myself. About 3 P. M. the enemy began to threaten both brigades. Had these demonstrations been made earlier, and vigorously, we could not have gotten over the river. Fortunately by this time we had taken over the 6th Kentucky and 9th Tennessee of my brigade—aggregating nearly six hundred men—and also the two pieces of artillery. These regiments were moved beyond Burkesville and placed in a position which served all the purposes of an ambuscade. When the enemy approached, one or two volleys caused his column to recoil in confusion. General Morgan instantly charged it with Quirk's scouts and some companies of the 9th Tennessee, and not only prevented it from rallying, but drove it all the way back to Marrowbone, entering the encampment there with the troops he was pursuing in a pell-mell dash. He was soon driven back, however, by the enemy's infantry and artillery.

The effect of this blow was to keep the enemy quiet for the rest of the day and night. The forces threatening Colonel Johnson were also withdrawn, and we both accomplished the passage of the river without further molestation. That night the division marched out on the Columbia road and encamped about two miles from Burkesville. On the next day Judah concentrated the three brigades of his cavalry command in that region, while orders were sent to all the other Federal detachments in Kentucky to close in upon our line of march.

General Bragg had sent with the expedition a large party of commissaries of subsistence, who were directed to collect cattle north of the Cumberland and drive them, guarded by one of our regiments, to Tullahoma. I have never understood how he expected us to be able, under the circumstances, to collect the cattle, or the foragers to drive them out. The commissaries did not attempt to carry out their instructions, but followed us the entire distance and pulled up in prison. They were gallant fellows and made no complaint of danger or hardship, seeming rather to enjoy it.

THE FARMER FROM CALFKILLER CREEK.

There was one case, however, which excited universal pity. An old farmer and excellent man, who lived near Sparta, had accompanied us to Burkesville; that is, he meant to go no farther, and thought we would not. He wished to procure a barrel of salt, as the supply of that commodity was exhausted in his part of the country. He readily purchased the salt, but learned, to his consternation, that the march to Burkesville was a mere preliminary canter. He was confronted with the alternative of going on a dangerous raid or of returning alone through a region swarming with the fierce bushwhackers of "Tinker Dave" Beattie, who never gave quarter to Confederate soldier or Southern sympathizer. He knew that if he fell into their hands they would pickle him with his own salt. So this old man sadly yet wisely resolved to follow the fortunes of Morgan. He made the grand tour, was hurried along day after day through battle and ambush, dragged night after night on the remorseless march, ferried over the broad Ohio under fire of the militia and gunboats, and lodged at last in a "loathsome dungeon." On one occasion, in Ohio, when the home guards were peppering us in rather livelier fashion than usual, he said to Captain C. H. Morgan, with tears in his voice: "I sw'ar if I would n't give all the salt in Kaintucky to stand once more safe and sound on the banks of Calfkiller Creek."

Pushing on before dawn of the 3d, we reached Columbia in the afternoon. The place was occupied by a detachment of Colonel Frank Wolford's brigade, which was quickly driven out. Encamping that evening some eight miles from Columbia, we could hear all night the ringing of the axes near Green River bridge, on the road from Columbia to Campbellsville. Three or four hundred of the 25th Michigan Infantry were stationed at the bridge to protect it;

GENERAL DUKE TESTS THE PIES.

but the commander, Colonel Orlando H. Moore, deliberately quitting the elaborate stockade erected near the bridge,—in which nine officers out of ten would have remained, but where we could have shelled him into surrender without losing a man ourselves,—selected one of the strongest natural positions I ever saw, and fortified it skilfully although simply. The Green River makes here an immense horseshoe sweep, with the bridge at the toe of the horseshoe; and more than a mile south of it was the point where Colonel Moore elected to make his fight. The river there wound back so nearly upon its previous course that the peninsula, or "neck," was scarcely a hundred yards wide. This narrow neck was also very short, the river bending almost immediately to the west again. At that time it was thickly covered with trees and undergrowth, and Colonel Moore, felling the heaviest timber, had constructed a formidable abatis across the narrowest part of it. Just in front of the abatis there was open ground for perhaps two hundred yards. South of the open was a deep ravine. The road ran on the east side of the cleared place, and the banks of the river were high and precipitous. The center of the open space rose into a swell, sloping gently away both to the north and south. On the crest of the swell Moore had thrown up a slight earthwork, which was manned when we approached. An officer was promptly despatched with a flag to demand his surrender. Colonel Moore responded that an officer of the United States ought not to surrender on the Fourth of July, and he must therefore decline. Captain "Ed" Byrne had planted one of the Parrott guns about six hundred yards from the earthwork, and on the return of the bearer of the flag opened fire, probing the work with a round shot. One man in the trench was killed by this shot, and the others ran back to the abatis.

Colonel Johnson, whose brigade was in advance, immediately dashed forward with the 3d and 11th Kentucky to attack the main position. Artillery could not be used, for the guns could bear upon the abatis only from the crest of which I have spoken, and if posted there the cannoneers, at the very short range, would not have been able to serve their pieces. The position could be won only by direct assault. The men rushed up to the fallen timber, but became entangled in the network of trunks and branches, and were shot down while trying to climb over or push through them. I reinforced Johnson with a part of Smith's regiment, the 5th Kentucky, but the jam and confusion incident to moving in so circumscribed an area and through the dense undergrowth broke the force of the charge. The enemy was quite numerous enough to defend a line so short and strong and perfectly protected on both flanks. We had not more than six hundred men actually engaged, and the fighting lasted not longer than fifteen or twenty minutes. Our loss was about ninety, nearly as many killed as wounded. Afterward we learned that Colonel Moore's loss was six killed and twenty-three wounded. When General Morgan ordered the attack he was not aware of the strength of the position; nor had he anticipated a resistance so spirited and so skilfully planned. He reluctantly drew off without another assault, convinced that to capture the abatis and its defenders would cost him half his command. Among the killed were Colonel D. W. Chenault and Captain Alexander Treble of the 11th Kentucky, Lieutenant Robert Cowan of the 3d, and Major Thomas Y. Brent, Jr., and Lieutenants Holloway and Ferguson of the 5th. These officers were all killed literally at the muzzles of the rifles.

Colonel Moore's position might easily have been avoided; indeed, we passed around it immediately afterward, crossing the river at a ford about two miles below the bridge. Morgan assailed it merely in accordance with his habitual policy when advancing of attacking all in his path except very superior forces.

On the same afternoon Captain William M. Magenis, assistant adjutant-general of the division, a valuable officer, was murdered by a Captain Murphy, whom he had placed under arrest for robbing a citizen. Murphy made his escape from the guard two or three days subsequently, just as the court-martial which was to have tried him was convening.

On the morning of July 5th the column reached Lebanon, which was garrisoned by the 20th Kentucky Infantry, commanded by Colonel Charles S. Hanson. The 8th and 9th Michigan Cavalry and the 11th Michigan Battery, under command of Colonel James I. David, were approaching by the Danville road to reinforce the garrison, necessitating a large detachment to observe them. Morgan's demand for surrender having been refused, artillery fire was directed upon the railroad depot and other buildings in which the enemy had established himself; but, as the Federals endured it with great firmness, it became necessary to carry the town by assault. Our loss was some forty in killed and wounded, including several excellent officers. One death universally deplored was that of the General's brother, Lieutenant Thomas H. Morgan. He was a bright, handsome, and very gallant lad of nineteen, the favorite of the division. He was killed in front of the 2d Kentucky in the charge upon the depot. The Federal loss was three killed and sixteen wounded, and three hundred and eighty were prisoners.

Without delay we passed through Springfield and Bardstown, crossing the Louisville and Nashville Railroad at Lebanon Junction, thirty miles from Louisville, on the evening of the 6th. At Springfield two companies of about ninety men were sent toward Harrodsburg and Danville to occupy the attention of the Federal cavalry in that quarter. From Bardstown, Captain W. C. Davis, acting assistant adjutant-general of the First Brigade, was sent with a detachment of one hundred and thirty men to scout in the vicinity of Louisville, to produce the impression that the city was about to be attacked, and to divert attention from the passage of the Ohio by the main body at Brandenburg. He was instructed to cross the river somewhere east of Louisville and to rejoin the column on its line of march through Indiana. He executed the first part of the program perfectly, but was unable to get across the river. Tapping the wires at Lebanon Junction, we learned from intercepted despatches that the garrison at Louisville was much alarmed, and in expectation of an immediate attack.

The detachments I have just mentioned, with some smaller ones previously sent off on similar service, aggregated not less than two hundred and sixty men permanently separated from the division; which, with a loss in killed and wounded, in Kentucky, of about one hundred and fifty, had reduced our effective strength, at the Ohio, by more than four hundred.

The rapid and constant marching already began to tell upon both horses and men, but we reached the Ohio at Brandenburg at 9 A. M. on the 8th. Captains Samuel Taylor and H. C. Meriwether of the 10th Kentucky had been sent forward the day before, with their companies, to capture steamboats. We found them in possession of two large craft. One had been surprised at the wharf, and steaming out on her, they had captured the other. Preparations for crossing were begun; but, just as the first boat was about to push off, an unexpected musketry fire was opened from the Indiana side by a party of home-guards collected behind some houses and haystacks. They were in pursuit of Captain Thomas H. Hines, who had that morning returned from Indiana to Kentucky, after having undertaken a brief expedition of his own. This fire did no harm, the river here being eight hundred or a thousand yards wide. But in a few minutes the bright gleam of a field-piece spouted through the low-hanging mist on the farther bank. Its shell pitched into a group near the wharf, severely wounding Captain W. H. Wilson, acting quartermaster of the First Brigade. Several shots from this piece followed in quick succession, but it was silenced by Lieutenant Lawrence with his Parrotts. The 2d Kentucky and 9th Tennessee were speedily ferried over without their horses, and forming under the bluff

HOSPITALITIES OF THE FARM

they advanced upon the militia, which had retired to a wooded ridge some six hundred yards from the river-bank, abandoning the gun. The two regiments were moving across some open ground, toward the ridge, sustaining no loss from the volleys fired at them, and the boats had scarcely returned for further service when a more formidable enemy appeared. A gunboat, the *Elk*, steamed rapidly round the bend, and began firing alternately upon the troops in the town and those already across. The situation was now extremely critical. We could not continue the ferriage while this little vixen remained, for one well-directed shot would have sent either of the boats to the bottom. Delay was exceedingly hazardous, affording the enemy opportunity to cut off the regiments we had already sent over, and giving the cavalry in pursuit of us time to come up. If forced to give up the attempt to cross the river, we must also abandon our comrades on the other side. So every piece of artillery was planted and opened on the gunboat, and after an hour or two of vigorous cannonading she was driven off. By midnight all our troops were over.

About noon of the 9th the column reached the little town of Corydon, Indiana, which proved not nearly so gentle as its name. Our advance-guard, commanded by Colonel R. C. Morgan, found a body of militia there, ensconced behind stout barricades of fence rails, stretching for some distance on each side of the road. Colonel Morgan charged the barricade, his horses could not leap it, the militia stood resolutely, and he lost sixteen men. A few dismounted skirmishers thrown upon the flanks, and a shot or two from one of the pieces which accompanied the advance-guard, quickly dispersed them, however, and we entered the town without further resistance.

Our progress, quite rapid in Kentucky, was now accelerated, and we were habitually twenty-one hours out of the twenty-four in the saddle, very frequently not halting at night or going into camp at all. For the first three or four days we saw nothing of the inhabitants save in their character as militia, when they forced themselves on our attention much more frequently than we desired. The houses were entirely deserted. Often we found the kitchen fire blazing, the keys hanging in the cupboard lock, and the chickens sauntering about the yard with a confidence which proved that they had never before seen soldiers.

As the first scare wore off, however, we found the women and children remaining at home, while the men went to the muster. When a thirsty cavalryman rode up to a house to inquire for buttermilk, he was generally met by a buxom dame, with a half-dozen or more small children peeping out from her voluminous skirts, who, in response to a question about the "old man," would say: "The men hev all gone to the 'rally'; you 'll see 'em soon." We experienced little difficulty in procuring food for man and horse. Usually upon our raids it was much easier to obtain meat than bread. But in Indiana and Ohio we always found bread ready baked at every house. In Ohio, on more than one occasion, in deserted houses we found pies, hot from the oven, displayed upon tables conveniently spread. The first time that I witnessed this sort of hospitality was when I rode up to a house where a party of my men were standing around a table garnished as I have described, eyeing the pies hungrily, but showing no disposition to touch them. I asked, in astonishment, why they were so abstinent. One of them replied that they feared the pies might be poisoned. I was quite sure, on the contrary, that they were intended as a propitiatory offering. I have always been fond of pies,—these were of luscious apples,—so I made the spokesman hand me one of the largest, and proceeded to eat it. The men watched me vigilantly for two or three minutes, and then, as I seemed much better after my repast, they took hold ravenously.

The severe marching made an exchange of horses a necessity, though as a rule the horses we took were very inferior to the Kentucky and Tennessee stock we had brought with us, and which had generally a large infusion of thoroughbred blood. The horses we impressed were for the most part heavy, sluggish beasts, barefooted and grass-fed, and gave out after a day or two, sometimes in a few hours. A strong provost guard, under Major Steele of the 3d Kentucky, had been organized to prevent the two practices most prejudicial to discipline and efficiency—straggling and pillage. There were very good reasons, independent of the provost guard, why the men should not straggle far from the line of march; but the well-filled stores and gaudy shop-windows of the Indiana and Ohio towns seemed to stimulate, in men accustomed to impoverished and unpretentious Dixie, the propensity to appropriate beyond limit or restraint. I had never before seen anything like this disposition to plunder.

Our perilous situation only seemed to render the men more reckless. At the same time, anything more ludicrous than the manner in which they indulged their predatory tastes can scarcely be imagined. The weather was intensely warm,— the hot July sun burned the earth to powder, and we were breathing superheated dust,— yet one man rode for three days with seven pairs of skates slung about his neck; another loaded himself with sleigh-bells. A large chafing-dish, a medium-sized Dutch clock, a green glass decanter with goblets to match, a bag of horn buttons, a chandelier, and a bird-cage containing three canaries were some of the articles I saw borne off and jealously fondled. The officers usually waited a reasonable period, until the novelty had worn off, and then had this rubbish thrown away. Baby shoes and calico, however, were the staple articles of appropriation. A fellow would procure a bolt of calico, carry it carefully for a day or two, then cast it aside and get another.

From Corydon our route was *via* Salem, Vienna, Lexington, Paris, Vernon, Dupont, and Sumanville to Harrison, near the Ohio State line and twenty-five miles from Cincinnati. Detachments were sent to Madison, Versailles, and other points, to burn bridges, bewilder and confuse those before and behind us, and keep bodies of military stationary that might otherwise give trouble. All were drawn in before we reached Harrison. At this point Morgan began demonstrations intended to convey the impression that he would cross the Cincinnati, Hamilton, and Dayton Railroad at Hamilton. He had always anticipated difficulty in getting over this road; fearing that the troops from

Kentucky would be concentrated at or near Cincinnati, and that every effort would be made to intercept him there. If these troops lined the railroad and were judiciously posted, he knew it would be extremely difficult to elude them or cut his way through them. He believed that if he could pass this ordeal safely, the success of the expedition would be assured, unless the river should be so high that the boats would be able to transport troops to intercept him at the upper fords.

After remaining at Harrison two or three hours, and sending detachments in the direction of Hamilton, he moved with the entire column on the Hamilton road. But as soon as he was clear of the town, he cut the telegraph-wires — previously left intact with the hope that they might be used to convey intelligence of his apparent movement toward Hamilton — and, turning across the country, gained the direct road to Cincinnati. He hoped that, deceived by his demonstrations at Harrison, the larger part of the troops at Cincinnati would be sent to Hamilton, and that it would be too late to recall them when his movement toward Cincinnati was discovered. He trusted that those remaining would be drawn into the city, under the impression that he meant to attack, leaving the way clear for his rapid transit. He has been criticized for not attempting the capture of Cincinnati, but he had no mind to involve his handful of wearied men in a labyrinth of streets. We felt very much more at home amid rural surroundings. But if he had taken Cincinnati, and had safely crossed the river there, the raid would have been so much briefer, and its principal

LOOKING FOR THE FOOTPRINTS OF THE VAN.

object to that extent defeated by the release of the troops pursuing us.

We reached the environs of Cincinnati about ten o'clock at night, and were not clear of them until after daybreak. My brigade was marching in the rear, and the guides were with General Morgan in the front. The continual straggling of some companies in the rear of Johnson's brigade caused me to become separated from the remainder of the column by a wide gap, and I was for some time entirely ignorant of what direction I should take. The night was pitch-dark, and I was compelled to light torches and seek the track of the column by the foam dropped from the mouths of the horses and the dust kicked up by their feet. At every halt which this groping search necessitated, scores of tired men would fall asleep and drop out of their saddles. Daylight appeared after we had crossed all of the principal suburban roads, and were near the Little Miami Railroad. I never welcomed the fresh, invigorating air of morning more gratefully. That afternoon we reached Williamsburg, twenty-eight miles east of Cincinnati.

The Ohio militia were more numerous and aggressive than those of Indiana. We had frequent skirmishes with them daily, and although hundreds were captured, they resumed operations as soon as they were turned loose. What excited in us more astonishment than all else we saw were the crowds of able-bodied men. The contrast with the South, drained of adult males to recruit her armies, was striking, and suggestive of anything but confidence on our part in the result of the struggle.

At Piketon we learned that Vicksburg had fallen, and that General Lee, having been repulsed at Gettysburg, had retreated across the Potomac. Under the circumstances this information was peculiarly disheartening. As we approached Pomeroy the militia began to embarrass our march by felling trees and erecting barricades across the roads. In passing near that town we were assailed by regular troops,—as we called the volunteers, in contradistinction to the militia,—and forced a passage only by some sharp fighting. At 1 P. M. on the 18th we reached Chester, eighteen miles from Buffington's Island. A halt here of nearly two hours proved disastrous, as it caused us to arrive at the river after nightfall, and delayed any attempt at crossing until the next morning. Morgan thoroughly appreciated the importance of crossing the river at once, but it was impossible. The darkness was intense, we were ignorant of the ford and without guides, and were encumbered with nearly two hundred wounded, whom we were unwilling to abandon. By instruction I placed the 5th and 6th Kentucky in position to attack, as soon as day broke, an earthwork commanding the ford, and which we learned was mounted with two guns and manned by three hundred infantry. At dawn I moved upon the work, and found it had been evacuated and the guns thrown over the bluff. Pressing on a few hundred yards to reconnoiter the Pomeroy road, we suddenly encountered the enemy. It proved to be General Judah's advance. The 5th and 6th Kentucky instantly attacked and dispersed it, taking a piece of artillery and forty or fifty prisoners, and inflicting some loss in killed and wounded.

The position in which we found ourselves, now that we had light enough to examine the ground, was anything but favorable. The valley we had entered, about a mile long and perhaps eight hundred yards wide at its southern extremity,—the river running here nearly due north and south,—gradually narrows, as the ridge which is its western boundary closely approaches the river-bank, until it becomes a mere ravine. The Chester road enters the valley at a point about equidistant from either end. As the 5th Kentucky fell back that it might be aligned on the 6th Kentucky, across the southern end of the valley, into which Judah's whole force was now pouring, it was charged by the 8th and 9th Michigan and a detachment of the 5th Indiana. A part of the 5th Kentucky was cut off by this charge, the gun we had taken was recaptured, and our Parrotts also fell into the hands of the enemy. They were so clogged with dust, however, as to be almost unserviceable, and their ammunition was expended. Bringing up a part of the 2d Kentucky, I succeeded in checking and driving back the regiments that first bore down on us, but they were quickly reinforced and immediately returned to the attack. In the mean time Colonel Johnson's videttes on the Chester road had been driven in, and the cavalry under Hobson, which had followed us throughout our long march, deployed on the ridge, and attacked on that side. I sent a courier to General Morgan, advising that he retreat up the river and out of the valley with all the men he could extricate, while Colonel Johnson and I, with the troops already engaged, would endeavor to hold the enemy in check. The action was soon hot from both directions, and the gunboats, steaming up the river abreast of us, commenced shelling vigorously. We were now between three assailants. A sharp artillery fire was opened by each, and the peculiar formation we were compelled to adopt exposed us to a severe cross-fire of small arms.

We were in no condition to make a successful or energetic resistance. The men were worn out and demoralized by the tremendous march, and the fatigue and lack of sleep for the ten days that had elapsed since they had crossed the Ohio. Having had no opportunity to replenish their cartridge-boxes, they were almost destitute of ammunition, and after firing two or three rounds were virtually unarmed. To this fact is attributable the very small loss our assailants sustained. Broken down as we were, if we had been supplied with cartridges we could have piled the ground with Judah's men as they advanced over the open plain into the valley. As the line, seeking to cover the withdrawal of the troops taken off by General Morgan, was rolled back by the repeated charges of the enemy, the stragglers were rushing wildly about the valley, with bolts of calico streaming from their saddles, and changing direction with every shrieking shell. When the rear-guard neared the northern end of the valley,—out of which General Morgan with the greater part of the command had now passed,—and perceived that the only avenue of escape was through a narrow gorge, a general rush was made for it. The Michigan regiments dashed into the mass of fugitives, and the gunboats swept the narrow pass with grape. All order was lost in a wild tide of flight.

About seven hundred were captured here, and perhaps a hundred and twenty killed and wounded. Probably a thousand men got out with General Morgan. Of these some three hundred succeeded in swimming the river at a point twenty miles above Buffington, while many were drowned in the attempt. The arrival of the gunboats prevented others from crossing. General Morgan had gotten nearly over, when, seeing that the bulk of his command must remain on the Ohio side, he returned. For six more days Morgan taxed energy and ingenuity to the utmost to escape the toils. Absolutely exhausted, he surrendered near the Pennsylvania line, on the 26th day of July, with three hundred and sixty-four men.

The expedition was of immediate benefit, since a part of the forces that would otherwise have harassed Bragg's retreat and swollen Rosecrans's muster-roll at Chickamauga were carried by the pursuit of Morgan so far northward that they were kept from participating in that battle.

But Morgan's cavalry was almost destroyed, and his prestige impaired. Much the larger number of the captured men lingered in the Northern prisons until the close of the war. That portion of his command which had remained in Tennessee became disintegrated; the men either were incorporated in other organizations, or, attracted by the fascinations of irregular warfare, were virtually lost to the service. Morgan, after four or five months' imprisonment in the Ohio penitentiary, effected an escape which has scarcely a parallel for ingenuity and daring. He was received in the South enthusiastically. The authorities at Richmond seemed at first to share the popular sympathy and admiration. But it soon became apparent that his infraction of discipline in crossing the Ohio was not forgiven. Placed for a short time in practical command of the Department of Southwestern Virginia, he was given inadequate means for its defense, and bound with instructions which accorded neither with his temperament nor with his situation. The troops he commanded were not, like his old riders, accustomed to his methods, confident in his genius, and devoted to his fortunes. He attempted aggressive operations with his former energy and self-reliance, but not with his former success. He drove out of West Virginia two invading columns, and then made an incursion into the heart of Kentucky—known as his last Kentucky raid—in the hope of anticipating and deterring a movement into his own territory. Very successful at first, this raid ended, too, in disaster. After capturing and dispersing Federal forces in the aggregate much larger than his own, he encountered at Cynthiana a vastly superior force, and was defeated. Two months later, September 4, 1864, he was killed at Greeneville, Tennessee, while advancing to attack the Federal detachments stationed in front of Knoxville.[1]

[1] E. W. Doran of Greeneville. Tenn., gives the following particulars of General Morgan's death:

General Morgan came to Greeneville on September 3, and stationed his troops on a hill overlooking the town from the east, while he and his staff were entertained at the "Williams Mansion," the finest residence in town. At this time Captain Robert C. Carter, in command of a company of Colonel Crawford's regiment, was stationed three or four miles north of the town. He got accurate information of Morgan's whereabouts, and sent a messenger at once to General A. C. Gillem, at Bull's Gap, sixteen miles distant. This message was

The remnant of his old command served during the gloomy winter of 1864–65 in the region where their leader met death, fighting often on the same ground. When Richmond fell, and Lee surrendered, they marched to join Joseph E. Johnston. After his capitulation they were part of the escort that guarded Jefferson Davis in his aimless retreat from Charlotte, and laid down their arms at Woodville, Georgia, by order of John C. Breckinridge, when the armies of the Confederacy were disbanded, and its President became a fugitive.

II. THE CAPTURE

BY ORLANDO B. WILLCOX

WHEN it was known at Indianapolis that General Morgan, with a large force, had crossed the Ohio, the city was panic-stricken. The State had intrusted to John Davis and two other young men of his company, who rode through a fearful storm, picking their way by the lightning-flashes and arriving there some time before midnight. Other messages were probably sent to Gillem that night from Greeneville, but this was the first received. The report usually given in the histories to the effect that Mrs. Joseph Williams carried the news is not correct, as she was known to be in an opposite direction several miles, and knew nothing of the affair. In an hour after the message was delivered Gillem's forces were hurrying on their way to Greeneville, where they arrived about daylight, and surrounded the house where Morgan was. He ran out, without waiting to dress, to conceal himself in the shrubbery and grape arbors, but was seen from the street and shot by Andrew G. Campbell, a private in the 13th Tennessee. Campbell was promoted to a lieutenancy. Morgan's body was afterward secured by his friends and given decent burial. But little firing was done by either army; and after Morgan was killed his forces marched out of town while the Union forces marched in, in easy range of each other, yet not a shot was fired on either side.

been literally depleted of troops to assist Kentucky, and everybody knew it. The very worst was apprehended—that railways would be cut up, passenger and freight trains robbed, bridges and depots burned, our arsenal pillaged, two thousand Confederate prisoners at Camp Morton liberated, and Jeffersonville, with all its Government stores, and possibly Indianapolis itself, destroyed.

Nor was this all. It had been reported, and partly believed, as afterward indeed proved to be the fact, that the State was literally undermined with rebel sympathizers banded together in secret organizations. The coming of Morgan had been looked for, and his progress through Kentucky watched with considerable anxiety. It was gloomily predicted that hundreds, perhaps thousands, of "Knights of the Golden Circle" and of "Sons of Liberty" would flock to his standard and endeavor to carry the State over to the Confederacy.

Morgan probably had fair reason to believe that his ranks would be at least largely recruited in the southern counties of Indiana. The governor of Indiana, Oliver P. Morton, went to work with all his tremendous energy and indomitable will, in the face of the greatest opposition that had been encountered in any Northern State, amounting, just before, almost to open rebellion. He proclaimed martial law, though not in express terms, and ordered out the "Legion," or militia, and called upon the loyal citizens of the State to enroll themselves as minute-men, to organize and report for arms and for martial duty. Thousands responded to the call within twenty-four hours—many within two hours.[1] Everything possible was done by telegraph, until the lines were cut. Some arms were found in the State Arsenal, and more, with accoutrements and ammunition, together with whole batteries of artillery, were procured from Chicago and St. Louis.

The disposition of the State levies that came thronging in was left to me as fast as they were armed. The three great junctions of the Ohio and Mississippi Railroad in Indiana, over which troops and supplies were shipped from all points to Rosecrans at Chattanooga,—viz., Mitchell, Seymour, and Vernon,—were first to be made secure; for surely Morgan must have some military objectives, and these appeared to be the most likely. The westerly junction was Mitchell. This was quickly occupied and guarded by General James Hughes, with Legion men, reinforced by the new organizations rising in that quarter. Seymour was the most central, and lay directly on the road to Cincinnati and Indianapolis from Louisville; and at Seymour a brigade was assembled from the center of the State, with General John Love, a skilful old army officer, to command it, with instructions to have an eye to Vernon likewise. To this last point Burnside ordered a battery from Cincinnati; and what few

---

[1] According to the report of the adjutant-general of Indiana, 30,000 militia assembled within thirty-six hours, and about the time Morgan was leaving the state 65,000 men were in the field. In Ohio, according to a report made to the adjutant-general, 55,000 militia turned out; many of them refused pay, yet $232,000 were disbursed for services during the raid. It would appear, therefore, that 120,000 militia took the field against Morgan, in addition to the three brigades of General Judah's United States cavalry.—EDITOR.

troops I had in Michigan, though half organized, came down to Vernon and to General Love. Besides these thus rendezvoused, the people of the southern counties were called upon to bushwhack the enemy, to obstruct roads, to guard trains, bridges, etc., and to make themselves generally useful and pestiferous.

Our militia first came in contact with the enemy opposite Brandenburg, where he crossed; but it made the stand at Corydon Junction, where the road runs between two abrupt hills, across which Colonel Lewis Jordan threw up some light intrenchments. Morgan's advance attempted to ride over these "rail-piles" roughshod, but lost some twenty troopers unhorsed. They brought up their reserve and artillery, flanked, and finally surrounded Colonel Jordan, who, after an hour's resolute resistance, surrendered.

This gave the raiders the town, and the citizens the first taste of Morgan's style, which somewhat disgusted the numerous class of Southern sympathizers. The shops were given up to plunder, and the ladies levied on for meals for the whole command.

Throwing out columns in various directions, Morgan pushed for Mitchell, where no doubt he expected to cut the Ohio and Mississippi Railroad, got as far as Salem in that direction, captured or dispersed a few squads of badly armed minute-men who were guarding depots and bridges, which he burned, and doubtless hearing from his scouts, sent out in citizens' clothes, of Hughes's force collected at Mitchell, he discreetly turned off northeastward, apparently aiming next for Seymour. This I heard with great satisfaction.

The panic at Indianapolis began to subside. Still I

felt uneasy for Seymour, as I next heard of Morgan at Vienna, where he tapped the telegraph-lines and learned what he could of all our plans to catch him. He came within nine miles of Seymour. General Love sent out a reconnaissance of sharpshooters under Colonel C. V. De Land, with a couple of field-pieces. They found that Morgan had turned off eastward. Love divined his object, and started De Land and two Indiana regiments of militia for Vernon. Here Morgan next turned up, planted his Parrotts, and demanded surrender. He was defied until Love's arrival with the rest of his militia, and then he swept off in a hurry from Vernon, followed by our men, who captured his pickets and rear-guard, but who, having no cavalry, were soon outmarched.

Morgan secured a great advantage by seizing all the horses within reach,[1] leaving none for the militia or for General E. H. Hobson, which enabled him to gain on his pursuers, and he would then have left Hobson far out of sight but for the home guard, who obstructed the roads somewhat, and bushwhacked his men from every hedge, hill, or tree, when it could be done. But the trouble was that we could not attack him with sufficient organized numbers.

After he left Vernon we felt safe at Indianapolis. "Defensive sites" were abandoned, and the banks

---

[1] General J. M. Schackelford says in his official report: "Our pursuit was much retarded by the enemy's burning all the bridges in our front. He had every advantage. His system of horse-stealing was perfect. He would despatch men from the head of each regiment, on each side of the road, to go five miles into the country, seizing every horse, and then fall in at the rear of the column. In this way he swept the country for ten miles of all the horses."—EDITOR.

brought back their deposits which they had sent off by express to Chicago and the North. Some fears, or hopes, were entertained as to Madison, toward which Morgan next bent his way — fears for the safety of that city, and hopes that, with the help of Judah's troops and the gunboats now on the way up the river, we might put an end to the raid. From Indianapolis we started General Lew Wallace with a good brigade of minute-men, and with high hopes that at either Madison or Lawrenceburg, farther up the river, he might "capture them." The people ahead were asked by telegraph to coöperate. But after going down that line as far as Dupont, Morgan turned northeast for Versailles, where we next heard of him threatening the Cincinnati and Indianapolis Railway. This was a nice bit of work. He baffled all our calculations, and did some damage on both the Ohio and Mississippi and Cincinnati railroads, sending off flying columns in a dozen directions at a time for the purpose, as well as to throw Hobson off the scent. Some of these columns looked like traveling circuses adorned with useless plunder and an excess of clowns. Thus they went through Pierceville and Milan to Harrison, on White River, and on the Ohio line. Here Hobson's advance came upon them, but unfortunately it paused to plant artillery, instead of dashing across the bridge and engaging the raiders until the main body should arrive. This lost us the bridge, which was burned before our eyes, and many hours' delay, marching round by the ford. Their next demonstration was toward Hamilton. Here there was a fine railway bridge over the Big Miami. Hobson followed in such close pursuit through New

Baltimore, Glendale, and Miamiville that the raiders did little damage. Their attempt to burn a bridge at Miamiville was repulsed by the home guard. My last troops were despatched from Indianapolis to head them off at Hamilton, after five hours' delay caused by the intoxication of their commander. His successor in command was General Hascall, who swore like a trooper to find himself "just in time to be too late." He proceeded through Hamilton, Ohio, as far as Loveland. But Morgan had sent only a detachment toward Hamilton to divert attention from Cincinnati, toward which he made a rapid march with his whole united force.

Governor Tod of Ohio had already called out the militia and proclaimed martial law. He raised men enough, but Burnside had to organize and arm them. Morgan found the great city guarded, but he passed through the very suburbs by a night march around it, unmolested. He crossed the Little Miami Railroad at daylight, and came north in sight of Camp Dennison, where Colonel Neff half armed his convalescents, threw out pickets, dug rifle-pits, and threw up intrenchments. His fiery old veterans saved a railway bridge, and actually captured a lieutenant and others before they sheered off and went some ten miles northward to Williamsburg. From that point they seemed to be steering for the great bend of the Ohio at Pomeroy.

In the vicinity of Cincinnati, Colonel W. P. Sanders, the splendid raider of East Tennessee, came up from Kentucky with some Michigan cavalry, and joined Hobson in pursuit, and these were about the only fresh horses in the chase. Sanders had come by steamer, and, landing at Cincinnati, had been thrown out from there, it was hoped, ahead of Morgan, who, however, was too quick for him. They met later on.

Under the good management of Colonel A. V. Kautz in advance, with his brigade, and of Sanders, the men now marched more steadily and gained ground. Kautz had observed how the other brigade commanders had lost distance and blown their horses by following false leads, halting and closing up rapidly at the frequent reports of "enemy in front," and by stopping to plant artillery. Marching in his own way, at a steady walk, his brigade forming the rear-guard, he had arrived at Batavia two hours before the main body, that had been " cavorting round the country " all day, "misled by two citizen guides"—possibly Morgan's own men.

Not stopping to draw the rations sent out to him from Cincinnati, Hobson urged his jaded horses through Brown, Adams, and Pike counties, now under the lead of Kautz, and reached Jasper, on the Scioto, at midnight of the 16th, Morgan having passed there at sundown. The next day they raced through Jackson. On the 18th, Hobson, at Rutland, learned that Morgan had been turned off by the militia at Pomeroy, and had taken the Chester road for Portland and the fords of the Ohio. The chase became animated. Our troopers made a march of fifty miles that day and still had twenty-five miles to reach Chester. They arrived there without a halt at eleven at night, and had still fifteen miles to reach the ford. They kept on, and at dawn of the 19th struck the enemy's pickets. Two miles out from Portland, Morgan was brought to bay —and not by Hobson alone. First came the militia, then came Judah. His division had pushed up the river in steamers parallel with Morgan's course. Lieutenant John O'Neil, afterward of Fenian fame, with a troop of Indiana cavalry, kept up the touch on Morgan's right flank by a running fight, stinging it at every vulnerable point, and reporting Morgan's course to Judah in the neck-and-neck race. Aided by the local militia, O'Neil now dashed ahead and fearlessly skirmished with the enemy's flankers from every coign of vantage. He reached the last descent to the river-bottom near Buffington Bar, and near the historical Blennerhasset's Island, early on the morning of the 19th.

The Ohio River was up. It had risen unexpectedly. But here Morgan must cross, if at all. It could not be forded by night, when he got here. He tried the ford at Blennerhasset. Failing in this, his men collected flatboats, and set to work calking them, meantime sending a party to Buffington Bar, where they found a small earthwork and captured its guard; and these things delayed them until morning. General Judah attempted a reconnaissance, resulting in a fight, which he describes as follows in his report:

> Before leaving Pomeroy I despatched a courier to General Hobson, apprising him of my direction, and requesting him to press the enemy's rear with all the forces he could bring up. Traveling all night, I reached the last descent to the river-bottom at Buffington Bar at 5.30 A. M. on the 19th. Here, halting my force, and placing my artillery in a commanding position, I determined to make a reconnaissance in person, for the purpose of ascertaining if a report

just made to me — that the gunboats had left on a previous evening, the home guards had retreated, and that the enemy had been crossing all night — was true. A very dense fog enveloped everything, confining the view of surrounding objects to a radius of about fifty yards. I was accompanied by a small advance-guard, my escort, and one piece of Henshaw's battery, a section of which, under Captain Henshaw, I had ordered to join my force. I advanced slowly and cautiously along a road leading toward the river. . . . when my little force found itself enveloped on three sides — front and both flanks — by three regiments, dismounted, and led by Colonel Basil [W.] Duke, just discernible through the fog, at a distance of from fifty to a hundred yards. This force, as I afterward learned, had been disposed for the capture of the home guards, intrenched on the bank of the river. To use Colonel Duke's own expression after his capture, "He could not have been more surprised at the presence of my force if it had been dropped from the clouds." As soon as discovered the enemy opened a heavy fire, advancing so rapidly that before the piece of artillery could be brought into battery it was captured, as were also Captain R. C. Kise, my assistant adjutant-general, Captain Grafton, volunteer aide-de-camp, and between twenty and thirty of my men. Two privates were killed, Major McCook (since dead), paymaster and volunteer aide-de-camp,[1] Lieutenant F. G. Price, aide-de-camp, and ten men were wounded. Searching in vain for an opening through which to charge and temporarily beat back the enemy, I was compelled to fall back upon the main body, which I rapidly brought up into position, and opened a rapid and beautifully accurate artillery fire from the pieces of the 5th Indiana upon a battery of two pieces which the enemy had opened upon me, as well as upon his deployed dismounted force in line. Obstructing fences prevented a charge by my cavalry. In less than half an hour the enemy's lines were broken and in retreat. The advance of my artillery, and a charge of cavalry made by Lieutenant O'Neil, 5th Indiana Cavalry, with

[1] Major Daniel McCook, father of the famous fighting family, who pushed himself in, against remonstrance, to find the slayer of his son General Robert L. McCook, reported to be with Morgan.

only fifty men, converted his retreat into a rout, and drove him upon General Hobson's forces, which had engaged him upon the other road. His prisoners, the piece of artillery lost by me, all of his own artillery (five pieces), his camp equipage, and transportation and plunder of all kinds, were abandoned and captured. We also captured large numbers of prisoners, including Colonels Basil [W.] Duke, Dick [R. C.] Morgan, and Allen [Ward?], and the most of General Morgan's staff.

Yet with a considerable force Morgan succeeded in making his escape, and started into the interior like a fox for cover. Passing around the advanced column of his enemy, he suddenly came upon the end of Shackelford's column, under Wolford, whom he at once attacked with his usual audacity. Shackelford reversed his column, selected his best horses, and gave pursuit. He overtook the enemy at Backum Church, where Wolford's Kentucky fellows rushed upon Morgan's men with drawn sabers and Kentucky yells, and chased them until next afternoon, when they were found collected on a high bluff, where some hundreds surrendered; but Morgan again escaped, and with over six hundred horsemen gave our fellows a long chase yet by the dirt road and by rail. Continuing north through several counties, he veered northwest toward the Pennsylvania line, even now burning buildings, car-loads of freight, and bridges by the way, though hotly hounded by Shackelford, and flanked and headed off by troops in cars.

Among the latter was Major W. B. Way, of the 9th Michigan, with a battalion of his regiment. Way had left the cars at Mingo and marched over near to

Steubenville,[1] where he began a skirmish which lasted over twenty-five miles toward Salineville, away up in Columbiana County. Here he brought Morgan to bay. The latter still fought desperately, losing 200 prisoners, and over 70 of his men killed or wounded, and skipped away. Another Union detachment came up by rail under Major George W. Rue, of the 9th Kentucky Cavalry, joined Shackelford at Hammondsville, and took the advance with 300 men.

---

[1] Mr. E. E. Day makes the following statement in regard to Morgan's brief stay at Wintersville:

Defeated at Buffington Bar, Morgan abandoned his plan of making a watering trough of Lake Erie, and fled north through the tier of river counties, keeping within a few miles of the Ohio. The river was low, but not fordable except at Coxe's Riffle, a few miles below Steubenville. Headed at this point also, he struck across the country and passed through Wintersville, a small village five miles west of Steubenville. That was a memorable Saturday in Wintersville. Morgan's progress across the State had been watched with the most feverish anxiety, and the dread that the village might lie in his path filled the hearts of many. The wildest rumors passed current. Morgan and his "guerrillas," it was said, would kill all the men, lay the village in ashes, and carry off the women and children. The militia, or "hundred-day men," who lived in or near the village, drilled in the village streets, and fired rattling volleys of blank cartridges at a board fence, in preparation for the coming conflict. On Friday evening word came that Morgan would attempt to force a passage at Coxe's Riffle the next morning, and the militia marched to Steubenville to help intercept him. A bloody battle was expected. About the middle of the forenoon a horseman dashed into the village shouting, "Morgan's coming! He's just down at John Hanna's!" and galloped on to warn others. Mr. Hanna was a farmer living about a mile south of the village. He had shouldered his musket and gone with the militia, leaving his wife and two children at home. About ten o'clock Morgan's men were seen coming up the road. Mrs. Hanna with her children attempted to reach a neighbor's house, but they were overtaken and ordered to the house, which they found full of soldiers. Morgan and his officers were stretched, dusty clothes, boots, and all, upon her beds, and a negro was getting dinner. While the third table was eating, a squad of militiamen appeared on a neighboring hill. Morgan ordered their capture, saying, "What will those Yankees do with the thousand men I have?" A number of Morgan's men started to carry out their chief's command, but the militia made good their escape. Soon after, word came that Shackelford's men were near, and Morgan left so hurriedly that he neglected to take the quilts and blankets his men had selected.

In the village all was consternation. Many of the women and children gathered at the Maxwell Tavern. Their

At Salineville he found Morgan, pursued by Major Way, pushing for Smith's Ford on the Ohio. Breaking into trot and gallop, he outmarched and intercepted the fugitives at the cross-roads near Beaver Creek, and had gained the enemy's front and flank when a flag of truce was raised, and Morgan coolly demanded his surrender. Rue's threat to open fire brought Morgan to terms, when another issue was

terror upon hearing that Morgan was "just down at Hanna's" cannot be described. Word had been sent to Steubenville, and Colonel James Collier marched out with a force of about eight hundred militia, sending a squad under command of Captain Prentiss to reconnoiter. They galloped through the village, and as Morgan's advance came in sight began firing. The fire was returned, and a private named Parks, from Steubenville, was wounded. Morgan's men charged the scouting party, sending them through the village back to the main body in a very demoralized condition. The frightened women, and still worse frightened children, no sooner saw the "dust-brown ranks" of the head of Morgan's column than they beat a hasty retreat down the alley to the house of Dr. Markle, the village physician. This change of base was made under fire, as Morgan's men were shooting at the retreating militia, and also at a house owned by William Fisher, in which they had heard there were a number of militiamen. At the doctor's house all crowded into one room, and were led in prayer by the minister's wife. The retreat of the scouting party did not have a very cheering effect upon the advancing militia. As they passed a field of broom-corn several men suddenly disappeared, their swift course through the cane being easily followed by the swaying of the tassels. The militia were met by rumors that the village was in ashes. Morgan did not set fire to the village, but his men found time to explore the village store, and to search the Fisher house, in the second story of which they found a flag. Morgan's men were hardly out of sight on the Richmond road when Colonel Collier and the militia appeared. They formed line of battle on a hill east of the village just in time to see Shackelford's advance coming along the road over which they were expecting Morgan. The colonel at once opened fire with his six-pounder loaded with scrap-iron. The first shot did little damage. One piece of scrap-iron found its way to the right, and struck with a resounding thwack against the end of the Maxwell Tavern. The second shot did not hit anything. One of Shackelford's officers rode across the field and inquired, "What are you fools shooting at!" The colonel then learned, to his astonishment, that Morgan was at least two miles out on the Richmond road. Many who had been conspicuously absent then showed themselves, and the daring deeds and hairbreadth escapes which came to light are not to be lightly referred to. At least a dozen dead rebels, it was said, would be discovered in the fields when the farmers came to cut their oats, but for some reason the bodies were never found.

raised. It was now claimed that Morgan had already surrendered, namely, to a militia officer, and had been by him paroled. This "officer" turned out to be "Captain" James Burbick, of the home guard.[1] Rue held Morgan, with 364 officers and men and 400 horses, till General Shackelford came up, who held them as prisoners of war.

And thus ended the greatest of Morgan's raids. By it Bragg lost a fine large division of cavalry, that, if added to Buckner's force,— already equal to Burnside's in East Tennessee,— might have defeated Burnside; or, if thrown across Rosecrans's flanks or long lines of supply and communication, or used in reconnaissance on the Tennessee River, might have baffled Rosecrans's plans altogether. As it was, Rosecrans was able to deceive Bragg by counterfeit movements that could easily have been detected by Morgan.

---

[1] General W. T. H. Brooks says in his report:

Morgan had passed a company of citizens from New Lisbon, and agreed not to fire upon them if they would not fire upon him. He had taken two or three of their men prisoners, and was using them as guides. Among them was a Mr. Burbick, of New Lisbon, who had gone out at the head of a small squad of mounted men. When Morgan saw that his advance was about to be cut off by Major Rue, he said to this Captain Burbick: "I would prefer to surrender to the militia rather than to United States troops. I will surrender to you if you will agree to respect private property and parole the officers and men as soon as we get to Cincinnati." Burbick replied that he knew nothing about this business. Morgan said, "Give me an answer, yes or no." Burbick, evidently in confusion, said, "Yes."

James Burbick sent a statement to Governor Tod, in which he said that he was not a prisoner with Morgan, but that he was guiding him voluntarily away from the vicinity of New Lisbon, after Morgan had agreed not to pass through that town. Burbick reported that he accepted Morgan's surrender, and started for the rear with a handkerchief tied to a stick to intercept the advancing troops, while Lieutenant C. D. Maus, a prisoner with Morgan, was sent with another flag of truce across the fields.

III. THE ESCAPE [1]

BY THOMAS H. HINES

ON the 31st of July and the 1st of August, 1863, General John H. Morgan, General Basil W. Duke, and sixty-eight other officers of Morgan's command, were, by order of General Burnside, confined in the Ohio State Penitentiary at Columbus. Before entering the main prison we were searched and relieved of our pocket-knives, money, and of all other articles of value, subjected to a bath, the shaving of our faces, and the cutting of our hair. We were placed each in a separate cell in the first and second tiers on the south side in the east wing of the prison. General Morgan and General Duke were on the second range, General Morgan being confined in the last cell at the east end, those who escaped with General Morgan having their cells in the first range.

From five o'clock in the evening until seven o'clock in the morning we were locked into our cells, with no possible means of communication with one another; but in the day, between these hours, we were permitted to mingle together in the narrow hall, twelve feet wide and one hundred and sixty long, which was cut off from the other portion of the building, occupied by the convicts, by a plank partition, in one end of which was a wooden door. At each end of the hall, and within the partitions, was an armed military sentinel, while the civil guards of the prison passed at irregular inter-

[1] Condensed from "The Bivouac" of June, 1885.

vals among us, and very frequently the warden or his deputy came through in order to see that we were secure and not violating the prison rules. We were not permitted to talk with or in any way to communicate with the convicts, nor were we permitted to see any of our relatives or friends that might come from a distance to see us, except upon the written order of General Burnside, and then only in the presence of a guard. Our correspondence underwent the censorship of the warden, we receiving and he sending only such as met his approbation; we were not permitted to have newspapers, or to receive information of what was going on in the outside busy world.

Many plans for escape, ingenious and desperate, were suggested, discussed, and rejected because deemed impracticable. Among them was bribery of the guards. This was thought not feasible because of the double set of guards, military and civil, who were jealous and watchful of each other, so that it was never attempted, although we could have commanded, through our friends in Kentucky and elsewhere, an almost unlimited amount of money.

On a morning in the last days of October I was rudely treated, without cause, by the deputy warden. There was no means of redress, and it was not wise to seek relief by retort, since I knew, from the experience of my comrades, that it would result in my confinement in a dark dungeon, with bread and water for diet. I retired to my cell, and closed the door with the determination that I would neither eat nor sleep until I had devised some means of escape. I ate nothing and drank nothing during the day, and by nine o'clock

I had matured the plan that we carried into execution. It may be that I owed something to the fact that I had just completed the reading of Victor Hugo's "Les Misérables," containing such vivid delineations of the wonderful escapes of Jean Valjean, and of the subterranean passages of the city of Paris. This may have led me to the line of thought that terminated in the plan of escape adopted. It was this: I had observed that the floor of my cell was upon a level with the ground upon the outside of the building, which was low and flat, and also that the floor of the cell was perfectly dry and free from mold. It occurred to me that, as the rear of the cell was to a great extent excluded from the light and air, this dryness and freedom from mold could not exist unless there was underneath something in the nature of an air-chamber to prevent the dampness from rising up the walls and through the floor. If this chamber should be found to exist, and could be reached, a tunnel might be run through the foundations into the yard, from which we might escape by scaling the outer wall, the air-chamber furnishing a receptacle for the earth and stone to be taken out in running the tunnel. The next morning, when our cells were unlocked, and we were permitted to assemble in the hall, I went to General Morgan's cell, he having been for several days quite unwell, and laid before him the plan as I have sketched it. Its feasibility appeared to him unquestioned, and to it he gave a hearty and unqualified approval. If, then, our supposition was correct as to the existence of the air-chamber beneath the lower range of cells, a limited number of those occupying that range could escape, and only a limited number, because the greater the number the longer the time required to complete the work, and the greater the danger of discovery while prosecuting it, in making our way over the outer wall, and in escaping afterward.

With these considerations in view, General Morgan and myself agreed upon the following officers, whose cells were nearest the point at which the tunnel was to begin, to join us in the enterprise: Captain J. C. Bennett, Captain L. D. Hockersmith, Captain C. S. Magee, Captain Ralph Sheldon, and Captain Samuel B. Taylor. The plan was then laid before these gentlemen, and received their approval. It was agreed that work should begin in my cell, and continue from there until completed. In order, however, to do this without detection, it was necessary that some means should be found to prevent the daily inspection of that cell, it being the custom of the deputy warden, with the guards, to visit and have each cell swept every morning. This end was accomplished by my obtaining permission from the warden to furnish a broom and sweep my own cell. For a few mornings thereafter the deputy warden would pass, glance into my cell, compliment me on its neatness, and go on to the inspection of the other cells. After a few days my cell

CORRIDOR AND CELLS IN THE EAST WING. A, CAPTAIN HINES'S CELL.

was allowed to go without any inspection whatever, and then we were ready to begin work, having obtained, through some of our associates who had been sent to the hospital, some table-knives made of flat steel files. In my cell, as in the others, there was a narrow iron cot, which could be folded and propped up to the cell wall. I thought the work could be completed within a month.

On the 4th of November work was begun in the back part of my cell, under the rear end of my cot. We cut through six inches of cement, and took out six layers of brick put in and cemented with the ends up. Here we came to the air-chamber, as I had calculated, and found it six feet wide by four feet high, and running the entire length of the range of cells. The cement and brick taken out in effecting an entrance to the chamber were placed in my bed-tick, upon which I slept during the progress of this portion of the work, after which the material was removed to the chamber. We found the chamber heavily grated at the end, against which a large quantity of coal had been heaped, cutting off any chance of exit in that way. We then began a tunnel, running it at right angles from the side of the chamber, and almost directly beneath my cell. We cut through the foundation wall, five feet thick, of the cell block; through twelve feet of grouting, to the outer wall of the east wing of the prison; through this wall, six feet in thickness; and four feet up near the surface of the yard, in an unfrequented place between this wing and the female department of the prison.

During the progress of the work, in which we were

greatly assisted by several of our comrades who were not to go out, notably among them Captain Thomas W. Bullitt of Louisville, Kentucky, I sat at the entrance to my cell studiously engaged on Gibbon's Rome and in trying to master French. By this device

EXTERIOR OF THE PRISON. B—EXIT FROM TUNNEL.

I was enabled to be constantly on guard without being suspected, as I had pursued the same course during the whole period of my imprisonment. Those who did the work were relieved every hour. This was accomplished, and the danger of the guards overhearing the work as they passed obviated, by adopting a system of signals, which consisted in giving taps on the floor over the chamber. One knock was to suspend work, two to proceed, and three to come out. On one occasion, by oversight, we came near being discovered. The prisoners were taken out to their meals by ranges, and on this day those confined in the first range were called for dinner while Captain Hockersmith was in the tunnel. The deputy warden, on calling the roll, missed Hockersmith, and came back to inquire for him. General Morgan engaged the attention of the warden by asking his opinion as to the propriety of a remonstrance that the general had prepared to be sent to General Burnside. Flattered by the deference shown to his opinion by General Morgan, the warden unwittingly gave Captain Hockersmith time to get out and fall into line for dinner. While the tunnel was being run, Colonel R. C. Morgan, a brother of General Morgan, made a rope, in links, of bed-ticking, thirty-five feet in length, and from the iron poker of the hall stove we made a hook, in the nature of a grappling-iron, to attach to the end of the rope.

The work was now complete with the exception of making an entrance from each of the cells of those who were to go out. This could be done with safety only by working from the chamber upward, as the cells were daily inspected. The difficulty presented in doing this was the fact that we did not know at what point to begin in order to open the holes in the cells at the proper place. To accomplish this a measurement was necessary, but we had nothing to measure with. Fortunately the deputy warden again ignorantly aided us. I got into a discussion with him as to the length of the hall, and to convince me of my error he sent for his measuring-line, and after the hall had been measured, and his statement verified, General Morgan occupied his attention, while I took the line, measured the distance from center to center of the cells,—all being of uniform size,—and marked it upon the stick used in my cell for propping up my cot. With this stick, measuring from the middle of the hole in my cell, the proper distance was marked off in the chamber for the holes in the other cells. The chamber was quite dark, and light being necessary for the work, we had obtained candles and matches through our sick comrades in the hospital. The hole in my cell during the progress of the work was kept covered with a large handsatchel containing my change of clothing. We cut from underneath upward until there was only a thin crust of the cement left in each of the cells. Money was necessary to pay expenses of transportation and for other contingencies as they might arise. General Morgan had some money that the search had not discovered, but it was not enough. Shortly after we began work I wrote to my sister in Kentucky a letter, which through a trusted convict I sent out and mailed, requesting her to go to my library and get certain books, and in the back of a designated one, which she was to open with a thin knife, place a certain amount of Federal money, repaste the back, write my name across the inside of the back where the money was concealed, and send the box by express. In due course of time the books with the money came to hand. It only remained now to get information as to the time of the running of the trains and to await a cloudy night, as it was then full moon. Our trusty convict was again found useful. He was quite an old man, called Heavy, had been in the penitentiary for many years, and as he had been so faithful, and his time having almost expired, he was permitted to go on errands for the officials to the city. I gave him ten dollars to bring us a daily paper and six ounces of French brandy. Neither he nor any one within the prison or on the outside had any intimation of our contemplated escape.

It was our first thought to make our way to the Confederacy by way of Canada; but, on inspecting the time-table in the paper, it was seen that a knowledge of the escape would necessarily come to the prison officials before we could reach the Canadian border. There was nothing left, then, but to take the train south, which we found, if on time, would reach Cincinnati, Ohio, before the cells were opened in the morning, at which time we expected our absence to be discovered. One thing more remained to be done, and that was to ascertain the easiest and safest place at which to scale the outside wall of the prison. The windows opening outward were so high that we could not see the wall. In the hall was a ladder resting against the wall, fifty feet long, that had been used for sweeping down the wall. A view from the top of the ladder would give us a correct idea of the outside, but the difficulty was to get that view without exciting suspicion.

Fortunately the warden came in while we were discussing the great strength and activity of Captain Samuel B. Taylor, who was very small of stature, when it was suggested that Taylor could go hand over hand on the under side of the ladder to the top, and, with a moment's rest, return in the same way. To the warden this seemed impossible, and, to convince him,

Taylor was permitted to make the trial, which he did successfully. At the top of the ladder he rested for a minute and took a mental photograph of the wall. When the warden had left, Taylor communicated the fact that directly south of and at almost right angles from the east end of the block in which we were confined there was a double gate to the outer wall, the inside one being of wooden uprights four inches apart, and the outside one as solid as the wall; the wooden gate being supported by the wing wall of the female department, which joined to the main outer wall.

WITHIN THE WOODEN GATE.

On the evening of the 27th of November the cloudy weather so anxiously waited for came; and prior to being locked in our cells it was agreed to make the attempt at escape that night. Cell No. 21, next to my cell, No. 20, on the first range, was occupied by Colonel R. C. Morgan, a brother of General Morgan. That cell had been prepared for General Morgan by opening a hole to the chamber, and when the hour for locking up came, General Morgan stepped into Cell 21, and Colonel Morgan into General Morgan's cell in the second range. The guard did not discover the exchange, as General Morgan and Colonel Morgan were of about the same physical proportions, and each stood with his back to the cell door when it was being locked.

At intervals of two hours every night, beginning at eight, the guards came around to each cell and passed a light through the grating to see that all was well with the prisoners. The approach of the guard was often so stealthily made that a knowledge of his presence was first had by seeing him at the door of the cell. To avoid a surprise of this kind we sprinkled fine coal along in front of the cells, walking upon which would give us warning. By a singular coincidence that might have been a fatality, on the day we had determined upon for the escape General Morgan received a letter from Lexington, Kentucky, begging and warning him not to attempt to escape, and by the same mail I received a letter from a member of my family saying that it was rumored and generally believed at home that I had escaped. Fortunately these letters did not put the officials on their guard. We ascertained from the paper we had procured that a train left for Cincinnati at 1.15 A. M., and as the regular time for the guard to make his round of the cells was twelve o'clock, we arranged to descend to the chamber immediately thereafter. Captain Taylor was to descend first, and, passing under each cell, notify the others. General Morgan had been permitted to keep his watch, and this he gave to Taylor that he might not mistake the time to go.

At the appointed hour Taylor gave the signal, each of us arranged his cot with the seat in his cell so as to represent a sleeping prisoner, and, easily breaking the thin layer of cement, descended to the chamber, passed through the tunnel, breaking through the thin stratum of earth at the end. We came out near the wall of the female prison,—it was raining slightly,—crawled by the side of the wall to the wooden gate, cast our grappling-iron attached to the rope over the gate, made it fast, ascended the rope to the top of the gate, drew up the rope, and made our way by the wing wall to the outside wall, where we entered a sentry-box and divested ourselves of our soiled outer garments. In the daytime sentinels were placed on this wall, but at night they were on the inside of the walls and at the main entrance to the prison. On the top of the wall we found a cord running along the outer edge and connecting with a bell in the office of the prison. This cord General Morgan cut with one of the knives we had used in tunneling. Before leaving my cell I wrote and left, addressed to N. Merion, the warden, the following:

CASTLE MERION, CELL NO. 20, November 27, 1863.— Commencement, November 4, 1863; conclusion, November 24, 1863; number of hours for labor per day, five; tools, two small knives. *La patience est amère, mais son fruit est doux.* By order of my six honorable Confederates. THOMAS H. HINES, *Captain, C. S. A.*

Having removed all trace of soil from our clothes and persons, we attached the iron hook to the railing on the outer edge of the wall, and descended to the ground within sixty yards of where the prison guards were sitting round a fire and conversing. Here we separated, General Morgan and myself going to the depot, about a quarter of a mile from the prison, where I purchased two tickets for Cincinnati, and entered the car that just then came in. General Morgan took a seat beside a Federal major in uniform, and I sat immediately in their rear. The general entered into conversation with the major, who was made the more talkative by a copious drink of my French brandy. As the train passed near the prison-wall where we had descended, the major remarked, "There is where the rebel General Morgan and his officers are put for safe-keeping." The general replied, "I hope they will keep him as safe as he is now." Our train passed through Dayton, Ohio, and there, for some unknown reason, we were delayed an hour. This rendered it extra hazardous to go to the depot in the city of Cincinnati, since by that time the prison officials would, in all probability, know of our escape, and telegraph to intercept us. In fact, they did telegraph in every direction, and offered a reward for our recapture. Instead, then, of going to the depot in Cincinnati, we got off, while the train was moving slowly, in the outskirts of the city, near Ludlow Ferry, on the Ohio River. Going directly to the ferry we were crossed over in a skiff and landed immediately in front of the residence of Mrs. Ludlow. We rang the door-bell, a servant came, and General Morgan wrote upon a visiting-card, "General Morgan and Captain Hines, escaped." We were warmly received, took a cup of coffee with the family, were furnished a guide, and walked some three miles in the country, where we were furnished horses. Thence we went through Florence to Union, in Boone County, Kentucky, where we took supper with Daniel Piatt. On making ourselves known to Mr. Piatt, who had two sons in our command, we were treated with the most

OVER THE PRISON WALL.

cordial hospitality and kindness by the entire family. We there met Dr. John J. Dulaney of Florence, Kentucky, who was of great benefit in giving us information as to the best route. That night we went to Mr. Corbin's, near Union,—who also had gallant sons in our command,—where we remained concealed until the next night, and where friends supplied us with fresh horses and a pair of pistols each.

On the evening of the 29th of November we left Union with a voluntary guide, passed through the eastern edge of Gallatin County, and after traveling all night spent the day of the 30th at the house of a friend on the Owen County line. Passing through New Liberty, in Owen County, and crossing the Kentucky River at the ferry on the road to New Castle, in Henry County, we stopped at the house of Mr. Pollard at 2 A. M., December 1. Our guide did not know the people nor the roads farther than the ferry, at which point he turned back. Not knowing the politics of Mr. Pollard, it was necessary to proceed with caution. On reaching his house we aroused him and made known our desire to spend the remainder of the night with him. He admitted us and took us into the family room, where there was a lamp dimly burning on a center-table. On the light being turned up I discovered a Cincinnati "Enquirer" with large displayed head-lines, announcing the escape of General Morgan, Captain Hines, and five other officers from the Ohio penitentiary. The fact that this newspaper was taken by Mr. Pollard was to me sufficient evidence that he was a Southern sympathizer. Glancing at the paper, I looked up and remarked, "I see that General Morgan, Hines, and other officers have escaped from the penitentiary." He responded, "Yes; and you are Captain Hines, are you not?" I replied, "Yes; and what is your name?" "Pollard," he answered. "Allow me, then, to introduce General Morgan." I found that I had not made a mistake.

After rest and a late breakfast and a discussion of the situation, it was deemed inexpedient to remain during the day, as the house was immediately on a public highway, besides the danger of such unexplained delay exciting the suspicion of the negroes on the place. We assumed the character of cattle-buyers, Mr. Pollard furnishing us with cattle-whips to make the assumption plausible. Our first objective point was the residence of Judge W. S. Pryor, in the outskirts of New Castle. After dinner Judge Pryor rode with us some distance, and put us in charge of a guide, who conducted us that night to Major Helm's, near Shelbyville, where we remained during the day of the 2d, and were there joined by four of our command in citizen's dress. That night we passed through Taylorsville, and stopped on the morning of the 3d near Bardstown.

The night of the 4th we resumed our journey, and stopped on the morning of the 5th at Mr. McCormack's at Rolling Fork Creek, in Nelson County, thence through Taylor, Green (passing near Greensburg), Adair, and Cumberland counties, crossing Cumberland River some nine miles below Burkesville. We crossed the Cumberland, which was quite high, by swimming our horses by the side of a canoe. Near the place of crossing, on the south side, we stopped overnight with a private in Colonel R. T. Jacob's Federal cavalry, passing ourselves as citizens on the lookout for stolen horses. Next morning, in approaching the road from Burkesville to Sparta, Tennessee, we came out of a byway immediately in the rear of and some hundred yards from a dwelling fronting on the Burkesville-

Sparta road, and screening us from view on the Burkesville end. As we emerged from the woodland a woman appeared at the back door of the dwelling and motioned us back. We withdrew from view, but kept in sight of the door from which the signal to retire was given, when after a few minutes the woman again appeared and signaled us to come forward. She informed us that a body of Federal cavalry had just passed, going in the direction of Burkesville, and that the officer in command informed her that he was trying to intercept General Morgan. We followed the Burkesville road something like a mile, and in sight of the rear-guard. We crossed Obey's River near the mouth of Wolf, and halted for two days in the hills of Overton County, where we came upon forty of our men, who had been separated from the force on the expedition into Indiana and Ohio. These men were placed under my command, and thence we moved directly toward the Tennessee River, striking it about fifteen miles below Kingston, at Bridges's Ferry, December 13. There was no boat to be used in crossing, and the river was very high and angry, and about one hundred and fifty yards wide. We obtained an ax from a house near by, and proceeded to split logs and make a raft on which to cross, and by which to swim our horses. We had learned that two miles and a half below us was a Federal cavalry camp. This stimulated us to the utmost, but notwithstanding our greatest efforts we were three hours in crossing over five horses and twenty-five men. At this juncture the enemy appeared opposite, and began to fire on our men.

Here General Morgan gave characteristic evidence

of devotion to his men. When the firing began he insisted on staying with the dismounted men and

"HURRY UP, MAJOR!"

taking their chances, and was dissuaded only by my earnest appeal and representation that such a course would endanger the men as well as ourselves. The men, by scattering in the mountains, did ultimately make their way to the Confederacy.

General Morgan, myself, and the four mounted men crossed over a spur of the mountains and descended by a bridle-path to a ravine or gulch upon the opposite side, and halted in some thick underbrush about ten steps from a path passing along the ravine. Not knowing the country, it was necessary to have information or a guide, and observing a log cabin about a hundred yards up the ravine, I rode there to get directions, leaving General Morgan and the others on their horses near the path. I found at the house a woman and some children. She could not direct me over the other spur of the mountain, but consented that her ten-year-old son might go with me and show the way. He mounted behind me, and by the time he was seated I heard the clatter of hoofs down the ravine, and, looking, I saw a body of about seventy-five cavalry coming directly toward me, and passing within ten steps of where the general and his men were sitting on their horses. I saw that my own escape was doubtful, and that any halt or delay of the cavalry would certainly result in the discovery and capture of General Morgan. I lifted the boy from behind me and dashed to the head of the column, exclaiming, "Hurry up, Major, or the rebels will escape!" He responded, "Who are you?" I answered, "I belong to the home-guard company in the bend: hurry, or they are gone." We dashed on, I riding by the major at the head of the column about half a mile, when we came to where a dry branch crossed the road, and, as it had been raining that day, it was easily seen from the soil that had washed down from the side of the mountain that no one had passed there since the rain. Seeing this, the command was halted, and the major again demanded to know who I was. I replied that I was a member of General Morgan's command. "Yes, —— you! You have led me off from Morgan; I have a notion to hang you for it." "No, that was not General Morgan. I have served under him two years and know him well, and have no object in deceiving you; for if it was Morgan, he is now safe." "You lie, for he was recognized at the house where you got the ax. I would not have missed getting him for ten thousand dollars. It would have been a brigadier's commission to me. I will hang you for it." Up to this time I had taken the situation smilingly and pleasantly, because I did not apprehend violence; but the officer, livid with rage from disappointment, directed one of his men to take the halter from his horse and hang me to a designated limb of a tree. The halter was adjusted around my neck, and thrown over the limb. Seeing that the officer was desperately in earnest, I said, "Major, before you perform this operation, allow me to make a suggestion." "Be quick about it, then." "Suppose that *was* General Morgan, as you insist, and I have led you astray, as you insist, would n't I, being a member of his command, deserve to be hung if I had not done what you charge me with?" He dropped his head for a moment, looked up with a more pleasant expression, and said, "Boys, he is right; let him alone."

I was placed under guard of two soldiers and sent

across the river to camp, while the officer in command took his men over the mountain in search of

CAPTAIN HINES OBJECTS.

General Morgan, who succeeded in making good his escape. The next evening the major returned with his command from his unsuccessful pursuit. He questioned me closely, wanting to know my name, and if I was a private in the command, as I had stated to him at the time of my capture. Remembering that in prison the underclothing of Captain Bullitt had been exchanged for mine, and that I then had on his with his name in ink, I assumed the name of Bullitt.

On the evening of the second day in this camp the major invited me to go with him and take supper at the house of a Unionist half a mile away. We spent the evening with the family until nine o'clock, when the major suggested that we should go back to camp. On reaching the front gate, twenty steps from the front veranda, he found that he had left his shawl in the house, and returned to get it, requesting me to await his return. A young lady of the family was standing in the door, and when he went in to get the shawl, she closed the door. I was then perfectly free, but I could not get my consent to go. For a moment of time while thus at liberty I suffered intensely in the effort to determine what was the proper thing to do. Upon the one hand was the tempting offer of freedom, that was very sweet to me after so many months of close confinement; while on the other hand was the fact that the officer had treated me with great kindness, more as a comrade than as a prisoner, that the acceptance of his hospitality was a tacit parole and my escape would involve him in trouble. I remained until his return. He was greatly agitated, evidently realizing for the first time the extent of his indiscretion, and surprised undoubtedly at finding me quietly awaiting him. I had determined not to return to prison, but rather than break faith I awaited some other occasion for escape. Notwithstanding all this, something excited suspicion of me; for the next morning, while lying in the tent apparently asleep, I heard the officer direct the sergeant to detail ten men and guard me to Kingston, and he said to the sergeant, "Put him on the meanest horse you have and be watchful or he will escape." I was taken to Kingston and placed in jail, and there met three of our party who had been captured on the north side of the Tennessee River at the time we attempted to cross. They were R. C. Church, William Church, and —— Smith. After two days' confinement there, we were sent under guard of twelve soldiers to the camp of the 3d Kentucky Federal Infantry, under command of Colonel Henry C. Dunlap. The camp was opposite the town of Loudon, and was prepared for winter quarters. The large forest trees had been felled for a quarter of a mile around the camp, and log huts built in regular lines for the occupation of the troops. We were placed in one of these huts with three guards on the inside, while the guards who delivered us there were located around a camp-fire some ten steps in front of the only door to our hut, and around the whole encampment was the regular camp guard. The next day, as we had learned, we were to be sent to Knoxville, Tennessee, which was then General Burnside's headquarters; and as I knew I would there be recognized, and, on account of my previous escape, that my chances for freedom would be reduced to a minimum, we determined to escape that night.

It was perfectly clear, the moon about full, making the camp almost as light as day; and as the moon did not go down until a short time before daylight, we concluded to await its setting. The door of the cabin was fastened by a latch on the inside. The night was cold. We had only pretended to sleep, awaiting our opportunity. When the moon was down we arose, one after another, from our couches, and went to the fire to warm us. We engaged the guards in pleasant conversation, detailing incidents of the war. I stood with my right next the door, facing the fire and the three guards, and my comrades standing immediately on my left. While narrating some incident in which the guards were absorbed, I placed my right hand upon the latch of the door, with a signal to the other prisoners, and, without breaking the thread of the narrative, bade the guards good night, threw the door open, ran through the guards in front of the door, passed the sentinel at the camp limits, and followed the road we had been brought in to the mountains. The guards in front of the door fired upon me, as did the sentinel on his beat, the last shot being so close to me that I felt the fire from the gun. Unfortunately and unwittingly I threw the door open with such force that it rebounded and caught my comrades on the inside. The guards assaulted them and attempted to bayonet them, but they grappled, overpowered, and disarmed the guards, and made terms with them before they would let them up. All three of these prisoners, by great daring, escaped before they were taken North to prison.

In running from the camp to the mountains I passed two sentinel fires, and was pursued some distance at the point of the bayonet of the soldier who had last fired at me. All was hurry and confusion in the camp. The horses were bridled, saddled, and mounted, and rapidly ridden out on the road I had taken; but by the time the pursuers reached the timber I was high up the mountain side, and complacently watched them as they hurried by. As I ran from my prison-house I fixed my eye upon Venus, the morning star, as my guide, and traveled until daylight, when I reached the summit of the mountain, where I found a sedge-grass field of about twenty acres, in the middle of which I lay down on the frozen ground and remained until the sun had gone down and darkness was gathering. During the day the soldiers in search of me frequently passed within thirty steps, so close that I could hear their conjectures as to where I was most likely to be found. I remained so long in one position that I thawed into the frozen earth; but the cool of the evening coming on, the soil around me froze again, and I had some difficulty in releasing myself.

As it grew dark I descended the mountain, and cautiously approached a humble dwelling. Seeing no one but a woman and some children, I entered and asked for supper. While my supper was being prepared, no little to my disappointment, the husband, a strapping, manly-looking fellow, with his rifle on his shoulder, walked in. I had already assumed a character, and that was as agent to purchase horses for the Federal Government. I had come down that evening on the train from Knoxville, and was anxious to get a canoe and some one to paddle me down to Kingston, where I had an engagement for the next day to meet some gentlemen who were to have horses there, by agreement with me, for sale. Could the gentleman tell me where I could get a canoe and some one to go with me? He said the rebels were so annoying that all boats and canoes had been destroyed to keep them from crossing. He knew of but one canoe, owned by a good Union man some two miles down the river. Would he be kind enough to show me the way there, that I might get an early start and keep my engagement?

After supper my hospitable entertainer walked with me to the residence of the owner of the canoe. The family had retired, and when the owner of the premises came out, there came with him a Federal soldier who was staying overnight with him. This was not encouraging. After making my business known and offering large compensation, the owner of the canoe agreed to start with me by daylight. During my walk down there, my guide had mentioned that a certain person living opposite the place where the canoe was owned had several horses that he would like to sell. I suggested that, in order to save time and get as early a start as possible for Kingston, the canoe-owner should take me over to see to the purchase of these horses that night. The river was high and dangerous to cross at night, but by promises of compensation I was taken over and landed some quarter of a mile from the house. With an injunction to await me, when the canoe landed I started toward the house; but when out of sight I changed my course and took to the mountains.

For eight days I traveled by night, taking my course by the stars, lying up in the mountains by day, and getting food early in the evening wherever I could find a place where there were no men. On the 27th of December I reached the Confederate lines near Dalton, Georgia.

COLONEL ROSE'S TUNNEL AT LIBBY PRISON

BY FRANK E. MORAN

AMONG all the thrilling incidents in the history of Libby Prison, none exceeds in interest the celebrated tunnel escape which occurred on the night of February 9, 1864. I was one of the 109 Union officers who passed through the tunnel, and one of the ill-fated 48 that were retaken. I and two companions — Lieutenant Charles H. Morgan of the 21st Wisconsin regiment, who has since served several terms in Congress from Missouri, and Lieutenant William L. Watson of the same company and regiment — when recaptured by the Confederate cavalry were in sight of the Union picket posts. Strange as it may appear, no accurate and complete account has ever been given to the public of this, the most ingenious and daring escape made on either side during the civil war. Twelve of the party of fifteen who dug the tunnel are still living, including their leader.

Thomas E. Rose, colonel of the 77th Pennsylvania Volunteers, the engineer and leader in the plot throughout,— now a captain in the 16th United States Infantry,— was taken prisoner at the battle of Chickamauga, September 20, 1863. On his way to Richmond he escaped from his guards at Weldon, N. C., but, after a day's wandering about the pine forests with a broken foot, was retaken by a detachment of Confederate cavalry and sent to Libby Prison, Richmond, where he arrived October 1, 1863.

Libby Prison fronts on Carey street, Richmond, and stands upon a hill which descends abruptly to the

COLONEL THOMAS E. ROSE.

canal, from which its southern wall is divided only by a street, and having a vacant lot on the east. The building was wholly detached, making it a comparatively easy matter to guard the prison securely with a small force and keep every door and window in full view from without. As an additional measure of safety, prisoners were not allowed on the ground-floor, except that in the daytime they were permitted to use the first floor of the middle section for a cook-room. The interior embraced nine large warehouse-rooms, 105 x 45, with eight feet from each floor to ceiling, except the upper floor, which gave more room, owing to the pitch of the gable roof. The abrupt slant of the hill gives the building an additional story on the south side. The whole building really embraces three sections, and these were originally separated by heavy blank walls. The Confederates cut doors through the walls of the two upper floors, which comprised the prisoners' quarters, and they were thus permitted to mingle freely with each other; but there was no communication whatever between the three large rooms on the first floor. Beneath these floors were three cellars of the same dimensions as the rooms above them, and, like them, divided from each other by massive blank walls. For ready comprehension, let these be designated the east, middle, and west cellars. Except in the lofts known as "Streight's room" and "Milroy's room," which were occupied by the earliest inmates of Libby in 1863, there was no furniture in the building, and only a few of the early comers possessed such a luxury as an old army blanket or a knife, cup, and tin plate. As a rule, the prisoner, by the time he reached Libby, found himself devoid of earthly goods save the meager and dust-begrimed summer garb in which he had made his unlucky campaign.

At night the six large lofts presented strange war-pictures, over which a single tallow candle wept copious and greasy tears that ran down over the petrified loaf of corn-bread, Borden's condensed-milk can, or bottle in which it was set. The candle flickered on until "taps," when the guards, with unconscious irony shouted, "Lights out!"—at which signal it usually disappeared amid a shower of boots and such other missiles as were at hand. The sleepers covered

the six floors, lying in ranks, head to head and foot to foot, like prostrate lines of battle. For the general good, and to preserve something like military precision, these ranks (especially when cold weather compelled them to lie close for better warmth) were subdivided into convenient squads under charge of a "captain," who was invested with authority to see that every man lay "spoon fashion."

No consideration of personal convenience was permitted to interfere with the general comfort of the "squad." Thus, when the hard floor could no longer be endured on the right side,—especially by the thin men, —the captain gave the command, "Attention, Squad Number Four! Prepare to spoon! One—two—spoon!" And the whole squad flopped over on the left side.

The first floor on the west of the building was used by the Confederates as an office and for sleeping-quarters for the prison officials, and a stairway guarded by sentinels led from this to Milroy's room just above it. As before explained, the middle room was shut off from the office by a heavy blank wall. This room, known as the "kitchen," had two stoves in it, one of which stood about ten feet from the heavy door that opened on Carey street sidewalk, and behind the door was a fireplace. The room contained also several long pine tables with permanent seats attached, such as may be commonly seen at picnic grounds. The floor was constantly inundated here by several defective and overworked water-faucets and a leaky trough.

A stairway without banisters led up on the southwest end of the floor, above which was a room known as the "Chickamauga room," being chiefly occupied by Chickamauga prisoners. The sentinel who had formerly been placed at this stairway at night, to prevent the prisoners from entering the kitchen, had been withdrawn when, in the fall of 1863, the horrible condition of the floor made it untenable for sleeping purposes.

The uses to which the large ground-floor room east of the kitchen was put varied during the first two years of the war; but early in October of 1863, and thereafter, it was permanently used and known as the hospital, and it contained a large number of cots, which were never unoccupied. An apartment had been made at the north or front of the room, which served as a doctor's office and laboratory. Like those adjoining it on the west, this room had a large door opening on Carey street, which was heavily bolted and guarded on the outside.

The arrival of the Chickamauga prisoners greatly crowded the upper floors, and compelled the Confed-

LIBBY PRISON IN 1865.

erates to board up a small portion of the east cellar at its southeast corner as an additional cook-room, several large caldrons having been set in a rudely built furnace; so, for a short period, the prisoners were allowed down there in the daytime to cook. A stairway led from this cellar to the room above, which subsequently became the hospital.

Such, in brief, was the condition of things when Colonel Rose arrived at the prison. From the hour of his coming, a means of escape became his constant and eager study; and, with this purpose in view, he made a careful and minute survey of the entire premises.

From the windows of the upper east or "Gettysburg room" he could look across the vacant lot on the east and get a glimpse of the yard between two adjacent buildings which faced the canal and Carey street respectively, and he estimated the intervening space at about seventy feet. From the south windows he looked out across a street upon the canal and James River, running parallel with each other, the two streams at this point being separated by a low and narrow strip of land. This strip periodically disappeared when protracted seasons of heavy rain came, or when spring floods so rapidly swelled the river that the latter invaded the cellars of Libby. At such times it was common to see enormous swarms of rats come out from the lower doors and windows of the prison and make head for dry land in swimming platoons amid the cheers of the prisoners in the upper windows. On one or two occasions Rose observed workmen descending from the middle of the south-side street into a sewer running through its center, and concluded that this sewer must have various openings to the canal both to the east and west of the prison.

The north portion of the cellar contained a large quantity of loose packing-straw, covering the floor to an average depth of two feet; and this straw afforded

MAJOR A. G. HAMILTON.

shelter, especially at night, for a large colony of rats, which gave the place the name of "Rat Hell."

In one afternoon's inspection of this dark end, Rose suddenly encountered a fellow-prisoner, Major A. G. Hamilton, of the 12th Kentucky Cavalry. A confiding friendship followed, and the two men entered at once upon the plan of gaining their liberty. They agreed that the most feasible scheme was a tunnel, to begin in the rear of the little kitchen-apartment at the southeast corner of Rat Hell. Without more ado they secured a broken shovel and two case-knives and began operations.

Within a few days the Confederates decided upon certain changes in the prison for the greater security of their captives. A week afterward the cook-room was abandoned, the stairway nailed up, the prisoners sent to the upper floors, and all communication with the east cellar was cut off. This was a sore misfortune, for this apartment was the only possible base of successful tunnel operations. Colonel Rose now began to study other practicable means of escape, and spent night after night examining the posts and watching the movements of the sentinels on the four sides of Libby. One very dark night, during a howling storm, Rose again unexpectedly met Hamilton in a place where no prisoner could reasonably be looked for at such an hour. For an instant the impenetrable darkness made it impossible for either to determine whether he had met a friend or foe: neither had a weapon, yet each involuntarily felt for one, and each made ready to spring at the other's throat, when a flash of lightning revealed their identity. The two men had availed themselves of the darkness of the night and the roar of the storm to attempt an escape from a window of the upper west room to a platform that ran along the west outer wall of the prison, from which they hoped to reach the ground and elude the sentinels, whom they conjectured would be crouched in the shelter of some doorway or other partial refuge that might be available; but so vivid and frequent were the lightning flashes that the attempt was seen to be extremely hazardous.

Rose now spoke of the entrance from the south-side street to the middle cellar, having frequently noticed the entrance and exit of workmen at that point, and expressed his belief that if an entrance could be effected to this cellar it would afford them the only chance of slipping past the sentinels.

He hunted up a bit of pine-wood which he whittled into a sort of wedge, and the two men went down into the dark, vacant kitchen directly over this cellar. With the wedge Rose pried a floor-board out of its place, and made an opening large enough to let himself through. He had never been in this middle cellar, and was wholly ignorant of its contents or whether it was occupied by Confederates or workmen; but as he had made no noise, and the place was in profound darkness, he decided to go down and reconnoiter.

He wrenched off one of the long boards that formed a table-seat in the kitchen, and found that it was long enough to touch the cellar base and protrude a foot or so above the kitchen floor. By this means he easily descended, leaving Hamilton to keep watch above.

The storm still raged fiercely, and the faint beams of a street-lamp revealed the muffled form of the sentinel slowly pacing his beat and carrying his musket at "secure" arms. Creeping softly toward him along the cellar wall, he now saw that what he had supposed was a door was simply a naked opening to the street; and further inspection disclosed the fact that there was but one sentinel on the south side of the prison. Standing in the dark shadow, he could easily have touched this man with his hand as he repeatedly passed him. Groping about, he found various appurtenances indicating that the south end of this cellar was used for a carpenter's shop, and that the north end was partitioned off into a series of small cells with padlocked doors, and that through each door a square hole, a foot in diameter, was cut. Subsequently it was learned that these dismal cages were alternately used for the confinement of "troublesome prisoners"— *i. e.*, those who had distinguished themselves by ingenious attempts to escape—and also for runaway slaves, and Union spies under sentence of death.

At the date of Rose's first reconnaissance to this cellar, these cells were vacant and unguarded. The night was far spent, and Rose proceeded to return to the kitchen, where Hamilton was patiently waiting for him.

The very next day a rare good fortune befell Rose. By an agreement between the commissioners of exchange, several bales of clothing and blankets had been sent by our government to the famishing Union prisoners on Belle Isle, a number of whom had already frozen to death. A committee of Union officers then confined in Libby, consisting of General Neal Dow, Colonel Alexander von Shrader, Lieut.-Colonel Joseph F. Boyd, and Colonel Harry White, having been selected by the Confederates to supervise the distribution of the donation, Colonel White had, by a shrewd bit of finesse, "confiscated" a fine rope by which one of the bales was tied, and this he now presented to Colonel Rose. It was nearly a hundred feet long, an inch thick, and almost new.

It was hardly dark the following night before Rose and Hamilton were again in the kitchen, and as soon as all was quiet Rose fastened his rope to one of the supporting posts, took up the floor-plank as before, and both men descended to the middle cellar. They were not a little disappointed to discover that where there had been but one sentinel on the south side there were now two. On this and for several nights they contented themselves with sly visits of observation to this cellar, during which Rose found and secreted various tools, among which were a broad-ax, a saw, two chisels, several files, and a carpenter's square. One dark night both men went down and determined to try their luck at passing the guards. Rose made the attempt and succeeded in passing the first man, but unluckily was seen by the second. The latter called lustily for the corporal of the guard, and the first excitedly cocked his gun and peered into the dark door through which Rose swiftly retreated. The guard called, "Who goes there?" but did not enter the dark cellar. Rose and Hamilton mounted the rope and had just succeeded in replacing the plank when the corporal and a file of men entered the cellar with a lantern. They looked into every barrel and under every bench, but no sign of Yankees appeared; and as on this night it happened that several workmen were sleeping in an apartment at the north end, the corporal concluded that the man seen by the sentinel was one of these, notwithstanding their denial when awakened and questioned. After a long parley the Confederates withdrew, and Hamilton and Rose, depressed in spirits, went to bed, Rose as usual concealing his rope.

Before the week was out they were at it again. On

one of these nights Rose suddenly came upon one of the workmen, and, swift as thought, seized the hidden broad-ax with the intention of braining him if he attempted an alarm; but the poor fellow was too much paralyzed to cry out, and when finally he did recover his voice and his wits, it was to beg Rose, "for God's sake," not to come in there again at night. Evidently the man never mentioned the circumstance, for Rose's subsequent visits, which were soon resumed, disclosed no evidence of a discovery by the Confederates.

Hamilton agreed with Rose that there remained apparently but one means of escape, and that was by force. To overpower the two sentinels on the south side would have been an easy matter, but how to do it and not alarm the rest of the guard, and, in consequence, the whole city, was the problem. To secure these sentinels, without alarming their comrades on the east, west, and north sides of the prison, would require the swift action of several men of nerve acting in concert. Precious time was passing, and possibly further alterations might be decided upon that would shut them off from the middle cellar, as they had already been from their original base of operations. Moreover, a new cause of anxiety now appeared. It soon transpired that their nocturnal prowlings and close conferences together had already aroused the belief among many observant prisoners that a plan of escape was afoot, and both men were soon eagerly plied with guarded inquiries, and besought by their questioners to admit them to their confidence.

Hamilton and Rose now decided to organize an escaping party. A number of men were then sworn to secrecy and obedience by Colonel Rose, who was the only recognized leader in all operations that followed.

LIBBY PRISON IN 1861.

This party soon numbered seventy men. The band was then taken down by Rose in convenient details to the middle cellar or carpenter's shop on many nights, to familiarize each man with the place and with his special part in the plot, and also to take advantage of any favoring circumstances that might arise.

When all had by frequent visits become familiar with the rendezvous, Rose and the whole party descended one night with the determination to escape at whatever hazard. The men were assigned to their several stations as usual, and a selected few were placed by the leader close to the entrance, in front of which the sentinel was regularly passing. Rose commanded strict silence, and placed himself near the exit preparatory to giving the signal. It was an exciting moment, and the bravest heart beat fast. A signal came, but not the one they looked for. At the very moment of action, the man whom Rose had left at the floor-opening in the kitchen gave the danger-signal! The alert leader had, with consummate care, told every man beforehand that he must never be surprised by this signal,—it was a thing to be counted upon,—and that noise and panic were of all things to be avoided as fatal folly in their operations. As a consequence, when this signal came, Rose quietly directed the men to fall in line and reascend to the kitchen rapidly, but without noise, which they did by the long rope which now formed the easy means of communication from the kitchen to the cellar.

Rose remained below to cover the retreat, and when the last man got up he followed him, replaced the board in the floor, and concealed the rope. He had barely done so when a detail of Confederate guards entered the kitchen from the Carey street door, and, headed by an officer, marched straight in his direction. Meantime the party had disappeared up the stairway and swiftly made their way over their prostrate comrades' forms to their proper sleeping-places. Rose, being the last up, and having the floor to fix, had now no time to disappear like his companions, at least without suspicious haste. He accordingly took a seat at one of the tables, and, putting an old pipe in his mouth, coolly awaited the approach of the Confederates. The officer of the guard came along, swinging his lantern almost in his face, stared at him for a second, and without a remark or a halt marched past him and ascended with his escort to the Chickamauga room. The entrance of a guard and their march around the prison, although afterward common enough after taps, was then an unusual thing, causing much talk among the prisoners, and to the mind of Rose and his fellow-plotters was indicative of aroused suspicion on the part of the Confederates.

The whispering groups of men next day, and the number of his eager questioners, gave the leader considerable concern; and Hamilton suggested, as a measure of safety rather than choice, that some of the mischievous talk of escape would be suppressed by increasing the party. This was acted upon; the men, like the rest, were put under oath by Rose, and the party was thus increased to four hundred and twenty. This force would have been enough to overpower the prison guard in a few minutes, but the swift alarm certain to ensue in the streets and spread like wild-fire over Richmond, the meager information possessed by the prisoners as to the strength and position of the nearest Federal troops, the strongly guarded labyrinth of breastworks that encircled the city, and the easy facilities for instant pursuit at the command of the Confederates, put the success of such an undertaking clearly out of the range of probability, unless, indeed, some unusual favoring contingency should arise, such as the near approach of a coöperating column of Federal cavalry.

Nor was this an idle dream, as the country now knows, for even at this period General Kilpatrick was maturing his plans for that bold expedition for the rescue of the prisoners at Richmond and Belle Isle in which the lamented and heroic young cripple, Colonel Ulric Dahlgren, lost his life. Rose saw that a break out of Libby without such outside assistance promised nothing but a fruitless sacrifice of life and the savage punishment of the survivors. Hence the project, although eagerly and exhaustively discussed, was prudently abandoned.

All talk of escape by the general crowd now wholly ceased, and the captives resigned themselves to their fate and waited with depressed spirits for the remote contingency of an exchange. The quiet thus gained was Rose's opportunity. He sought Hamilton and told him that they must by some stratagem regain access to Rat Hell, and that the tunnel project must be at once revived. The latter assented to the proposition, and the two began earnestly to study the means of gaining an entrance without discovery into this coveted base of operations.

They could not even get into the room above the cellar they wanted to reach, for that was the hospital, and the kitchen's heavy wall shut them off therefrom. Neither could they break the heavy wall that divided this cellar from the carpenter's shop, which had been the nightly rendezvous of the party while the breakout was under consideration, for the breach certainly would be discovered by the workmen or Confederates, some of whom were in there constantly during daylight.

There was, in fact, but one plan by which Rat Hell could be reached without detection, and the conception of this device and its successful execution were due to the stout-hearted Hamilton. This was to cut a hole in the back of the kitchen fireplace; the incision must be just far enough to preserve the opposite or hospital side intact. It must then be cut downward to a point below the level of the hospital floor, then eastward into Rat Hell, the completed opening thus to describe the letter "S." It must be wide enough to let a man through, yet the wall must not be broken on the hospital side above the floor, nor marred on the carpenter's-shop side below it. Such a break would be fatal, for both of these points were conspicuously exposed to the view of the Confederates every hour in the day. Moreover, it was imperatively necessary that all trace of the beginning of the opening should be concealed, not only from the Confederate officials and guards, who were constantly passing the spot every day, but from the hundreds of uninitiated prisoners who crowded around the stove just in front of it from dawn till dark.

Work could be possible only between the hours of ten at night, when the room was generally abandoned by the prisoners because of its inundated condition, and four o'clock in the morning, when the earliest risers were again astir. It was necessary to do the work with an old jack-knife and one of the chisels previously secured by Rose. It must be done in darkness and without noise, for a vigilant sentinel paced on the Carey street sidewalk just outside the door and within ten feet of the fireplace. A rubber blanket was procured, and the soot from the chimney carefully swept into it. Hamilton, with his old knife, cut the mortar between the bricks and pried a dozen of them out, being careful to preserve them whole.

The rest of the incision was made in accordance with the design described, but no conception could have been formed beforehand of the sickening tediousness of cutting an S-shaped hole through a heavy wall with a feeble old jack-knife, in stolen hours of darkness. Rose guarded his comrade against the constant danger of interruption by alert enemies on one side and by blundering friends on the other; and, as frequently happens in human affairs, their friends gave them more trouble than their foes. Night after night passed, and still the two men got up after taps from their hard beds, and descended to the dismal and reeking kitchen to bore for liberty. When the sentinel's call at Castle Thunder and at Libby announced four o'clock, the dislodged bricks were carefully replaced, and the soot previously gathered in the gum blanket was flung in handfuls against the restored wall, filling the seams between the bricks so thoroughly as to defy detection. At last, after many weary nights, Hamilton's heroic patience and skill were rewarded, and the way was open to the coveted base of operations, Rat Hell.

Now occurred a circumstance that almost revealed the plot and nearly ended in a tragedy. When the opening was finished, the long rope was made fast to one of the kitchen supporting posts, and Rose proceeded to descend and reconnoiter. He got partly through with ease, but lost his hold in such a manner that his body slipped through so as to pinion his arms and leave him wholly powerless either to drop lower or return—the bend of the hole being such as to cramp his back and neck terribly and prevent him from breathing. He strove desperately, but each effort only wedged him more firmly in the awful vise. Hamilton sprang to his aid and did his utmost to effect his release; but, powerful as he was, he could not budge him. Rose was gasping for breath and rapidly getting fainter, but even in this fearful strait he refrained from an outcry that would certainly alarm the guards just outside the door. Hamilton saw that without speedy relief his comrade must soon smother. He dashed through the long, dark room up the stairway, over the forms of several hundred men, and disregarding consequences and savage curses in the dark and crowded room, he trampled upon arms, legs, faces, and stomachs, leaving riot and blasphemy in his track among the rudely awakened and now furious lodgers of the Chickamauga room. He sought the sleeping-place of Major George H. Fitzsimmons, but he was missing. He, however, found Lieutenant F. F. Bennett, of the 18th Regulars (since a major in the 9th United States Cavalry), to whom he told the trouble in a few hasty words. Both men fairly flew across the room, dashed down the stairs, and by their united efforts Rose, half dead and quite speechless, was drawn up from the fearful trap.

Hamilton managed slightly to increase the size of the hole and provide against a repetition of the accident just narrated, and all being now ready, the two men entered eagerly upon the work before them. They appropriated one of the wooden spittoons of the prison, and to each side attached a piece of clothes-line which they had been permitted to have to dry clothes on. Several bits of candle and the larger of the two chisels were also taken to the operating-cellar. They kept this secret well, and worked alone for many nights. In fact, they would have so continued, but they found that after digging about four feet their candle would go out in the vitiated air. Rose did the digging, and Hamilton fanned air into him with his hat: even then he had to emerge into the cellar every few minutes to breathe. Rose could dig, but needed the light and air; and Hamilton could not fan, and drag out and deposit the excavated earth, and meantime keep a lookout. In fact, it was demonstrated that there was slim chance of succeeding without more assistance, and it was decided to organize a party large enough for effective work by reliefs. As a preliminary step, and to afford the means of more rapid communication with the cellar from the fireplace opening, the long rope obtained from Colonel White was formed by Hamilton into a rope-ladder with convenient wooden rungs. This alteration considerably increased its bulk, and added to Rose's difficulty in concealing it from curious eyes.

He now made a careful selection of thirteen men

besides himself and Hamilton, and bound them by a solemn oath to secrecy and strict obedience. To form this party as he wanted it required some diplomacy, as it was known that the Confederates had on more than one occasion sent cunning spies into Libby disguised as Union prisoners, for the detection of any contemplated plan of escape. Unfortunately, the complete list of the names of the party now formed has not been preserved; but among the party, besides Rose and Hamilton, were Captain John Sterling, 30th Indiana; Captain John Lucas, 5th Kentucky Cavalry; Captain Isaac N. Johnson, 6th Kentucky Cavalry; and Lieutenant F. F. Bennett, 18th Regulars.

The party, being now formed, were taken to Rat Hell and their several duties explained to them by Rose, who was invested with full authority over the work in hand. Work was begun in rear of the little kitchen-room previously abandoned at the southeast corner of the cellar. To systematize the labor, the party was divided into squads of five each, which gave the men one night on duty and two off, Rose assigning each man to the branch of work in which experiments proved him the most proficient. He was himself, by long odds, the best digger of the party; while Hamilton had no equal for ingenious mechanical skill in contriving helpful little devices to overcome or lessen the difficulties that beset almost every step of the party's progress.

The first plan was to dig down alongside the east wall and under it until it was passed, then turn southward and make for the large street sewer next the canal and into which Rose had before noticed workmen descending. This sewer was a large one, believed to be fully six feet high, and, if it could be gained, there could be little doubt that an adjacent opening to the canal would be found to the eastward. It was very soon revealed, however, that the lower side of Libby was built upon ponderous timbers, below which they could not hope to penetrate with their meager stock of tools—such, at least, was the opinion of nearly all the party. Rose nevertheless determined that the effort should be made, and they were soon at work with old penknives and case-knives hacked into saws. After infinite labor they at length cut through the great logs, only to be met by an unforeseen and still more formidable barrier. Their tunnel, in fact, had penetrated below the level of the canal. Water began to filter in — feebly at first, but at last it broke in with a rush that came near drowning Rose, who barely had time to make his escape. This opening was therefore plugged up; and to do this rapidly and leave no dangerous traces put the party to their wit's end.

An attempt was next made to dig into a small sewer that ran from the southeast corner of the prison into the main sewer. After a number of nights of hard labor, this opening was extended to a point below a brick furnace in which were incased several caldrons. The weight of this furnace caused a cave-in near the sentinel's path outside the prison wall. Next day, a group of officers were seen eying the break curiously. Rose, listening at a window above, heard the words "rats" repeated by them several times, and took comfort. The next day he entered the cellar alone, feeling that if the suspicions of the Confederates were really awakened a trap would be set for him in Rat Hell, and determined, if such were really the case, that he would be the only victim caught. He therefore entered the little partitioned corner room with some anxiety, but there was no visible evidence of a visit by the guards, and his spirits again rose.

The party now reassembled, and an effort was made to get into the small sewer that ran from the cook-room to the big sewer which Rose was so eager to reach; but soon it was discovered, to the utter dismay of the weary party, that this wood-lined sewer was too small to let a man through it. Still it was hoped by Rose that by removing the plank with which it was lined the passage could be made. The spirits of the party were by this time considerably dashed by their repeated failures and sickening work; but the undaunted Rose, aided by Hamilton, persuaded the men to another effort, and soon the knives and toy saws were at work again with vigor. The work went on so swimmingly that it was confidently believed that an entrance to the main sewer would be gained on the night of January 26, 1864.

On the night of the 25th two men had been left down in Rat Hell to cover any remaining traces of a tunnel, and when night came again it was expected that all would be ready for the escape between eight and nine o'clock. In the mean time, the two men were to enter and make careful examination of the main sewer and its adjacent outlets. The party, which was now in readiness for its march to the Federal camps, waited tidings from these two men all next day in tormenting anxiety, and the weary hours went by on leaden wings. At last the sickening word came that the planks yet to be removed before they could enter the main sewer were of seasoned oak—hard as bone, and three inches thick. Their feeble tools were now worn out or broken; they could no longer get air to work, or keep a light in the horrible pit, which was reeking with cold mud; in short, any attempt at further progress with the utensils at hand was foolish.

Most of the party were now really ill from the foul stench in which they had lived so long. The visions of liberty that had first lured them to desperate efforts under the inspiration of Rose and Hamilton had at last faded, and one by one they lost heart and hope, and frankly told Colonel Rose that they could do no more. The party was therefore disbanded, and the yet sanguine leader, with Hamilton for his sole helper, continued the work alone. Up to this time thirty-nine nights had been spent in the work of excavation. The two men now made a careful examination of the northeast corner of the cellar, at which point the earth's surface outside the prison wall, being eight or nine feet higher than at the canal or south side, afforded a better place to dig than the latter, being free from water and with clay-top enough to support itself. The unfavorable feature of this point was that the only possible terminus of a tunnel was a yard between the buildings beyond the vacant lot on the east of Libby. Another objection was that, even when the tunnel should be made to that point, the exit of any escaping party must be made through an arched wagon-way under the building that faced the street on the canal side, and every man must emerge on the sidewalk in sight of the sentinel on the south side of the prison, the intervening space being in the full glare of the gas-lamp. It was carefully noted, however, by Rose, long before this, that the west end of the beat of the nearest sentinel was between fifty and sixty feet from the point of egress, and it was concluded that by walking away at the moment the sentinel commenced his pace westward, one would be far enough into the shadow to make it improbable that the color of his clothing could be made out by the sentinel when he faced about to return toward the eastern end of his beat, which terminated ten to fifteen feet east of the prison wall. It was further considered that as these sentinels had for their special duty the guarding of the prison, they would not be eager to burden themselves with the duty of molesting persons seen in the vicinity outside of their jurisdiction, provided, of course, that the retreating forms—many of which they must certainly see—were not recognized as Yankees. All others they might properly leave for the challenge and usual examination of the provost guard who patrolled the streets of Richmond.

The wall of that east cellar had to be broken in three places before a place was found where the earth was firm enough to support a tunnel. The two men worked on with stubborn patience, but their progress was painfully slow. Rose dug assiduously, and Hamilton alternately fanned air to his comrade and dragged out and hid the excavated dirt, but the old difficulty confronted him. The candle would not burn, the air could not be fanned fast enough with a hat, and the dirt hidden, without better contrivances or additional help.

Rose now reassembled the party, and selected from them a number who were willing to renew the attempt.[1] Against the east wall stood a series of stone fenders abutting inward, and these, being at uniform intervals of about twenty feet, cast deep shadows that fell toward the prison front. In one of these dark recesses the wall was pierced, well up toward the Carey street end. The earth here has very densely compressed sand, that offered a strong resistance to the broad-bladed chisel, which was their only effective implement, and it was clear that a long turn of hard work must be done to penetrate under the fifty-foot lot to the objective point. The lower part of the tunnel was about six inches above the level of the cellar floor, and its top about two and a half feet. Absolute accuracy was of course impossible, either in giving the hole a perfectly horizontal direction or in preserving uniform dimensions; but a fair level was preserved, and the average diameter of the tunnel was a little over two feet. Usually one man would dig, and fill the spittoon with earth; upon the signal of a gentle pull, an assistant would drag the load into the

---

[1] The party now consisted of Colonel Thomas E. Rose, 77th Pennsylvania; Major A. G. Hamilton, 12th Kentucky; Captain Terrance Clark, 79th Illinois; Major George H. Fitzsimmons, 30th Indiana; Captain John F. Gallagher, 2d Ohio; Captain W. S. B. Randall, 2d Ohio; Captain John Lucas, 5th Kentucky; Captain I. N. Johnson, 6th Kentucky; Major B. B. McDonald, 101st Ohio; Lieutenant N. S. McKean, 21st Illinois; Lieutenant David Garbett, 77th Pennsylvania; Lieutenant J. C. Fislar, 7th Indiana Artillery; Lieutenant John D. Simpson, 10th Indiana; Lieutenant John Mitchell, 79th Illinois; and Lieutenant Eli Foster, 30th Indiana. This party was divided into three reliefs, as before, and the work of breaking the cellar wall was successfully done the first night by McDonald and Clark.

cellar by the clothes-lines fastened to each side of this box, and then hide it under the straw; a third constantly fanned air into the tunnel with a rubber blanket stretched across a frame, the invention of the ingenious Hamilton; a fourth would give occasional relief to the last two; while a fifth would keep a lookout.

The danger of discovery was continual, for the guards were under instructions from the prison commandant to make occasional visits to every accessible part of the building; so that it was not unusual for a sergeant and several men to enter the south door of Rat Hell in the daytime, while the diggers were at labor in the dark north end. During these visits the digger would watch the intruders with his head sticking out of the tunnel, while the others would crouch behind the low stone fenders, or crawl quickly under the straw. This was, however, so uninviting a place that the Confederates made this visit as brief as a nominal compliance with their orders permitted, and they did not often venture into the dark north end. The work was fearfully monotonous, and the more so because absolute silence was commanded, the men moving about mutely in the dark. The darkness caused them frequently to become bewildered and lost; and as Rose could not call out for them, he had often to hunt all over the big dungeon to gather them up and pilot them to their places.

The difficulty of forcing air to the digger, whose body nearly filled the tunnel, increased as the hole was extended, and compelled the operator to back often into the cellar for air, and for air that was itself foul enough to sicken a strong man.

But they were no longer harassed with the water and timbers that had impeded their progress at the south end. Moreover, experience was daily making each man more proficient in the work. Rose urged them on with cheery enthusiasm, and their hopes rose high, for already they had penetrated beyond the sentinel's beat and were nearing the goal.

The party off duty kept a cautious lookout from the upper east windows for any indications of suspicion on the part of the Confederates. In this extreme caution was necessary, both to avert the curiosity of prisoners in those east rooms, and to keep out of the range of bullets from the guards, who were under a standing order to fire at a head if seen at a window, or at a hand if placed on the bars that secured them. A sentinel's bullet one day cut a hole in the ear of Lieutenant Hammond; another officer was wounded in the face by a bullet, which fortunately first splintered against one of the window-bars; and a captain of an Ohio regiment was shot through the head and instantly killed while reading a newspaper. He was violating no rule whatever, and when shot was from eight to ten feet inside the window through which the bullet came. This was a wholly unprovoked and wanton murder; the cowardly miscreant had fired the shot while he was off duty, and from the north sidewalk of Carey street. The guards (home guards they were) used, in fact, to gun for prisoners' heads from their posts below, pretty much after the fashion of boys after squirrels; and the whizz of a bullet through the windows became too common an occurrence to occasion remark unless some one was shot.

Under a standing rule, the twelve hundred prisoners were counted twice each day, the first count being made about nine in the morning, and the last about four in the afternoon. This duty was habitually done by the clerk of the prison, E. W. Ross, a civilian employed by the commandant. He was christened "Little Ross"[1] by the prisoners, because of his diminutive size. Ross was generally attended by either "Dick" Turner, Adjutant Latouche, or Sergeant George Stansil, of the 18th Georgia, with a small guard to keep the prisoners in four closed ranks during the count. The commandant of the prison, Major Thomas P. Turner (no relative of Dick's), seldom came up-stairs.

To conceal the absence of the five men who were daily at work at the tunnel, their comrades of the party off digging duty resorted, under Rose's supervision, to a device of "repeating." This scheme, which was of vital importance to hoodwink the Confederates and avert mischievous curiosity among the uninformed prisoners, was a hazardous business that severely taxed the ingenuity and strained the nerve of the leader and his coadjutors. The manner of the fraud varied with circumstances, but in general it was worked by five of Rose's men, after being counted at or near the head of the line, stooping down and running toward the foot of the ranks, where a few moments later they were counted a second time, thus making Ross's book balance. The whole five, however, could not always do this undiscovered, and perhaps but three of the number could repeat. These occasional mishaps threatened

[1] "Little Ross" was burned to death, with other guests, at the Spotswood House, Richmond, in 1873.

to dethrone the reason of the puzzled clerk; but in the next count the "repeaters" would succeed in their game, and for the time all went well, until one day some of the prisoners took it into their heads, "just for the fun of the thing," to imitate the repeaters. Unconscious of the curses that the party were mentally hurling at them, the meddlers' sole purpose was to make "Little Ross" mad. In this they certainly met with signal success, for the reason of the mystified clerk seemed to totter as he repeated the count over and over in the hope of finding out how one careful count would show that three prisoners were missing and the next an excess of fifteen. Finally Ross, lashed into uncontrollable fury by the sarcastic remarks of his employers and the heartless merriment of the grinning Yanks before him, poured forth his goaded soul as follows:

"Now, gentlemen, look yere. I can count a hundred as good as any blank man in this yere town, but I'll be blank blanked if I can count a hundred of you blanked Yankees. Now, gentlemen, there's one thing sho: there's eight or ten of you-uns yere that ain't yere!"

This extraordinary accusation "brought down the house," and the Confederate officers and guards, and finally Ross himself, were caught by the resistless contagion of laughter that shook the rafters of Libby.

The officials somehow found a balance that day on the books, and the danger was for this once over, to the infinite relief of Rose and his anxious comrades. But the Confederates appeared dissatisfied with something, and came up-stairs next morning with more officers and with double the usual number of guards; and some of these were now stationed about the room so as to make it next to impossible to work the repeating device successfully. On this day, for some reason, there were but two men in the cellar, and these were Major B. B. McDonald and Captain I. N. Johnson.

The count began as usual, and despite the guard in rear, two of the party attempted the repeating device by forcing their way through the center of the ranks toward the left; but the "fun of the thing" had now worn out with the unsuspecting meddlers, who resisted the passage of the two men. This drew the attention of the Confederate officers, and the repeaters were threatened with punishment. The result was inevitable: the count showed two missing. It was carefully repeated, with the same result. To the dismay of Rose and his little band, the prison register was now brought up-stairs and a long, tedious roll-call by name was endured, each man passing through a narrow door as his name was called, and between a line of guards.

No stratagem that Rose could now invent could avert the discovery by the Confederates that McDonald and Johnson had disappeared, and the mystery of their departure would be almost certain to cause an inquiry and investigation that would put their plot in peril and probably reveal it.

At last the "J's" were reached, and the name of I. N. Johnson was lustily shouted and repeated, with no response. The roll-call proceeded until the name of B. B. McDonald was reached. To the increasing amazement of everybody but the conspirators, he also had vanished. A careful note was taken of these two names by the Confederates, and a thousand tongues were now busy with the names of the missing men and their singular disappearance.

The conspirators were in a tight place, and must choose between two things. One was for the men in the cellar to return that night and face the Confederates with the most plausible explanation of their absence that they could invent, and the other alternative was the revolting one of remaining in their horrible abode until the completion of the tunnel.

When night came the fireplace was opened, and the unlucky pair were informed of the situation of affairs and asked to choose between the alternatives presented. McDonald decided to return and face the music; but Johnson, doubtful if the Confederates would be hoodwinked by any explanation, voted to remain where he was and wait for the finish of the tunnel.

As was anticipated, McDonald's return awakened almost as much curiosity among the inhabitants of Libby as his disappearance, and he was soon called to account by the Confederates. He told them he had fallen asleep in an out-of-the-way place in the upper west room, where the guards must have overlooked him during the roll-call of the day before. McDonald was not further molested. The garrulous busybodies, who were Rose's chief dread, told the Confederate officials that they had certainly slept near Johnson the night before the day he was missed. Lieutenant J. C. Fislar (of the working party), who also slept next to Johnson, boldly declared this a case of mistaken identity, and confidently expressed his belief to both Confederates and Federals who gathered around him that

Johnson had escaped, and was by this time, no doubt, safe in the Union lines. To this he added the positive statement that Johnson had not been in his accustomed sleeping-place for a good many nights. The busybodies, who had indeed told the truth, looked at the speaker in speechless amazement, but reiterated their statements. Others of the conspirators, however, took Fislar's bold cue and stoutly corroborated him.

Johnson was, of course, nightly fed by his companions, and gave them such assistance as he could at the work; but it soon became apparent that a man could not long exist in such a pestilential atmosphere. No tongue can tell how long were the days and nights the poor fellow passed among the squealing rats,— enduring the sickening air, the deathly chill, the horrible, interminable darkness. One day out of three was an ordeal for the workers, who at least had a rest of two days afterward. As a desperate measure of relief, it was arranged, with the utmost caution, that late each night Johnson should come up-stairs, when all was dark and the prison in slumber, and sleep among the prisoners until just before the time for closing the fireplace opening, about four o'clock each morning. As he spoke to no one and the room was dark, his presence was never known, even to those who lay next to him; and indeed he listened to many earnest conversations between his neighbors regarding his wonderful disappearance.[1]

As a matter of course, the incidents above narrated made day-work on the tunnel too hazardous to be in-

---

[1] In a volume entitled "Four Months in Libby," Captain Johnson has related his experience at this time, and his subsequent escape.

dulged in, on account of the increased difficulty of accounting for absentees; but the party continued the night-work with unabated industry.

When the opening had been extended nearly across the lot, some of the party believed they had entered under the yard which was the intended terminus; and one night, when McDonald was the digger, so confident was he that the desired distance had been made, that he turned his direction upward, and soon broke through to the surface. A glance showed him his nearly fatal blunder, against which, indeed, he had been earnestly warned by Rose, who from the first had carefully estimated the intervening distance between the east wall of Libby and the terminus. In fact, McDonald saw that he had broken through in the open lot which was all in full view of a sentinel who was dangerously close. Appalled by what he had done, he retreated to the cellar and reported the disaster to his companions. Believing that discovery was now certain, the party sent one of their number up the rope to report to Rose, who was asleep. The hour was about midnight when the leader learned of the mischief. He quickly got up, went down cellar, entered the tunnel, and examined the break. It was not so near the sentinel's path as McDonald's excited report indicated, and fortunately the breach was at a point whence the surface sloped downward toward the east. He took off his blouse and stuffed it into the opening, pulling the dirt over it noiselessly, and in a few minutes there was little surface evidence of the hole. He then backed into the cellar in the usual crab fashion, and gave directions for the required depression of the tunnel and vigorous resumption of the work. The hole made in the roof of the tunnel was not much larger than a rat-hole, and could not be seen from the prison. But the next night Rose shoved an old shoe out of the hole, and the day afterward he looked down through the prison bars and saw the shoe lying where he had placed it, and judged from its position that he had better incline the direction of the tunnel slightly to the left.

Meantime Captain Johnson was dragging out a wretched existence in Rat Hell, and for safety was obliged to confine himself by day to the dark north end, for the Confederates often came into the place very suddenly through the south entrance. When they ventured too close, Johnson would get into a pit that he had dug under the straw as a hiding-hole both for himself and the tunnelers' tools, and quickly cover himself with a huge heap of short packing-straw. A score of times he came near being stepped upon by the Confederates, and more than once the dust of the straw compelled him to sneeze in their very presence.

On Saturday, February 6, a larger party than usual of the Confederates came into the cellar, walked by the very mouth of the tunnel, and seemed to be making a critical survey of the entire place. They remained an unusually long time and conversed in low tones; several of them even kicked the loose straw about; and in fact everything seemed to indicate to Johnson—who was the only one of the working party now in the cellar—that the long-averted discovery had been made. That night he reported matters fully to Rose at the fireplace opening.

The tunnel was now nearly completed, and when Rose conveyed Johnson's message to the party it caused dismay. Even the stout-hearted Hamilton was for once excited, and the leader whose unflinching fortitude had thus far inspired his little band had his brave spirits dashed. But his buoyant courage rose quickly to its high and natural level. He could not longer doubt that the suspicions of the Confederates were aroused, but he felt convinced that these suspicions had not as yet assumed such a definite shape as most of his companions thought; still, he had abundant reason to believe that the success of the tunnel absolutely demanded its speedy completion, and he now firmly resolved that a desperate effort should be made to that end. Remembering that the next day was Sunday, and that it was not customary for the Confederates to visit the operating-cellar on that day, he determined to make the most in his power of the now precious time. He therefore caused all the party to remain upstairs, directing them to keep a close watch upon the Confederates from all available points of observation, to avoid being seen in whispering groups,—in short, to avoid all things calculated to excite the curiosity of friends or the suspicion of enemies,—and to await his return.

Taking McDonald with him, he went down through the fireplace before daylight on Sunday morning, and, bidding Johnson to keep a vigilant watch for intruders and McDonald to fan air into him, he entered the tunnel and began the forlorn hope. From this time forward he never once turned over the chisel to a relief.

All day long he worked with the tireless patience of

a beaver. When night came, even his single helper, who performed the double duty of fanning air and hiding the excavated earth, was ill from his hard, long task and the deadly air of the cellar. Yet this was as nothing compared with the fatigue of the duty that Rose had performed; and when at last, far into the night, he backed into the cellar, he had scarcely strength enough to stagger across to the rope-ladder.

He had made more than double the distance that had been accomplished under the system of reliefs on any previous day, and the non-appearance of the Confederates encouraged the hope that another day, without interruption, would see the work completed. He therefore determined to refresh himself by a night's sleep for the finish. The drooping spirits of his party were revived by the report of his progress and his unalterable confidence.

Monday morning dawned, and the great prison with its twelve hundred captives was again astir. The general crowd did not suspect the suppressed excitement and anxiety of the little party that waited through that interminable day, which they felt must determine the fate of their project.

Rose had repeated the instructions of the day before, and again descended to Rat Hell with McDonald for his only helper. Johnson reported all quiet, and McDonald taking up his former duties at the tunnel's mouth, Rose once more entered with his chisel. It was now the seventeenth day since the present tunnel was begun, and he resolved it should be the last. Hour after hour passed, and still the busy chisel was plied, and still the little wooden box with its freight of earth made its monotonous trips from the digger to his comrade and back again.

From the early morning of Monday, February 8, 1864, until an hour after midnight the next morning, his work went on. As midnight approached, Rose was nearly a physical wreck: the perspiration dripped from every pore of his exhausted body; food he could not have eaten if he had had it. His labors thus far had given him a somewhat exaggerated estimate of his physical powers. The sensation of fainting was strange to him, but his staggering senses warned him that to faint where he was meant at once his death and burial. He could scarcely inflate his lungs with the poisonous air of the pit; his muscles quivered with increasing weakness and the warning spasmodic tremor which their unnatural strain induced; his head swam like that of a drowning person.

By midnight he had struck and passed beyond a post which he felt must be in the yard. During the last few minutes he had directed his course upward, and to relieve his cramped limbs he turned upon his back. His strength was nearly gone; the feeble stream of air which his comrade was trying, with all his might, to send to him from a distance of fifty-three feet could no longer reach him through the deadly stench. His senses reeled; he had not breath or strength enough to move backward through his narrow grave. In the agony of suffocation he dropped the dull chisel and beat his two fists against the roof of his grave with the might of despair — when, blessed boon! the crust gave way and the loosened earth showered upon his dripping face purple with agony; his famished eye caught sight of a radiant star in the blue vault above him; a flood of light and a volume of cool, delicious air poured over him. At that very instant the sentinel's cry rang out like a prophecy — " Half-past one, and all 's well ! "

Recovering quickly under the inspiring air, he dragged his body out of the hole and made a careful

LIBERTY !

survey of the yard in which he found himself. He was under a shed, with a board fence between him and the east-side sentinels, and the gable end of Libby loomed grimly against the blue sky. He found the wagon-way under the south-side building closed from the street by a gate fastened by a swinging bar, which, after a good many efforts, he succeeded in opening. This was the only exit to the street. As soon as the nearest sentinel's back was turned he stepped out and walked quickly to the east. At the first corner he turned north, carefully avoiding the sentinels in front of the "Pemberton Buildings" (another military prison northeast of Libby), and at the corner above this he went westward, then south to the edge of the canal, and thus, by cautious moving, made a minute examination of Libby from all sides.

Having satisfied his desires, he retraced his steps to the yard. He hunted up an old bit of heavy plank, crept back into the tunnel feet first, drew the plank over the opening to conceal it from the notice of any possible visitors to the place, and crawled back to Rat Hell. McDonald was overjoyed, and poor Johnson almost wept with delight, as Rose handed one of them his victorious old chisel, and gave the other some trifle he had picked up in the outer world as a token that the Underground Railroad to God's Country was open.

Rose now climbed the rope-ladder, drew it up, rebuilt the fireplace wall as usual, and, finding Hamilton, took him over near one of the windows and broke the news to him. The brave fellow was almost speechless with delight, and quickly hunting up the rest of the party, told them that Colonel Rose wanted to see them down in the dining-room.

As they had been waiting news from their absent leader with feverish anxiety for what had seemed to them all the longest day in their lives, they instantly responded to the call, and flocked around Rose a few minutes later in the dark kitchen where he waited them. As yet they did not know what news he brought, and they could scarcely wait for him to speak out; and when he announced, "Boys, the tunnel is finished," they could hardly repress a cheer. They wrung his hand again and again, and danced about with childish joy.

It was now nearly three o'clock in the morning. Rose and Hamilton were ready to go out at once, and indeed were anxious to do so, since every day of late had brought some new peril to their plans. None of the rest, however, were ready; and all urged the advantage of having a whole night in which to escape through and beyond the Richmond fortifications, instead of the few hours of darkness which now preceded the day. To this proposition Rose and Hamilton somewhat reluctantly assented. It was agreed that each man of the party should have the privilege of taking one friend into his confidence, and that the second party of fifteen thus formed should be obligated not to follow the working party out of the tunnel until an hour had elapsed. Colonel H. C. Hobart, of the 21st Wisconsin, was deputed to see that the program was observed. He was to draw up the rope-ladder, hide it, and rebuild the wall; and the next night was himself to lead out the second party, deputing some trustworthy leader to follow with still another party on the third night; and thus it was to continue until as many as possible should escape.

On Tuesday evening, February 9, at seven o'clock, Colonel Rose assembled his party in the kitchen, and, posting himself at the fireplace, which he opened, waited until the last man went down. He bade Colonel Hobart good-by, went down the hole, and waited until he had heard his comrade pull up the ladder, and finally heard him replace the bricks in the fireplace and depart. He now crossed Rat Hell to the entrance into the tunnel, and placed the party in the order in which they were to go out. He gave each a parting caution, thanked his brave comrades for their faithful labors, and, feelingly shaking their hands, bade them Godspeed and farewell.

He entered the tunnel first, with Hamilton next, and was promptly followed by the whole party through the tunnel and into the yard. He opened the gate leading toward the canal, and signaled the party that all was clear. Stepping out on the sidewalk as soon as the nearest sentinel's back was turned, he walked briskly down the street to the east, and a square below was joined by Hamilton. The others followed at intervals of a few minutes, and disappeared in various directions in groups usually of three.

The plan agreed upon between Colonels Rose and Hobart was frustrated by information of the party's departure leaking out; and before nine o'clock the knowledge of the existence of the tunnel and of the departure of the first party was flashed over the crowded prison, which was soon a convention of excited and whispering men. Colonel Hobart made a brave effort to restore order, but the frenzied crowd that now fiercely struggled for precedence at the fireplace was beyond human control.

Some of them had opened the fireplace and were jumping down like sheep into the cellar one after another. The colonel implored the maddened men at least to be quiet, and put the rope-ladder in position and escaped himself.

My companion, Sprague, was already asleep when I lay down that night; but my other companion, Duenkel, who had been hunting for me, was very much awake, and, seizing me by the collar, he whispered excitedly the fact that Colonel Rose had gone out at the head of a party through a tunnel. For a brief moment the appalling suspicion that my friend's reason had been dethroned by illness and captivity swept over my mind; but a glance toward the window at the east end showed a quiet but apparently excited group of men from other rooms, and I now observed that several of them were bundled up for a march. The hope of regaining liberty thrilled me like a current of electricity. Looking through the window, I could see the escaping men appear one by one on the sidewalk below, opposite the exit yard, and silently disappear, without hindrance or challenge by the prison sentinels. While I was eagerly surveying this scene, I lost track of Duenkel, who had gone in search of further information, but ran against Lieutenant Harry Wilcox, of the 1st New York, whom I knew, and who appeared to have the "tip" regarding the tunnel. Wilcox and I agreed to unite our fortunes in the escape. My shoes were nearly worn out, and my clothes were thin and ragged. I was ill prepared for a journey in midwinter through the enemy's country: happily I had my old overcoat, and this I put on. I had not a crumb of food saved up, as did those who were posted; but as I was ill at the time, my appetite was feeble.

Wilcox and I hurried to the kitchen, where we found several hundred men struggling to be first at the opening in the fireplace. We took our places behind them, and soon two hundred more closed us tightly in the mass. The room was pitch-dark, and the sentinel could be seen through the door-cracks, within a dozen feet of us. The fight for precedence was savage, though no one spoke: but now and then fainting men begged to be released. They begged in vain: certainly some of them must have been permanently injured. For my own part, when I neared the stove I was nearly suffocated; but I took heart when I saw but three more men between me and the hole. At this moment a sound as of tramping feet was heard, and some idiot on the outer edge of the mob startled us with the cry, " The guards, the guards!" A fearful panic ensued, and the entire crowd bounded toward the stairway leading up to their sleeping-quarters. The stairway was unbanistered, and some of the men were forced off the edge and fell on those beneath. I was among the lightest in that crowd; and when it broke and expanded I was taken off my feet, dashed to the floor senseless, my head and one of my hands bruised and cut, and my shoulder painfully injured by the boots of the men who rushed over me. When I gathered my swimming wits I was lying in a pool of water. The room seemed darker than before; and, to my grateful surprise, I was alone. I was now convinced that it was a false alarm, and quickly resolved to avail myself of the advantage of having the whole place to myself. I entered the cavity feet first, but found it necessary to remove my overcoat and push it through the opening, and it fell in the darkness below.

I had now no comrade, having lost Wilcox in the stampede. Rose and his party, being the first out, were several hours on their journey; and I burned to be away, knowing well that my salvation depended on my passage beyond the city defenses before the pursuing guards were on our trail, when the inevitable discovery should come at roll-call. The fact that I was alone I regretted; but I had served with McClellan in the Peninsula campaign of 1862. I knew the country well from my frequent inspection of war maps, and the friendly north star gave me my bearings. The rope-ladder had either become broken or disarranged, but it afforded me a short hold at the top; so I balanced myself, trusted to fortune, and fell into Rat Hell, which was a rayless pit of darkness, swarming with squealing rats, several of which I must have killed in my fall. I felt a troop of them run over my face and hands before I could regain my feet. Several times I put my hand on them, and once I flung one from my shoulder. Groping around, I found a stout stick or stave, put my back to the wall, and beat about me blindly but with vigor.

In spite of the hurried instructions given me by Wilcox, I had a long and horrible hunt over the cold surface of the cellar walls in my efforts to find the entrance to the tunnel; and in two minutes after I began feeling my way with my hands I had no idea in what part of the place was the point where I had fallen; my bearings were completely lost, and I must have made the circuit of Rat Hell several times. At my entrance the rats seemed to receive me with cheers sufficiently hearty, I thought; but my vain efforts to find egress seemed to kindle anew their enthusiasm. They had received large reinforcements, and my march around was now received with deafening squeaks. Finally, my exploring hands fell upon a pair of heels which vanished at my touch. Here at last was the narrow road to freedom! The heels proved to be the property of Lieutenant Charles H. Morgan, 21st Wisconsin, a Chickamauga prisoner. Just ahead of him in the tunnel was Lieutenant William L. Watson, of the same company and regiment. With my cut

FIGHTING THE RATS.

hand and bruised shoulder, the passage through the cold, narrow grave was indescribably horrible, and when I reached the terminus in the yard I was sick and faint. The passage seemed to me to be a mile long; but the crisp, pure air and the first glimpse of freedom, the sweet sense of being out of doors, and the realization that I had taken the first step toward liberty and home, had a magical effect in my restoration.

I have related before, in a published reminiscence,[1] my experience and that of my two companions above named in the journey toward the Union lines, and our recapture; but the more important matter relating to the plot itself has never been published. This is the leading motive of this article, and therefore I will not intrude the details of my personal experience into the narrative. It is enough to say that it was a chapter of hairbreadth escapes, hunger, cold, suffering, and, alas! failure. We were run down and captured in a swamp several miles north of Charlottesville, and when we were taken our captors pointed out to us the smoke over a Federal outpost. We were brought back to Libby, and put in one of the dark, narrow dungeons. I was afterward confined in Macon, Georgia; Charleston and Columbia, South Carolina; and in Charlotte, North Carolina. After a captivity of just a year and eight months, during which I had made five escapes and was each time retaken, I was at last released on March 1, 1865, at Wilmington, North Carolina.

Great was the panic in Libby when the next morning's roll revealed to the astounded Confederates that 109 of their captives were missing; and as the fireplace had been rebuilt by some one and the opening of the hole in the yard had been covered by the last man who went out, no human trace guided the keepers toward a solution of the mystery. The Richmond papers having announced the "miraculous" escape of 109 Yankee officers from Libby, curious crowds flocked thither for

[1] "Philadelphia Times," October 28, 1882.

several days, until some one, happening to remove the plank in the yard, revealed the tunnel. A terrified negro was driven into the hole at the point of the bayonet, and thus made a trip to Rat Hell that nearly turned him white.

Several circumstances at this time combined to make this escape peculiarly exasperating to the Confederates. In obedience to repeated appeals from the Richmond newspapers, iron bars had but recently been fixed in all the prison windows for better security, and the guard had been considerably reinforced. The columns of these same journals had just been aglow with accounts of the daring and successful escape of the Confederate General John Morgan and his companions from the Columbus (Ohio) jail. Morgan had arrived in Richmond on the 8th of January, exactly a month prior to the completion of the tunnel, and was still the lion of the Confederate capital.

At daylight a plank was seen suspended on the outside of the east wall; this was fastened by a blanket-rope to one of the window-bars, and was, of course, a trick to mislead the Confederates. General John H. Winder, then in charge of all the prisoners in the Confederacy, with his headquarters in Richmond, was furious when the news reached him. After a careful external examination of the building, and a talk, not of the politest kind, with Major Turner, he reached the conclusion that such an escape had but one explanation —the guards had been bribed. Accordingly the sentinels on duty were marched off under arrest to Castle Thunder, where they were locked up and searched for "greenbacks." The thousand and more prisoners still

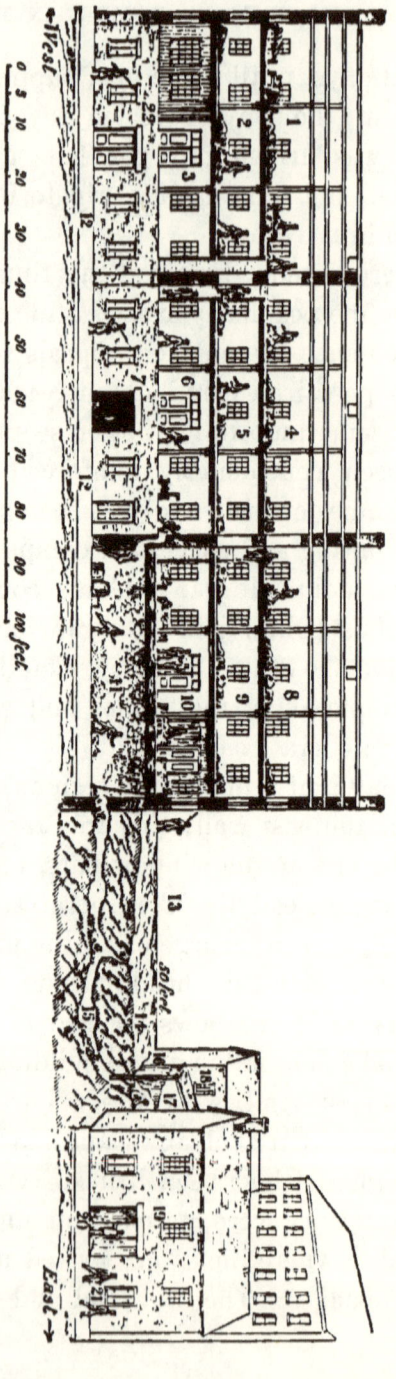

SECTION OF INTERIOR OF LIBBY PRISON AND TUNNEL.

1. Streight's room; 2. Milroy's room; 3. Commandant's office; 4. Chickamauga room (upper); 5. Chickamauga room (lower); 6. Dining-room; 7. Carpenter's shop (middle cellar); 8. Gettysburg room (upper); 9. Gettysburg room (lower); 10. Hospital room; 11. East or "Rat Hell" cellar; 12. South side Canal street, ten feet lower than Carey street; 13. North side Carey street, ground sloping toward Canal; 14. Open lot; 15. Tunnel; 16. Fence; 17. Shed; 18. Kerr's warehouse; 19. Office James River Towing Co.; 20. Gate; 21. Prisoners escaping; 22. West cellar.

in Libby were compensated, in a measure, for their failure to escape by the panic they saw among the "Rebs." Messengers and despatches were soon flying in all directions, and all the horse, foot, and dragoons of Richmond were in pursuit of the fugitives before noon. Only one man of the whole escaping party was retaken inside of the city limits.[1] Of the 109 who got out that night, 59 reached the Union lines, 48 were recaptured, and 2 were drowned.

Colonel Streight and several other officers who had been chosen by the diggers of the tunnel to follow them out, in accordance with the agreement already referred to, lay concealed for a week in a vacant house, where they were fed by loyal friends, and escaped to the Federal lines when the first excitement had abated.

After leaving Libby, Rose and Hamilton turned northward and cautiously walked on a few squares, when suddenly they encountered some Confederates who were guarding a military hospital. Hamilton retreated quickly and ran off to the east; but Rose, who was a little in advance, walked boldly by on the opposite walk, and was not challenged; and thus the two friends separated.

Hamilton, after several days of wandering and fearful exposure, came joyfully upon a Union picket squad, received the care he painfully needed, and was soon on his happy journey home.

Rose passed out of the city of Richmond to the York River Railroad, and followed its track to the Chickahominy bridge. Finding this guarded, he turned to the right, and as the day was breaking he came upon

---
[1] Captain Gates, of the 33d Ohio.

a camp of Confederate cavalry. His blue uniform made it exceedingly dangerous to travel in daylight in this region; and seeing a large sycamore log that was hollow, he crawled into it. The February air was keen and biting, but he kept his cramped position until late in the afternoon; and all day he could hear the loud talk in the camp and the neighing of the horses.

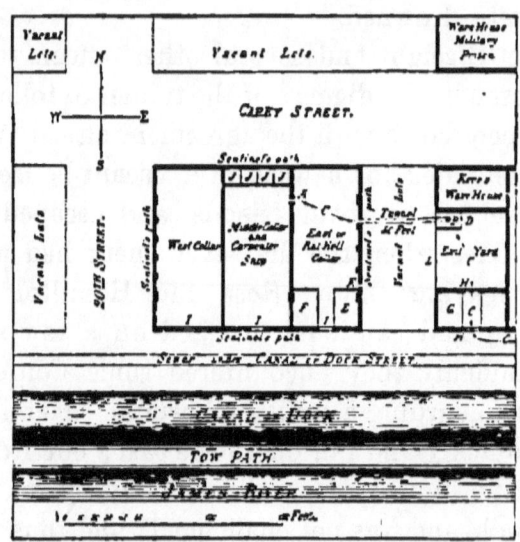

GROUND-PLAN OF LIBBY PRISON AND SURROUNDINGS.

A. Break in fireplace on floor above; B. End of tunnel; CCC. Course of party escaping; D. Shed; E. Cook-room (abandoned Oct., '63); F. Lumber-room; G. Office of James River Towing Company; HH. Gates; III. Doors; J. Cells for condemned prisoners; K. First tunnel (abandoned); L. Fence.

Toward night he came cautiously forth, and finding the Chickahominy fordable within a few hundred yards, he succeeded in wading across. The uneven bed of the river, however, led him into several deep holes, and before he reached the shore his scanty raiment was thoroughly soaked. He trudged on through the woods as fast as his stiffened limbs would bear him, borne up by the hope of early deliverance, and made a brave effort to shake off the horrible ague. He had not gone far, however, when he found himself again close to some Confederate cavalry, and was compelled once more to seek a hiding-place. The day seemed of interminable length, and he tried vainly in sleep to escape from hunger and cold. His teeth chattered in his head, and when he rose at dark to continue his journey his tattered clothes were frozen stiff. In this plight he pushed on resolutely, and was obliged to wade to his waist for hundreds of yards through one of those deep and treacherous morasses that proved such deadly fever-pools for McClellan's army in the campaign of 1862. Finally he reached the high ground, and as the severe exertion had set his blood again in motion and loosened his limbs, he was making better progress, when suddenly he found himself near a Confederate picket. This picket he easily avoided, and, keeping well in the shadow of the forest and shunning the roads, he pressed forward with increasing hopes of success. He had secured a box of matches before leaving Libby; and as the cold night came on and he felt that he was really in danger of freezing to death, he penetrated into the center of the cedar grove and built a fire in a small and secluded hollow. He felt that this was hazardous, but the necessity was desperate, since with his stiffened limbs he could no longer move along fast enough to keep the warmth of life in his body. To add to his trouble, his foot, which had been broken in Tennessee previous to his capture, was now giving him great pain, and threatened to cripple him wholly; indeed, it would stiffen and dis-able the best of limbs to compass the journey he had made in darkness over strange, uneven, and hard-frozen ground, and through rivers, creeks, and bogs, and this without food or warmth.

The fire was so welcome that he slept soundly — so soundly that waking in the early morning he found his boot-legs and half his uniform burned up, the ice on the rest of it probably having prevented its total destruction.

Resuming his journey much refreshed, he reached Crump's Cross-roads, where he successfully avoided another picket. He traveled all day, taking occasional short rests, and before dark had reached New Kent Court-house. Here again he saw some pickets, but by cautious flanking managed to pass them; but in crossing an open space a little farther on he was seen by a cavalryman, who at once put spurs to his horse and rode up to Rose, and, saluting him, inquired if he belonged to the New Kent Cavalry. Rose had on a gray cap, and seeing that he had a stupid sort of fellow to deal with, instantly answered, "Yes," whereupon the trooper turned his horse and rode back. A very few moments were enough to show Rose that the cavalryman's report had failed to satisfy his comrades, whom he could see making movements for his capture. He plunged through a laurel thicket, and had no sooner emerged than he saw the Confederates deploying around it in confidence that their game was bagged. He dashed on as fast as his injured foot would let him, and entered a tract of heavily timbered land that rose to the east of this thicket. At the border of the grove he found another picket post, and barely escaped the notice of several of the men. The only chance of escape lay through a wide, clear field before him, and even this was in full view from the grove that bordered it, and this he knew would soon swarm with his pursuers.

Across the center of this open field, which was fully half a mile wide, a ditch ran, which, although but a shallow gully, afforded a partial concealment. Rose, who could now hear the voices of the Confederates nearer and nearer, dove into the ditch as the only chance, and dropping on his hands and knees crept swiftly forward to the eastward. In this cramped position his progress was extremely painful, and his hands were torn by the briers and stones; but forward he dashed, fully expecting a shower of bullets every minute. At last he reached the other end of the half-mile ditch, breathless and half dead, but without having once raised his head above the gully.

Emerging from this field, he found himself in the Williamsburg road, and bordering the opposite side was an extensive tract thickly covered with pines. As he crossed and entered this tract he looked back and could see his enemies, whose movements showed that they were greatly puzzled and off the scent. When at a safe distance he sought a hiding-place and took a needed rest of several hours.

He then resumed his journey, and followed the direction of the Williamsburg road, which he found picketed at various points, so that it was necessary to avoid open spaces. Several times during the day he saw squads of Confederate cavalry passing along the road so near that he could hear their talk. Near nightfall he reached Diasen Bridge, where he successfully passed another picket. He kept on until nearly midnight, when he lay down by a great tree and, cold as he was, slept soundly until daylight. He now made a careful reconnoissance, and found near the road the ruins of an old building which, he afterward learned, was called "Burnt Ordinary."

He now found himself almost unable to walk with his injured foot, but, nerved by the yet bright hope of liberty, he once more went his weary way in the direction of Williamsburg. Finally he came to a place where there were some smoking fagots and a number of tracks, indicating it to have been a picket post of the previous night. He was now nearing Williamsburg, which, he was inclined to believe from such meager information as had reached Libby before his departure, was in possession of the Union forces. Still, he knew that this was territory that was frequently changing hands, and was therefore likely to be under a close watch. From this on he avoided the roads wholly, and kept under cover as much as it was possible; and if compelled to cross an open field at all, he did so in a stooping position. He was now moving in a southeasterly direction, and coming again to the margin of a wide opening, he saw, to his unutterable joy, a body of Union troops advancing along the road toward him.

Thoroughly worn out, Rose, believing that his deliverers were at hand, sat down to await their approach. His pleasant reverie was disturbed by a sound behind and near him, and turning quickly he was startled to see three soldiers in the road along which the troops first seen were advancing. The fact that these men had not been noticed before gave Rose some uneasiness for a moment; but as they wore blue uniforms, and moreover seemed to take no note of the approaching Federal troops, all things seemed to indicate that they were simply an advanced detail of the same body. This seemed to be further confirmed by the fact that the trio were now moving down the road, apparently with the intent of joining the larger body; and as the ground to the east rose to a crest, both of the bodies were a minute later shut off from Rose's view.

In the full confidence that all was right he rose to his feet and walked toward the crest to get a better view of everything and greet his comrades of the loyal blue. A walk of a hundred yards brought him again in sight of the three men, who now noticed and challenged him.

In spite of appearances a vague suspicion forced itself upon Rose, who, however, obeyed the summons and continued to approach the party, who now watched him with fixed attention. As he came closer to the group, the brave but unfortunate soldier saw that he was lost.

For the first time the three seemed to be made aware of the approach of the Federals, and to show consequent alarm and haste. The unhappy Rose saw before the men spoke that their blue uniform was a disguise, and the discovery brought a savage expression to his lips. He hoped and tried to convince his captors that he was a Confederate, but all in vain; they retained him as their prisoner, and now told him that they were Confederates. Rose, in the first bitter moment of his misfortune, thought seriously of breaking away to his friends so temptingly near; but his poor broken foot and the slender chance of escaping three bullets at a few yards made this suicide, and he decided to wait for a better chance, and this came sooner than he expected.

One of the men appeared to be an officer, who detailed one of his companions to conduct Rose to the rear in the direction of Richmond. The prisoner went quietly with his guard, the other two men tarried a little to watch the advancing Federals, and now Rose began to limp like a man who was unable to go farther. Presently the ridge shut them off from the view of the others. Rose, who had slyly been staggering closer and closer to the guard, suddenly sprang upon the man, and before he had time to wink had twisted his gun from his grasp, discharged it into the air, flung it down, and ran off as fast as his poor foot would let him toward the east and so as to avoid the rest of the Confederates. The disarmed Confederate made no attempt at pursuit, nor indeed did the other two, who were now seen retreating at a run across the adjacent fields.

Rose's heart bounded with new hope, for he felt that he would be with his advancing comrades in a few minutes at most. All at once a squad of Confederates, hitherto unseen, rose up in his very path, and beat him down with the butts of their muskets. All hands now rushed around and secured him, and one of the men called out excitedly, "Hurry up, boys; the Yankees are right here!" They rushed their prisoner into the wooded ravine, and here they were joined by the man whom Rose had just disarmed. He was in a savage mood, and declared it to be his particular desire to fill Rose full of Confederate lead. The officer in charge rebuked the man, however, and compelled him to cool down, and he went along with an injured air that excited the merriment of his comrades.

The party continued its retreat to Barhamsville, thence to the White House on the Pamunkey River, and finally to Richmond, where Rose was again restored to Libby, and, like the writer, was confined for a number of days in a narrow and loathsome cell. On the 30th of April his exchange was effected for a Confederate colonel, and on the 6th of July, 1864, he rejoined his regiment, in which he served with conspicuous gallantry to the close of the war.

As already stated, Hamilton reached the Union lines safely after many vicissitudes, and did brave service in the closing scenes of the rebellion. He is now a resident of Reedyville, Kentucky. Johnson, whose enforced confinement in Rat Hell gave him a unique fame in Libby, also made good his escape, and now lives at North Pleasantville, Kentucky.

Of the fifteen men who dug the successful tunnel, four are dead, viz.: Fitzsimmons, Gallagher, Garbett, and McDonald. Captain W. S. B. Randall lives at Hillsboro, Highland County, Ohio; Colonel Terrance Clark at Paris, Edgar County, Illinois; Captain Eli Foster at Chicago; Colonel N. S. McKean at Collinsville, Madison County, Illinois; and Captain J. C. Fislar at Lewiston, I. T. The addresses of Captains Lucas, Simpson, and Mitchell are unknown at this writing.

Colonel Rose has served faithfully almost since the end of the war with the 16th United States Infantry, in which he holds a captain's commission. No one meeting him now would hear from his reticent lips, or read in his placid face, the thrilling story that links his name in so remarkable a manner with the history of the famous Bastile of the Confederacy.

A HARD ROAD TO TRAVEL OUT OF DIXIE

BY W. H. SHELTON

IT was past noon of the first day of the bloody contest in the Wilderness. The guns of the Fifth Corps, led by Battery D of the 1st New York Artillery, were halted along the Orange turnpike, by which we had made the fruitless campaign to Mine Run. The continuous roar of musketry in front and to the left indicated that the infantry was desperately engaged, while the great guns filling every wooded road leading up to the battle-field were silent. Our drivers were lounging about the horses, while the cannoneers lay on the green grass by the roadside or walked by the pieces. Down the line came an order for the center section, under my command, to advance and pass the right section, which lay in front of us. General Warren, surrounded by his staff, sat on a gray horse at the right of the road where the woods bordered an open field dipping between two wooded ridges. The position we were leaving was admirable, while the one to which we were ordered, on the opposite side of the narrow field, was wholly impracticable. The captain had received his orders in person from General Warren, and joined my command as we passed.

We dashed down the road at a trot, the cannoneers running beside their pieces. At the center of the field we crossed by a wooden bridge over a deep, dry ditch, and came rapidly into position at the side of the turnpike and facing the thicket. As the cannoneers were not all up, the captain and I dismounted and lent a hand in swinging round the heavy trails. The air was full of Minié balls, some whistling by like mad hornets, and others, partly spent, humming like big nails. One of the latter struck my knee with force enough to wound the bone without penetrating the grained-leather boot-leg. In front of us the ground rose into the timber where our infantry was engaged. It was madness to continue firing here, for my shot must first plow through our own lines before reaching the enemy. So after one discharge the captain ordered the limbers to the rear, and the section started back at a gallop. My horse was cut on the flanks, and his plunging, with my disabled knee, delayed me in mounting, and prevented my seeing why the carriages kept to the grass instead of getting upon the roadway. When I overtook the guns they had come to a forced halt at the dry ditch, now full of skulkers, an angle of which cut the way to the bridge. Brief as the interval had been, not a man of my command was in sight. The lead horse of the gun team at my side had been shot and was reeling in the harness. Slipping to the ground, I untoggled one trace at the collar to release him, and had placed my hand on the other when I heard the demand "Surrender!" and turning found in my face two big pistols in the hands of an Alabama colonel. "Give me that sword," said he. I pressed the clasp and let it fall to the ground, where it remained. The colonel had taken me by the right arm, and as we turned toward the road I took in the whole situation at a glance. My chestnut horse and the captain's bald-faced brown were dashing frantically against the long, swaying gun teams. By the bridge stood a company of the 61st Alabama Infantry in butternut suits and slouch-hats, shooting straggling and wounded Zouaves from a Pennsylvania brigade as they appeared in groups of two or three on the road in front. The colonel as he handed me over to his men ordered his troops to take what prisoners they could and to cease firing. The guns which we were forced to abandon were a bone of contention until they were secured by the enemy on the third day, at which time but one of the twenty-four team horses was living.

With a few other prisoners I was led by a short detour through the woods. In ten minutes we had turned the flank of both armies and reached the same turnpike in the rear of our enemy. A line of ambulances was moving back on the road, all filled with wounded, and when we saw a vacant seat beside a driver I was hoisted up to the place. The boy driver was in a high state of excitement. He said that two shells had come flying down this same road, and showed where the trace of the near mule had been cut by a piece of shell, for which I was directly responsible.

The field hospital of General Jubal Early's corps was near Locust Grove Tavern, where the wounded Yankees were in charge of Surgeon Donnelly of the Pennsylvania Reserves. No guard was established, as no one was supposed to be in condition to run away. At the end of a week, however, my leg had greatly improved, although I was still unable to use it. In our party was another lieutenant, an aide on the staff of General James C. Rice, whose horse had been shot under him while riding at full speed with despatches. Lieutenant Hadley had returned to consciousness to find himself a prisoner in hospital, somewhat bruised, and robbed of his valuables, but not otherwise disabled. We two concluded to start for Washington by way of Kelly's Ford. I traded my penknife for a haversack of corn-bread with one of the Confederate nurses, and a wounded officer, Colonel Miller of a New York regiment, gave us a pocket compass. I provided myself with a stout pole, which I used with both hands in lieu of my left foot. At 9 P. M. we set out, passing during the night the narrow field and the dry ditch where I had left my guns. Only a pile of dead horses marked the spot.

On a grassy bank we captured a firefly and shut him in between the glass and the face of our pocket compass. With such a guide we shaped our course for the Rapidan. After traveling nearly all night we lay down exhausted upon a bluff within sound of the river, and slept until sunrise. Hastening to our feet again, we hurried down to the ford. Just before reaching the river we heard shouts behind us, and saw a man beckoning and running after us. Believing the man an enemy, we dashed into the shallow water, and after crossing safely hobbled away up the other side as fast as a man with one leg and a pole could travel. I afterward met this man, himself a prisoner, at Macon, Georgia. He was the officer of our pickets, and would have conducted us into our lines if we had permitted him to come up with us. As it was, we found a snug hiding-place in a thicket of swamp growth, where we lay in concealment all day. After struggling on a few miles in a chilling rain, my leg became so painful that it was impossible to go farther. A house was near by, and we threw ourselves on the mercy of the family. Good Mrs. Brandon had harbored the pickets of both armies again and again, and had luxuriated in real coffee and tea and priceless salt at the hands of our officers. She bore the Yankees only good-will, and after dressing my wound we sat down to breakfast with herself and daughters.

After breakfast we were conducted to the second half-story, which was one unfinished room. There was a bed in one corner, where we were to sleep. Beyond the stairs was a pile of yellow ears of corn, and from the rafters and sills hung a variety of dried herbs and medicinal roots. Here our meals were served, and the girls brought us books and read aloud to pass away the long days. I was confined to the bed, and my companion never ventured below stairs except on one dark night, when at my earnest entreaty he set out for Kelly's Ford, but soon returned unable to make his way in the darkness. One day we heard the door open at the foot of the stairs, a tread of heavy boots on the steps, and a clank, clank that sounded very much like a saber. Out of the floor rose a gray slouch-hat with the yellow cord and tassel of a cavalryman, and in another moment there stood on the landing one of the most astonished troopers that ever was seen. "Coot" Brandon was one of "Jeb" Stuart's rangers, and came every day for corn for his horse. Heretofore the corn had been brought down for him, and he was as ignorant of our presence as we were of his existence. On this day no pretext could keep him from coming up to help himself. His mother worked on his sympathies, and he departed promising her that he would leave us undisturbed. But the very next morning he turned up again, this time accompanied by another ranger of sterner mold. A parole was exacted from my able-bodied companion, and we were left for another twenty-four hours, when I was considered in condition to be moved. Mrs. Brandon gave us each a new blue overcoat from a plentiful store of Uncle Sam's clothing she had on hand, and I opened my heart and gave her my last twenty-dollar greenback — and wished I had it back again every day for the next ten months.

I was mounted on a horse, and with Lieutenant Hadley on foot we were marched under guard all day until we arrived at a field hospital established in the rear of Longstreet's corps, my companion being sent on to some prison for officers. Thence I was forwarded with a train-load of wounded to Lynchburg, on which General Hunter was then marching, and we had good reason to hope for a speedy deliverance. On more than one day we heard his guns to the north, where there was no force but a few citizens with bird-guns to oppose the entrance of his command. The slaves were employed on a line of breastworks which there was no adequate force to hold. It was our opinion that one well-disciplined regiment could have captured and held the town. It was several days before a portion of General Breckinridge's command arrived for the defense of Lynchburg.

I had clung to my clean bed in the hospital just as long as my rapidly healing wound would permit, but was soon transferred to a prison where at night the sleepers — Yankees, Confederate deserters, and negroes — were so crowded upon the floor that some lay under the feet of the guards in the doorways. The atmosphere was dreadful. I fell ill, and for three days lay with my head in the fireplace, more dead than alive.

A few days thereafter about three hundred prisoners were crowded into cattle-cars bound for Andersonville. We must have been a week on this railroad journey when an Irish lieutenant of a Rochester regiment and I, who had been allowed to ride in the baggage-car, were taken from the train at Macon, Georgia, where about sixteen hundred Union officers were confined at the fair-grounds. General Alexander Shaler, of Sedgwick's corps, also captured at the Wilderness, was the ranking officer, and to him was accorded a sort of interior command of the camp. Before passing through the gate we expected to see a crowd bearing some outward semblance of respectability. Instead, we were instantly surrounded by several hundred ragged, barefooted, frowzy-headed men shouting "Fresh fish!" at the top of their voices and eagerly asking for news. With rare exceptions all were shabbily dressed. There was, however, a little knot of naval officers who had been captured in the windings of the narrow Rappahannock by a force of cavalry, and who were the aristocrats of the camp. They were housed in a substantial fair-building in the center of the grounds, and by some special terms of surrender must have brought their complete wardrobes along. On hot days they appeared in spotless white duck, which they were permitted to send outside to be laundered. Their mess was abundantly supplied with the fruits and vegetables of the season. The ripe red tomatoes they were daily seen to peel were the envy of the camp. I well remember that to me, at this time, a favorite occupation was to lie on my back with closed eyes and imagine the dinner I would order if I were in a first-class hotel. It was no unusual thing to see a dignified colonel washing his lower clothes in a pail, clad only in his uniform dress-coat. Ladies sometimes appeared on the guard-walk outside the top of the stockade, on which occasions the cleanest and best-dressed men turned out to see and be seen. I was quite proud to appear in a clean gray shirt, spotless white drawers, and moccasins made of blue overcoat cloth.

On the Fourth of July, after the regular morning count, we repaired to the big central building and held an informal celebration. One officer had brought into captivity, concealed on his person, a little silk national flag, which was carried up into the cross-beams of the building, and the sight of it created the wildest enthusiasm. We cheered the flag and applauded the patriotic speeches until a detachment of the guard succeeded in putting a stop to our proceedings. They tried to capture the flag, but in this they were not successful. We were informed that cannon were planted commanding the camp, and would be opened on us if we renewed our demonstrations.

Soon after this episode the fall of Atlanta and the subsequent movements of General Sherman led to the breaking up of the camp at Macon, and to the transfer of half of us to a camp at Charleston, and half to Savannah. Late in September, by another transfer, we found ourselves together again at Columbia. We had no form of shelter, and there was no stockade around the camp, only a guard and a dead-line. During two hours of each morning an extra line of guards was stationed around an adjoining piece of pine woods, into which we were allowed to go and cut wood and timber to construct for ourselves huts for the approaching winter. Our ration at this time consisted of raw corn-meal and sorghum molasses, without salt or any provision of utensils for cooking. The camp took its name from our principal article of diet, and was by common consent known as "Camp Sorghum." A stream of clear water was accessible during the day by an extension of the guards, but at night the lines were so contracted as to leave the path leading to the water outside the guard. Lieutenant S. H. M. Byers, who had already written the well-known lyric "Sherman's March to the Sea," was sharing my tent, which consisted of a ragged blanket. We had been in the new camp but little more than a week when we determined to make an attempt at escape. Preparatory to starting we concealed two tin cups and two blankets in the pine woods to which we had access during the chopping hours, and here was to be our rendezvous in case we were separated in getting out. Covering my shoulders with an old gray blanket and providing myself with a stick, about the size of a gun, from the woodpile, I tried to smuggle myself into the relief guard when the line was contracted at six o'clock. Unfortunately an unexpected halt was called, and the soldier in front turned and discovered me. I was now more than ever determined on getting away. After a hurried conference with Lieutenant Byers, at which I promised to wait at our rendezvous in the woods until I heard the posting of the ten-o'clock relief, I proceeded alone up the side of the camp to a point where a group of low cedars grew close to the dead-line. Concealing myself in their dark shadow, I could observe at my leisure the movements of the sentinels. A full moon was just rising above the horizon to my left, and in the soft, misty light the guards were plainly visible for a long distance either way. An open field from which the small growth had been recently cut away lay beyond, and between the camp and the guard-line ran a broad road of soft sand — noiseless to cross, but so white in the moonlight that a leaf blown across it by the wind could scarcely escape a vigilant eye. The guards were bundled in their overcoats, and I soon observed that the two who met opposite to my place of concealment turned and walked their short beats without looking back. Waiting until they separated again, and regardless of the fact that I might with equal likelihood be seen by a dozen sentinels in either direction, I ran quickly across the soft sand road several yards into the open field, and threw myself down upon the uneven ground. First I dragged my body on my elbows for a few yards, then I crept on my knees, and so gradually gained in distance until I could rise to a standing position and get safely to the shelter of the trees. With some difficulty I found the cups and blankets we had concealed, and lay down to await the arrival of my companion. Soon I heard several shots which I understood too well; and, as I afterward learned, two officers were shot dead for attempting the feat I had accomplished, and perhaps in emulation of my success. A third young officer, whom I knew, was also killed in camp by one of the shots fired at the others.

At ten o'clock I set out alone and made my way across the fields to the bank of the Saluda, where a covered bridge crossed to Columbia. Hiding when it was light, wandering through fields and swamps by night, and venturing at last to seek food of negroes, I proceeded for thirteen days toward the sea.

In general I had followed the Columbia turnpike; at a quaint little chapel on the shore of Goose Creek, but a few miles out of Charleston, I turned to the north and bent my course for the coast above the city. About this time I learned that I should find no boats along the shore between Charleston and the mouth of the Santee, everything able to float having been destroyed to prevent the escape of the negroes and the desertion of the soldiers. I was ferried over the Broad River by a crusty old darky who came paddling across in response to my cries of "O-v-e-r," and who seemed so put out because I had no fare for him that I gave him my case-knife. The next evening I had the only taste of meat of this thirteen days' journey, which I got from an old negro whom I found alone in his cabin eating possum and rice.

I had never seen the open sea-coast beaten by the surf, and after being satisfied that I had no hope of escape in that direction it was in part my curiosity that led me on, and partly a vague idea that I would get

Confederate transportation back to Columbia and take a fresh start westward bound. The tide was out, and in a little cove I found an abundance of oysters bedded in the mud, some of which I cracked with stones and ate. After satisfying my hunger, and finding the sea rather unexpectedly tame inside the line of islands which marked the eastern horizon, I bent my steps toward a fire, where I found a detachment of Confederate coast-guards, to whom I offered myself as a guest as coolly as if my whole toilsome journey had been prosecuted to that end.

In the morning I was marched a few miles to Mount Pleasant, near Fort Moultrie, and taken thence in a sail-boat across the harbor to Charleston. At night I found myself again in the city jail, where with a large party of officers I had spent most of the month of August. My cell-mate was Lieutenant H. G. Dorr of the 4th Massachusetts Cavalry, with whom I journeyed by rail back to Columbia, arriving at "Camp Sorghum" about the 1st of November.

I rejoined the mess of Lieutenant Byers, and introduced to the others Lieutenant Dorr, whose cool assurance was a prize that procured us all the blessings possible. He could borrow frying-pans from the guards, money from his brother Masons at headquarters, and I believe if we had asked him to secure us a gun he would have charmed it out of the hand of a sentinel on duty.

Lieutenant Edward E. Sill, of General Daniel Butterfield's staff, whom I had met at Macon, during my absence had come to "Sorghum" from a fruitless trip to Macon for exchange, and I had promised to join him

LIEUTENANTS L. E. SILL AND A. T. LAMSON.

in an attempt to escape when he could secure a pair of shoes. On November 29 our mess had felled a big pine-tree and had rolled into camp a short section of the trunk, which a Tennessee officer was to split into shingles to complete our hut, a pretty good cabin with an earthen fireplace. While we were resting from our exertion, Sill appeared with his friend Lieutenant A. T. Lamson of the 104th New York Infantry, and reminded me of my promise. The prisoners always respected their parole on wood-chopping expeditions, and went out and came in at the main entrance. The guards were a particularly verdant body of back-country militia, and the confusion of the parole system enabled us to practise ruses. In our present difficulty we resorted to a new expedient and forged a parole. The next day all three of us were quietly walking down the guard-line on the outside. At the creek, where all the camp came for water, we found Dorr and Byers and West, and calling to one of them in the presence of the guard, asked for blankets to bring in spruce boughs for beds. When the blankets came they contained certain haversacks, cups, and little indispensable articles for the road. Falling back into the woods, we secured a safe hiding-place until after dark. Just beyond the village of Lexington we successfully evaded the first picket, being warned of its presence by the smoldering embers in the road. A few nights after this, having exposed ourselves and anticipating pursuit, we pushed on until we came to a stream crossing the road. Up this we waded for some distance, and secured a hiding-place on a neighboring hill. In the morning we looked out upon mounted men and dogs, at the very point where we had entered the stream, searching for our lost trail. We spent two days during a severe storm of rain and sleet in a farm-barn where the slaves were so drunk on applejack that they had forgotten us and left us with nothing to eat but raw turnips. One night, in our search for provisions, we met a party of negroes burning charcoal, who took us to their camp and sent out for a supply of food. While waiting a venerable "uncle" proposed to hold a prayer-meeting. So under the tall trees and by the light of the smoldering coal-pits the old man prayed long and fervently to the "bressed Lord and Massa Lincoln," and hearty amens echoed through the woods. Besides a few small potatoes, one dried goat ham was all our zealous friends could procure. The next day, having made our camp in the secure depths of a dry swamp, we lighted the only fire we allowed ourselves between Columbia and the mountains. The ham, which was almost as light as cork, was riddled with worm-holes, and as hard as a petrified sponge.

We avoided the towns, and after an endless variety of adventures approached the mountains, cold, hungry, ragged, and foot-sore. On the night of December 13 we were grouped about a guide-post, at a fork in the road, earnestly contending as to which way we should proceed. Lieutenant Sill was for the right, I was for the left, and no amount of persuasion could induce Lieutenant Lamson to decide the controversy. I yielded, and we turned to the right. After walking a mile in a state of general uncertainty, we came to a low white farm-house standing very near the road. It was now close upon midnight, and the windows were all dark; but from a house of logs, partly behind the other, gleamed a bright light. Judging this to be servants' quarters, two of us remained back while Lieutenant Sill made a cautious approach. In due time a negro appeared, advancing stealthily, and, beckoning to my companion and me, conducted us in the shadow of a hedge to a side window, through which we clambered into the cabin. We were made very comfortable in the glow of a bright woodfire. Sweet potatoes were already roasting in the ashes, and a tin pot of barley coffee was steaming on the coals. Rain and sleet had begun to fall, and it was decided that after having been warmed and refreshed we should be concealed in the barn until the following night. Accordingly we were conducted thither and put to bed upon a pile of cornshucks high up under the roof. Secure as this retreat seemed, it was deemed advisable in the morning to burrow several feet down in the mow, so that the children, if by any chance they should climb so high, might romp unsuspecting over our heads. We could still look out through the cracks in the siding and get sufficient light whereby to study a map of the Southern States, which had been brought us with our breakfast. A luxurious repast was in preparation, to be eaten at the quarters before starting; but a frolic being in progress, and a certain negro present of questionable fidelity, the banquet was transferred to the barn. The great barn doors were set open, and the cloth was spread on the floor by the light of the moon. Certainly we had partaken of no such substantial fare within the Confederacy. The central dish was a pork-pie, flanked by savory little patties of sausage. There were sweet potatoes, fleecy biscuits, a jug of sorghum, and a pitcher of sweet milk. Most delicious of all was a variety of corn-bread having tiny bits of fresh pork baked in it, like plums in a pudding.[1]

Filling our haversacks with the fragments, we took grateful leave of our sable benefactors and resumed our journey, retracing our steps to the point of disagreement of the evening before. Long experience in night marching had taught us extreme caution. We had advanced along the new road but a short way when we were startled by the barking of a house-dog. Apprehending that something was moving in front of us, we instantly withdrew into the woods. We had scarcely concealed ourselves when two cavalrymen passed along, driving before them a prisoner. Aware that it was high time to betake ourselves to the cross-roads and describe a wide circle around the military station at Pickensville, we first sought information. A ray of light was visible from a hut in the woods, and believing from its humble appearance that it sheltered friends,

---

[1] Major Sill contributes the following evidence of the impression our trio made upon one, at least, of the piccaninnies who looked on in the moonlight. The picture of Lieutenants Sill and Lamson which appears on page 255 was enlarged from a small photograph taken on their arrival at Chattanooga, before divesting themselves of the rags worn throughout the long journey. Years afterward Major Sill gave one of these pictures to Wallace Bruce of Florida, at one time United States consul at Glasgow. In the winter of 1888-89 Mr. Bruce, at his Florida home, was showing the photograph to his family when it caught the eye of a colored servant, who exclaimed: "O Massa Bruce, I know those gen'men. My father and mother hid 'em in Massa's barn at Pickensville and fed 'em; there was three of 'em; I saw 'em." This servant was a child barely ten years old in 1864, and could have seen us only through the barn door while we were eating our supper in the uncertain moonlight. Yet more than twenty years thereafter he greeted the photograph of the ragged Yankee officers with a flash of recognition.

my companions lay down in concealment while I advanced to reconnoiter. I gained the side of the house, and, looking through a crack in the boards, saw, to my surprise, a soldier lying on his back before the fire playing with a dog. I stole back with redoubled care. Thoroughly alarmed by the dangers we had already encountered, we decided to abandon the roads. Near midnight of December 16 we passed through a wooden gate on a level road leading into the forest. Believing that the lateness of the hour would secure us from further dangers, we resolved to press on with all speed, when two figures with lighted torches came suddenly into view. Knowing that we were yet unseen, we turned into the woods and concealed ourselves behind separate trees at no great distance from the path. Soon the advancing lights revealed two hunters, mere lads, but having at their heels a pack of mongrel dogs, with which they had probably been pursuing the coon or the possum. The boys would have passed unaware of our presence, but the dogs, scurrying along with their noses in the leaves, soon struck our trail, and were instantly yelping about us. We had possessed ourselves of the name of the commanding officer of the neighboring post at Pendleton, and advanced boldly, representing ourselves to be his soldiers. "Then where did you get them blue pantaloons?" they demanded, exchanging glances, which showed they were not ignorant of our true character. We coolly faced them down and resumed our march leisurely, while the boys still lingered undecided. When out of sight we abandoned the road and fled at the top of our speed. We had covered a long distance through forest and field before we heard in our wake the faint yelping of the pack. Plunging into the first stream, we dashed for some distance along its bed. Emerging on the opposite bank, we sped on through marshy fields, skirting high hills and bounding down through dry watercourses, over shelving stones and accumulated barriers of driftwood; now panting up a steep ascent, and now resting for a moment to rub our shoes with the resinous needles of the pine; always within hearing of the dogs, whose fitful cries varied in volume in accordance with the broken conformation of the intervening country. Knowing that in speed and endurance we were no match for our four-footed pursuers, we trusted to our precautions for throwing them off the scent, mindful that they were but an ill-bred kennel and the more easily to be disposed of. Physically we were capable of prolonged exertion. Fainter and less frequent came the cry of the dogs, until, ceasing altogether, we were assured of our escape.

At Oconee, on Sunday, December 18, we met a negro well acquainted with the roads and passes into North Carolina, who furnished us information by which we traveled for two nights, recognizing on the second objects which by his direction we avoided (like the house of Black Bill McKinney), and going directly to that of friendly old Tom Handcock. The first of these two nights we struggled up the foot-hills and outlying spurs of the mountains, through an uninhabited waste of rolling barrens, along an old stage road, long deserted, and in places impassable to a saddle-mule. Lying down before morning, high up on the side of the mountain, we fell asleep, to be awakened by thunder and lightning, and to find torrents of hail and sleet beating upon our blankets. Chilled to the bone, we ventured to build a small fire in a secluded place. After dark, and before abandoning our camp, we gathered quantities of wood, stacking it upon the fire, which when we left it was a wild tower of flame lighting up the whole mountain-side in the direction we had come, and seeming, in some sort, to atone for a long succession of shivering days in fireless bivouac. We followed the same stage road through the scattering settlement of Casher's Valley in Jackson County, North Carolina. A little farther on, two houses, of hewn logs, with verandas and green blinds, just fitted the description we had received of the home of old Tom Handcock. Knocking boldly at the door of the farther one, we were soon in the presence of the loyal mountaineer. He and his wife had been sleeping on a bed spread upon the floor before the fire. Drawing this to one side, they heaped the chimney with green wood, and were soon listening with genuine delight to the story of our adventures.

After breakfast next day, Tom, with his rifle, led us by a back road to the house of "'Squire Larkin C. Hooper," a leading loyalist, whom we met on the way, and together we proceeded to his house. Ragged and forlorn, we were eagerly welcomed at his home by Hooper's invalid wife and daughters. For several days we enjoyed a hospitality given as freely to utter strangers as if we had been relatives of the family.

Here we learned of a party about to start through the mountains for East Tennessee, guided by Emanuel Headen, who lived on the crest of the Blue Ridge. Our friend Tom was to be one of the party, and other refugees were coming over the Georgia border, where Headen, better known in the settlement as "Man Heady," was mustering his party. It now being near Christmas, and the squire's family in daily expectation of a relative, who was a captain in the Confederate

WE ARRIVE AT HEADEN'S.

army, it was deemed prudent for us to go on to Headen's under the guidance of Tom. Setting out at sunset on the 23d of December, it was late in the evening when we arrived at our destination, having walked nine miles up the mountain trails over a light carpeting of snow. Pausing in front of a diminutive cabin, through the chinks of whose stone fireplace and stick chimney the whole interior seemed to be red hot like a furnace, our guide demanded, "Is Man Heady to hum?" Receiving a sharp negative in reply, he continued. "Well, can Tom get to stay all night?" At this the door flew open and a skinny woman appeared, her homespun frock pendent with tow-headed urchins.

"In course you can," she cried, leading the way into the cabin. Never have I seen so unique a character as this voluble, hatchet-faced, tireless woman. Her skin was like yellow parchment, and I doubt if she knew by experience what it was to be sick or weary. She had built the stake-and-cap fences that divided the fields, and she boasted of the acres she had plowed. The cabin was very small. Two bedsteads, with a narrow alleyway between, occupied half the interior. One was heaped with rubbish, and in the other slept the whole family, consisting of father, mother, a daughter of sixteen, and two little boys. When I add that the room contained a massive timber loom, a table, a spinning-wheel, and a variety of rude seats, it will be understood that we were crowded uncomfortably close to the fire. Shrinking back as far as possible from the blaze, we listened in amused wonder to the tongue of this seemingly untamed virago, who, nevertheless, proved to be the kindest-hearted of women. She cursed, in her high, pitched tones, for a pack of fools, the men who had brought on the war. Roderic Norton, who lived down the mountain, she expressed a profane desire to "stomp through the turnpike" because at some time he had stolen one of her hogs, marked, as to the ear, with "two smooth craps an' a slit in the left." Once only she had journeyed into the low country, where she had seen those twin marvels, steam cars and brick chimneys. On this occasion she had driven a heifer to market, making a journey of forty miles, walking beside her horse and wagon, which she took along to bring back the corn-meal received in payment for the animal. Charged by her husband to bring back the heifer bell, and being denied that musical instrument by the purchaser, it immediately assumed more importance to her mind than horse, wagon, and corn-meal. Baffled at first, she proceeded to the pasture in the gray of the morning, cornered the cow, and cut off the bell, and, in her own picturesque language, "walked through the streets of Walhalla cussin'." Rising at midnight she would fall to spinning with all her energy. To us, waked from sleep on the floor by the humming of the wheel, she seemed by the light of the low fire like a witch in a sunbonnet, darting forward and back.

We remained there several days, sometimes at the cabin and sometimes at a cavern in the rocks such as abound throughout the mountains, and which are called by the natives "rock houses." Many of the men at that time were "outliers"—that is, they camped in the mountain fastnesses, receiving their food from some member of the family. Some of these men, as now, had their copper stills in the rock houses, while others, more wary of the recruiting sergeant, wandered from point to point, their only furniture a rifle and a bed-quilt. On December 29, we were joined at the cavern by Lieutenant Knapp and Captain Smith, Federal officers, who had also made their way from Columbia, and by three refugees from Georgia, whom I remember as Old Man Tigue and the two Vincent boys. During the night our party was to start across the mountains for Tennessee. Tom Handcock was momentarily expected to join us. Our guide was busy with preparations for the journey. The night coming on icy cold, and a cutting wind driving the smoke of the fire into our granite house, we abandoned it at nine o'clock and descended to the cabin. Headen and his wife had gone to the mill for a supply of corn-meal. Although it was time for their return, we were in nowise alarmed by their absence, and formed a jovial circle about the roaring chimney. About midnight came a rap on the door. Thinking it was Tom Handcock and some of his companions, I threw it open with an eager "Come in, boys!" The boys began to come in, stamping the snow from their boots and rattling their muskets on the floor, until the house was full, and yet others were on guard without and crowding the porch. "Man Heady" and his wife were already prisoners at the mill, and the house had been picketed for some hours awaiting the arrival of the other refugees, who had discovered the plot just in time to keep out of the toils. Marshaled in some semblance of military array, we were marched down the mountain, over the frozen ground, to the house of old Roderic Norton. The Yankee officers were sent to an upper room, while the refugees were guarded below, under the immediate eyes of the soldiery. Making the best of our misfortune, our original trio bounced promptly into a warm bed, which had been recently deserted by some members of the family, and secured a good night's rest.

Lieutenant Knapp, who had imprudently indulged in frozen chestnuts on the mountain-side, was attacked with violent cramps, and kept the household below stairs in commotion all night humanely endeavoring to assuage his agony. In the morning, although quite recovered, he cunningly feigned a continuance of his pains, and was left behind in the keeping of two guards, who, having no suspicion of his deep designs, left their guns in the house and went out to the spring to wash. Knapp, instantly on the alert, possessed himself of the muskets, and breaking the lock of one, by a powerful effort he bent the barrel of the other, and dashed out through the garden. His keepers, returning from the spring, shouted and rushed indoors only to find their disabled pieces. They joined our party later in the day, rendering a chapfallen account of their detached service.

We had but a moderate march to make to the headquarters of the battalion, where we were to spend the night. Our guards we found kindly disposed toward us, but bitterly upbraiding the refugees, whom they saluted by the ancient name of Tories. Lieutenant Cogdill, in command of the expedition, privately informed us that his sympathies were entirely ours, but as a matter of duty he should guard us jealously while under his military charge. If we could effect our escape thereafter we had only to come to his mountain home and he would conceal us until such time as he could despatch us with safety over the borders. These mountain soldiers were mostly of two classes, both opposed to the war, but doing home-guard duty in lieu of sterner service in the field. Numbers were of the outlier class, who, wearied of continual hiding in the laurel brakes, had embraced this service as a compromise. Many were deserters, some of whom had coolly set at defiance the terms of their furloughs, while others had abandoned the camps in Virginia, and, versed in mountain craft, had made their way along the Blue Ridge and put in a heroic appearance in their native valleys.

That night we arrived at a farm-house near the river, where we found Major Parker, commanding the battalion, with a small detachment billeted upon the family. The farmer was a gray-haired old loyalist, whom I shall always remember, leaning on his staff in the middle of the kitchen, barred out from his place in the chimney-corner by the noisy circle of his unbidden guests. Major Parker was a brisk little man, clad in brindle jeans of ancient cut, resplendent with brass buttons. Two small piercing eyes, deep-set beside a hawk's-beak nose, twinkled from under the rim of his brown straw hat, whose crown was defiantly surmounted by a cock's feather. But he was exceedingly jolly withal, and welcomed the Yankees with pompous good-humor, despatching a sergeant for a jug of apple-jack, which was doubtless as inexpensive to the major as his other hospitality. Having been a prisoner at Chicago, he prided himself on his knowledge of dungeon etiquette and the military courtesies due to our rank.

We were awakened in the morning by high-pitched voices in the room below. Lieutenant Sill and I had passed the night in neighboring caverns of the same miraculous feather-bed. We recognized the voice of the major, informing some culprit that he had just ten minutes to live, and that if he wished to send any dying message to his wife or children then and there was his last opportunity; and then followed the tramping of the guards as they retired from his presence with their victim. Hastily dressing, we hurried down to find what was the matter. We were welcomed with a cheery good-morning from the major, who seemed to be in the sunniest of spirits. No sign of commotion was visible. "Step out to the branch, gentlemen; your parole of honor is sufficient; you'll find towels — been a prisoner myself." And he restrained by a sign the sentinel who would have accompanied us. At the branch, in the yard, we found the other refugees trembling for their fate, and learned that Headen had gone to the orchard in the charge of a file of soldiers with a rope. While we were discussing the situation and endeavoring to calm the apprehensions of the Georgians, the executioners returned from the orchard, our guide marching in advance and looking none the worse for the rough handling he had undergone. The brave fellow had confided his last message and been thrice drawn up toward the branch of an apple-tree, and as many times lowered for the information it was supposed he would give. Nothing was learned, and it is probable he had no secrets to disclose or conceal.

Lieutenant Cogdill, with two soldiers, was detailed to conduct us to Quallatown, a Cherokee station at the foot of the Great Smoky Mountains. Two horses were allotted to the guard, and we set out in military order, the refugees two and two in advance, Headen and Old Man Tigue lashed together by the wrists, and the rear brought up by the troopers on horseback. It was the last day of the year, and although a winter morning, the rare mountain air was as soft as spring. We struck the banks of the Tuckasegee directly opposite to a feathery waterfall, which, leaping over a crag of the opposite cliff, was dissipated in a glittering sheet of spray before reaching the tops of the trees below. As the morning advanced we fell into a more negligent order of marching. The beautiful river, a wide, swift current, flowing smoothly between thickly wooded banks, swept by on our left, and on the right wild, uninhabited mountains closed in the road. The two Vincents were strolling along far in advance. Some distance behind them were Headen and Tigue; the remainder of us following in a general group, Sill mounted beside one of the guards. Advancing in this order, a cry from the front broke on the stillness of the woods, and we beheld Old Man Tigue gesticulating wildly in the center of the road and screaming, "He's gone! He's gone! Catch him!" Sure enough the old man was alone, the fragment of the parted strap dangling from his outstretched wrist. The guard, who was mounted, dashed off in pursuit, followed by the lieutenant on foot, but both soon returned, giving over the hopeless chase. Thoroughly frightened by the events of the morning, Headen[1] had watched his opportunity to make good his escape, and, as we afterward learned, joined by Knapp and Tom Handcock, he conducted a party safely to Tennessee.

At Webster, the court town of Jackson County, we were quartered for the night in the jail, but accompanied Lieutenant Cogdill to a venison breakfast at the

---

[1] A short time ago the writer received the following letter: "Casher's Valley, May 28, 1890. Old Manuel Headen and wife are living, but separated. Julia Ann is living with her mother. The old lady is blind. Old man Norton (Roderic), to whose house you were taken as prisoner, has been dead for years. Old Tom Handcock is dead.—W. R. HOOPER."

THE ESCAPE OF HEADEN.

parsonage with Mrs. Harris and her daughter, who had called on us the evening before. Snow had fallen during the night, and when we continued our march it was with the half-frozen slush crushing in and out, at every step, through our broken shoes. Before the close of this dreary New-Year's day we came upon the scene of one of those wild tragedies which are still of too frequent occurrence in those remote regions, isolated from the strong arm of the law. Our road led down and around the mountain-side, which on our right was a barren, rocky waste, sloping gradually up from the inner curve of the arc we were describing. From this direction arose a low wailing sound, and a little farther on we came in view of a dismal group of men, women, and mules. In the center of the gathering lay the lifeless remains of a father and his two sons; seated upon the ground, swaying and weeping over their dead, were the mother and wives of the young men. A burial party, armed with spades and picks, waited by their mules, while at a respectful distance from the mourners stood a circle of neighbors and passers-by, some gazing in silent sympathy, and others not hesitating to express a quiet approval of the shocking tragedy. Between two families, the Hoopers and the Watsons, a bitter feud had long existed, and from time to time men of each clan had fallen by the rifles of the other. The Hoopers were loyal Union men, and if the Watsons yielded any loyalty it was to the State of North Carolina. On one occasion shortly before the final tragedy, when one of the young Hoopers was sitting quietly in his door, a light puff of smoke rose from the bushes and a rifle-ball plowed through his leg. The Hoopers resolved to begin the new year by wiping out their enemies, root and branch. Before light they had surrounded the log cabin of the Watsons and secured all the male inmates, except one who, wounded, escaped through a window. The latter afterward executed a singular revenge by killing and skinning the dog of his enemies and elevating the carcass on a pole in front of their house.

After a brief stay at Quallatown we set out for Asheville, leaving behind our old and friendly guard. Besides the soldiers who now had us in charge, a Cherokee Indian was allotted to each prisoner, with instructions to keep his man constantly in view. To travel with an armed Indian, sullen and silent, trotting at your heels like a dog, with very explicit instructions to blow out your brains at the first attempt to escape, is neither cheerful nor ornamental, and we were a sorry-looking party plodding silently along the road. Detachments of prisoners were frequently passed over this route, and regular stopping-places were established for the nights. It was growing dusk when we arrived at the first cantonment, which was the wing of a great barren farm-house owned by Colonel Bryson. The place was already occupied by a party of refugees, and we were directed to a barn in the field beyond. We had brought with us uncooked rations, and while two of the soldiers went into the house for cooking utensils, the rest of the party, including the Indians, were leaning in a line upon the door-yard fence; Sill and Lamson were at the end of the line, where the fence cornered with a hedge. Presently the two soldiers reappeared, one of them with an iron pot in which to cook our meat, and the other swinging in his hand a burning brand. In the wake of these guides we followed down to the barn, and had already started a fire when word came from the house that for fear of rain we had best return to the corn-barn. It was not until we were again in the road that I noticed the absence of Sill and Lamson. I hastened to Smith and confided the good news. The fugitives were missed almost simultaneously by the guards, who first beat up the vicinity of the barn, and then, after securing the remainder of us in a corn-crib, sent out the Indians in pursuit. Faithful dogs, as these Cherokees had shown themselves during the day, they proved but poor hunters when the game was in the bush, and soon returned, giving over the chase. Half an hour later they were all back in camp, baking their hoecake in genuine aboriginal fashion, flattened on the surface of a board and inclined to the heat of the fire.[1]

That I was eager to follow goes without saying, but our keepers had learned our slippery character. All the way to Asheville, day and night, we were watched with sleepless vigilance. There we gave our parole, Smith and I, and secured thereby comfortable quarters in the court-house with freedom to stroll about the town. Old Man Tigue and the Vincents were committed to the county jail. We were there a week, part of my spare time being employed in helping a Confederate company officer make out a correct pay-roll.

---

[1] Sill and Lamson reached Loudon, Tennessee, in February. A few days after their escape from the Indian guard they arrived at the house of "Shooting John Brown," who confided them to the care of the young Hoopers and a party of their outlying companions. From a rocky cliff overlooking the valley of the Tuckasegee they could look down on the river roads dotted with the sheriff's posse in pursuit of the Hoopers. So near were they that they could distinguish a relative of the Watsons leading the sheriff's party. One of the Hooper boys, with characteristic recklessness and to the consternation of the others, stood boldly out on a great rock in plain sight of his pursuers (if they had chanced to look up), half resolved to try his rifle at the last of the Watsons.

When our diminished ranks had been recruited by four more officers from Columbia, who had been captured near the frozen summit of the Great Smoky Mountains, we were started on a journey of sixty miles to Greenville in South Carolina. The night before our arrival we were quartered at a large farm-house. The prisoners, together with the privates of the guard, were allotted a comfortable room, which contained, however, but a single bed. The officer in charge had retired to enjoy the hospitality of the family. A flock of enormous white pullets were roosting in the yard. Procuring an iron kettle from the servants, who looked with grinning approval upon all forms of chicken stealing, we sallied forth to the capture. Twisting the precious necks of half a dozen, we left them to die in the grass while we pierced the side of a sweet-potato mound. Loaded with our booty we retreated to the house undiscovered, and spent the night in cooking in one pot instead of sleeping in one bed. The fowls were skinned instead of plucked, and, vandals that we were, dressed on the backs of the picture-frames taken down from the walls.

At Greenville we were lodged in the county jail to await the reconstruction of railway-bridges, when we were to be transported to Columbia. The jail was a stone structure, two stories in height, with halls through the center on both floors and square rooms on each side. The lock was turned on our little party of six in one of these upper rooms, having two grated windows looking down on the walk. Through the door which opened on the hall a square hole was cut as high as one's face and large enough to admit the passage of a plate. Aside from the rigor of our confinement we were treated with marked kindness. We had scarcely walked about our dungeon before the jailer's daughters were at the door with their autograph albums. In a few days we were playing draughts and reading Bulwer, while the girls, without, were preparing our food and knitting for us warm new stockings. Notwithstanding all these attentions, we were ungratefully discontented. At the end of the first week we were joined by seven enlisted men, Ohio boys, who like ourselves had been found at large in the mountains. From one of these new arrivals we procured a case-knife and a gun screw-driver. Down on the hearth before the fire the screw-driver was placed on the thick edge of the knife and belabored with a beef bone until a few inches of its back were converted into a rude saw. The grate in the window was formed of cast-iron bars, passing perpendicularly through wrought-iron plates, bedded in the stone jambs. If one of these perpendicular bars, an inch and a half square, could be cut through, the plates might be easily bent so as to permit the egress of a man. With this end in view we cautiously began operations. Outside of the bars a piece of carpet had been stretched to keep out the raw wind, and behind this we worked with safety. An hour's toil produced but a few feathery filings on the horizontal plate, but many hands make light work, and steadily the cut grew deeper. We recalled the adventures of Claude Duval, Dick Turpin, and Sixteen-string Jack, and sawed away. During the available hours of three days and throughout one entire night the blade of steel was worrying, rasping, eating

GREENVILLE JAIL.

the iron bar. At last the grosser yielded to the temper and persistence of the finer metal. It was Saturday night when the toilsome cut was completed, and preparations were already under way for a speedy departure. The jail had always been regarded as too secure to require a military guard, although soldiers were quartered in the town; besides, the night was so cold that a crust had formed on the snow, and both citizens and soldiers, unused to such extreme weather, would be likely to remain indoors. For greater secrecy of movement, we divided into small parties, aiming to traverse different roads. I was to go with my former companion, Captain Smith. Lots were cast to determine the order of our going. First exit was allotted to four of the Ohio soldiers. Made fast to the grating outside were a bit of rope and strip of blanket, along which to descend. Our room was immediately over that of the jailer and his sleeping family, and beneath our opening was a window, which each man must pass in his descent. At eleven o'clock the exodus began. The first man was passed through the bars amid a suppressed buzz of whispered cautions. His boots were handed after him in a haversack. The rest of us, pressing our faces to the frosty grating, listened breathlessly for the success of the movement we could no longer see. Suddenly there was a crash, and in the midst of mutterings of anger we snatched in the rag ladder and restored the piece of carpeting to its place outside the bars. Our pioneer had hurt his hand against the rough stones, and, floundering in mid-air, had dashed his leg through sash and glass of the window below. We could see nothing of his further movements, but soon discovered the jailer standing in the door, looking up and down the street, seemingly in the dark as to where the crash came from. At last, wearied and worried and disappointed, we lay down in our blankets upon the hard floor.

At daylight we were awakened by the voice of Miss Emma at the hole in the door. "Who got out last night?" "Welty." "Well, you was fools you did n't all go; pap would n't 'a' stopped you. If you 'll keep the break concealed until night we 'll let you all out." The secret of the extreme kindness of our keepers was explained. The jailer, a loyalist, retained his position as a civil detail, thus protecting himself and sons from conscription. Welty had been taken in the night before, his bruises had been anointed, and he had been provisioned for the journey.

We spent the day repairing our clothing and preparing for the road. My long-heeled cowhides, "wife's shoes," for which I had exchanged a uniform waistcoat with a cotton-wooled old darky on the banks of the Saluda, were about parting soles from uppers, and I kept the twain together by winding my feet with stout cords. At supper an extra ration was given us. As soon as it was dark the old jailer appeared among us and gave us a minute description of the different roads leading west into the mountains, warning us of certain dangers. At eleven o'clock Miss Emma came with the great keys, and we followed her, in single file, down the stairs and out into the back yard of the jail. From the broken gratings in front, the bit of rope and strip of blanket were left dangling in the wind.

We made short work of leave-taking, Captain Smith and I separating immediately from the rest, and pushing hurriedly out of the sleeping town, by back streets, into the bitter cold of the country roads. We stopped once to warm at the pits of some negro charcoal-burners, and before day dawned had traveled sixteen miles. We found a sheltered nook on the side of the mountain open to the sun, where we made a bed of dry leaves and remained for the day. At night we set out again, due west by the stars, but before we had gone far my companion, who claimed to know something of the country, insisted upon going to the left, and within a mile turned into another left-hand road. I protested, claiming that this course was leading us back. While we were yet contending, we came to a bridgeless creek whose dark waters barred our progress, and at the same moment, as if induced by the thought of the fording, the captain was seized with rheumatic pains in his knees, so that he walked with difficulty. We had just passed a house where lights were still showing, and to this we decided to return, hoping at least to find shelter for Smith. Leaving him at the gate, I went to a side porch and knocked at the door, which was opened by a woman who proved to be friendly to our cause, her husband being in the rebel army much against his will. We were soon seated to the right and left of her fireplace. Blazing pine-knots brilliantly lighted the room, and a number of beds lined the walls. A trundle-bed before the fire was occupied by a very old woman, who was feebly moaning with rheumatism. Our hostess shouted into the old lady's ear, "Granny, them 's Yankees." "Be they!" said she, peering at us with her poor old eyes. "Be ye sellin' tablecloths?" When it was explained that we were just from the war, she demanded, in an absent way, to know if we were Britishers. We slept in one of the comfortable beds, and, as a measure of prudence, passed the day in the woods, leaving at nightfall with well-filled haversacks. Captain Smith was again the victim of his rheumatism, and directing me to his friends at Cæsar's Head, where I was to wait for him until Monday (it then being Tuesday), he returned to the house, little thinking that we were separating forever.

I traveled very rapidly all night, hoping to make the whole distance, but day was breaking when I reached the head waters of the Saluda. Following up the stream, I found a dam on which I crossed, and although the sun was rising and the voices of children mingled with the lowing of cattle in the frosty air, I ran across the fields and gained a secure hiding-place on the side of the mountain. It was a long, solitary day, and glad was I when it grew sufficiently dark to turn the little settlement and get into the main road up the mountain. It was six zigzag miles to the top, the road turning on log abutments, well anchored with stones, and not a habitation on the way until I should reach Bishop's house, on the crest of the divide. Half-way up I paused before a big summer hotel, looming up in the woods like the ghost of a deserted factory, its broken windows and rotting gateways redoubling the solitude of the bleak mountain-side. Shortly before reaching Bishop's, "wife's shoes" became quite unmanageable. One had climbed up my leg half-way to the knee, and I knocked at the door with the wreck of the other in my hand. My visit had been preceded but a day by a squad of partizan raiders, who had carried away the bedding and driven off the cattle of my new friends, and for this reason the most generous hospitality could offer no better couch than the hard floor. Stretched thereon in close proximity to the dying fire, the cold air coming up through the wide cracks between the hewn planks seemed to be cutting me in sections as with icy saws, so that I was forced to establish myself lengthwise on a broad puncheon at the side of the room and under the table.

In this family "the gray mare was the better horse," and poor Bishop, an inoffensive man, and a cripple withal, was wedded to a regular Xantippe. It was evident that unpleasant thoughts were dominant in the woman's mind as she proceeded sullenly and vigorously with preparations for breakfast. The bitter bread of charity was being prepared with a vengeance for the unwelcome guest. Premonitions of the coming storm flashed now and then in lightning cuffs on the ears of the children, or crashed venomously among the pottery in the fireplace. At last the repast was spread, the table still standing against the wall, as is the custom among mountain housewives. The good-natured husband now advanced cheerfully to lend a hand in removing it into the middle of the room. It was when one of the table-legs overturned the swill-pail that the long pent-up storm burst in a torrent of invective. The prospect of spending several days here was a very gloomy outlook, and the relief was great when it was proposed to pay a visit to Neighbor Case, whose house was in the nearest valley, and with whose sons Captain Smith had lain in concealment for some weeks on a former visit to the mountains. I was curious to see his sons, who were famous outliers. From safe cover they delighted to pick off a recruiting officer or a tax-in-kind collector, or tumble out of their saddles the last drivers of a wagon-train These lively young men had been in unusual demand of late, and their hiding-place was not known even to the faithful, so I was condemned to the society of an outlier of a less picturesque variety. Pink Bishop was a blacksmith, and just the man to forge me a set of shoes from the leather Neighbor Case had already provided. The little still-shed, concealed

PINK BISHOP AT THE STILL.

from the road only by a low hill, was considered an unsafe harbor, on account of a fresh fall of snow with its sensibility to tell-tale impressions. So we set up our shoe-factory in a deserted cabin, well back on the mountain and just astride of that imaginary line which divides the Carolinas. From the fireplace we dug away the corn-stalks, heaping the displaced bundles against broken windows and windy cracks, and otherwise secured our retreat against frost and enemies. Then ensued three days of primitive shoemaking. As may be inferred, the shoes made no pretension to style. I sewed the short seams at the sides, and split the pegs from a section of seasoned maple. Rudely constructed as these shoes were, they bore their wearer triumphantly into the promised land.

I restrained my eagerness to be going until Monday night, the time agreed upon, when, my disabled companion not putting in an appearance, I set out for my old friend's in Casher's Valley. I got safely over a long wooden bridge within half a mile of a garrisoned town. I left the road, and turned, as I believed, away from the town; but I was absolutely lost in the darkness of a snow-storm, and forced to seek counsel as well as shelter. In this plight I pressed on toward a light glimmering faintly through the blinding snow. It led me into the shelter of the porch to a small brown house, cut deeply beneath the low eaves, and protected at the sides by flanking bedrooms. My knock was answered by a girlish voice, and from the ensuing parley, through the closed door, I learned that she was the daughter of a Baptist exhorter, and that she was alone in the house, her brother being away at the village, and her father, who preached the day before at some distance, not being expected home until the next morning. Reassured by my civil-toned inquiries about the road, she unfastened the door and came out to the porch, where she proceeded to instruct me how to go on, which was just the thing I least desired to do. By this time I had discovered the political complexion of the family, and, making myself known, was instantly invited in, with the assurance that her father would be gravely

ARRIVAL HOME OF THE BAPTIST MINISTER.

displeased if she permitted me to go on before he returned. I had interrupted my little benefactress in the act of writing a letter, on a sheet of foolscap, which lay on an old-fashioned stand in one corner of the room, beside the ink-bottle and the candlestick. In the diagonal corner stood a tall bookcase, the crowded volumes nestling lovingly behind the glass doors—the only collection of the sort that I saw at any time in the mountains. A feather-bed was spread upon the floor, the head raised by means of a turned-down chair, and here I was reposing comfortably when the brother arrived. It was late in the forenoon when the minister reached home, his rickety wagon creaking through the snow, and drawn at a snail's pace by a long-furred, knock-kneed horse. The tall but not very clerical figure was wrapped in a shawl and swathed round the throat with many turns of a woolen tippet. The daughter ran out with eagerness to greet her father and tell of the wonderful arrival. I was received with genuine delight. It was the enthusiasm of a patriot eager to find a sympathetic ear for his long-repressed views.[1]

When night came and no entreaties could prevail to detain me over another day, the minister conducted me some distance in person, passing me on with ample

---

[1] The Rev. James H. Duckworth, now postmaster of Brevard, Transylvania County, North Carolina, and in 1868 member of the State Constitutional Convention, in his letter of June 24, 1890, says: "I have not forgotten those things of which you speak. I can almost see you (even in imagination) standing at the fire when I drove up to the gate and went into the house and asked you, 'Have I ever seen you before?' Just then I observed your uniform. 'Oh, yes,' said I; 'I know who it is now.' . . . This daughter of whom you speak married about a year after, and is living in Morgantown, North Carolina, about one hundred miles from here. Hattie (for that is her name) is a pious, religious woman."

directions to another exhorter, who was located for that night at the house of a miller who kept a ferocious dog. I came first to the pond and then to the mill, and got into the house without encountering the dog. Aware of the necessity of arriving before bedtime, I had made such speed as to find the miller's family still lingering about the fireplace with preacher number two seated in the lay circle. That night I slept with the parson, who sat up in bed in the morning, and after disencumbering himself of a striped extinguisher nightcap, electrified the other sleepers by announcing that this was the first time he had ever slept with a Yankee. After breakfast the parson, armed with staff and scrip, signified his purpose to walk with me during the day, as it was no longer dangerous to move by daylight. We must have been traveling the regular Baptist road, for we lodged that night at the house of another lay brother. The minister continued with me a few miles in the morning, intending to put me in the company of a man who was going toward Casher's Valley on a hunting expedition. When we reached his house, however, the hunter had gone; so, after parting with my guide, I set forward through the woods, following the tracks of the hunter's horse. The shoe-prints were sometimes plainly impressed in the snow, and again for long distances over dry leaves and bare ground but an occasional trace could be found. It was past noon when I arrived at the house where the hunters were assembled. Quite a number of men were gathered in and about the porch, just returned from the chase. Blinded by the snow over which I had been walking in the glare of the sun, I blundered up the steps, inquiring without much tact for the rider who had preceded me, and was no little alarmed at receiving a rude and gruff reception. I continued in suspense for some time, until my man found an opportunity to inform me that there were suspicious persons present, thus accounting for his unexpected manner. The explanation was made at a combination meal, serving for both dinner and supper, and consisting exclusively of beans. I set out at twilight to make a walk of thirteen miles to the house of our old friend Esquire Hooper. Eager for the cordial welcome which I knew awaited me, and nerved by the frosty air, I sped over the level wood road, much of the way running instead of walking. Three times I came upon bends of the same broad rivulet. Taking off my shoes and stockings and rolling up my trousers above my knees, I tried the first passage. Flakes of broken ice were eddying against the banks, and before gaining the middle of the stream my feet and ankles ached with the cold, the sharp pain increasing at every step until I threw my blanket on the opposite bank and springing upon it wrapped my feet in its dry folds. Rising a little knoll soon after making the third ford, I came suddenly upon the familiar stopping-place of my former journey. It was scarcely more than nine o'clock, and the little hardships of the journey from Cæsar's Head seemed but a cheap outlay for the joy of the meeting with friends so interested in the varied fortunes of myself and my late companions. Together we rejoiced at the escape of Sill and Lamson, and made merry over the vicissitudes of my checkered career. Here I first learned of the safe arrival in Tennessee of Knapp, Man Heady, and old Tom Handcock.

After a day's rest I climbed the mountains to the Headen cabin, now presided over by the heroine of the heifer-bell, in the absence of her fugitive husband. Saddling her horse, she took me the next evening to join a lad who was about starting for Shooting Creek. Young Green was awaiting my arrival, and after a brief delay we were off on a journey of something like sixty miles; the journey, however, was pushed to a successful termination by the help of information gleaned by the way. It was at the close of the last night's march, which had been long and uneventful, except that we had surmounted no fewer than three snow-capped ridges, that my blacksmith's shoes, soaked to a pulp by the wet snow, gave out altogether. On the top of the last ridge I found myself panting in the yellow light of the rising sun, the sad wrecks of my two shoes dangling from my hands, a wilderness of beauty spread out before me, and a sparkling field of frosty forms beneath my tingling feet. Stretching far into the west toward the open country of East Tennessee was the limitless wilderness of mountains, drawn like mighty furrows across the toilsome way, the pale blue of the uttermost ridges fading into an imperceptible union with the sky. A log house was in sight down in the valley, a perpendicular column of smoke rising from its single chimney. Toward this we picked our way, I in my stocking feet, and my boy guide confidently predicting that we should find the required cobbler. Of course we found him in a country where every family makes its own shoes as much as its own bread, and he was ready to serve the traveler without pay. Notwithstanding our night's work, we tarried only for the necessary repairs, and just before sunset we looked down upon the scattering settlement of Shooting Creek. Standing on the bleak brow of "Chunky Gall" Mountain, my guide recognized the first familiar object on the trip, which was the roof of his uncle's house. At Shooting Creek I was the guest of the Widow Kitchen, whose house was the chief one in the settlement, and whose estate boasted two slaves. The husband had fallen by an anonymous bullet while salting his cattle on the mountain in an early year of the war.

On the day following my arrival I was conducted over a ridge to another creek, where I met two professional guides, Quince Edmonston and Mack Hooper. As I came upon the pair parting a thicket of laurel, with their long rifles at a shoulder, I instantly recognized the coat of the latter as the snuff-colored sack in which I had last seen Lieutenant Lamson. It had been given to the man at Chattanooga, where these same guides had conducted my former companions in safety a month before. Quince Edmonston, the elder, had led numerous parties of Yankee officers over the Wacheesa trail for a consideration of a hundred dollars, pledged to be paid by each officer at Chattanooga or Nashville.

Two other officers were concealed near by, and a number of refugees, awaiting a convoy, and an arrangement was rapidly made with the guides. The swollen condition of the Valley River made it necessary to remain for several days at Shooting Creek before setting out. Mack and I were staying at the house of Mrs. Kitchen. It was on the afternoon of a memorable Friday, the rain still falling in torrents without, that I sat before the fire poring over a small Sunday-school book,—the only printed book in the

SURPRISED AT MRS. KITCHEN'S.

house, if not in the settlement. Mack Hooper was sitting by the door. Attracted by a rustling sound in his direction, I looked up just in time to see his heels disappearing under the nearest bed. Leaping to my feet with an instinctive impulse to do likewise, I was confronted in the doorway by a stalwart Confederate officer fully uniformed and armed. Behind him was his quartermaster-sergeant. This was a government party collecting the tax in kind, which at that time throughout the Confederacy was the tenth part of all crops and other farm productions. It was an ugly surprise. Seeing no escape, I ventured a remark on the weather: only a stare in reply. A plan of escape flashed through my mind like an inspiration. I seated myself quietly, and for an instant bent my eyes upon the printed pages. The two soldiers had advanced to the corner of the chimney nearest the door, inquiring for the head of the family, and keeping their eyes riveted on my hostile uniform. At this juncture I was seized with a severe fit of coughing. With one hand upon my chest, I walked slowly past the men, and laid my carefully opened book face down upon a chest. With another step or two I was in the porch, and bounding into the kitchen I sprang out through a window already opened by the women for my exit. Away I sped bareheaded through the pelting rain, now crashing through thick underbrush, now up to my waist in swollen streams, plunging on and on, only mindful to select a course that would baffle horsemen in pursuit. After some miles of running I took cover behind a stack, within view of the road which Mack must take in retreating to the other settlement; and sure enough here he was, coming down the road with my cap and haversack, which was already loaded for the western journey. Mack had remained undiscovered under the bed, an interested listener to the conversation that ensued. The officer had been assured that I was a friendly scout; but, convinced of the contrary by my flight, he had departed swearing he would capture that Yankee before morning if he had to search the whole settlement. So alarmed were we for our safety that we crossed that night into a third valley and slept in the loft of a horse-barn.

On Sunday our expedition assembled on a hillside overlooking Shooting Creek, where our friends in the secret of the movement came up to bid us adieu. With guides we were a party of thirteen or fourteen, but only three of us officers who were to pay for our safe conduct. Each man carried his supply of bread and meat and bedding. Some were wrapped in faded bed-quilts and some in tattered army blankets; nearly all wore ragged clothes, broken shoes, and had unkempt beards. We arrived upon a mountain-side overlooking the settlement of Peach Tree, and were awaiting the friendly shades of night under which to descend to the house of the man who was to put us across Valley River. Premature darkness was accompanied with torrents of rain, through which we followed our now uncertain guides. At last the light of the cabin we were seeking gleamed humidly through the trees. Most of the family fled into the outhouses at our approach, some of them not reappearing until we were disposed for sleep in a half-circle before the fire. The last arrivals were two tall women in homespun dresses and calico sunbonnets. They slid timidly in at the door, with averted faces, and then with a rush and a bounce covered themselves out of sight in a bed, where they had probably been sleeping in the same clothing when we approached the house. Here we learned that a cavalcade of four hundred Texan Rangers had advanced into Tennessee by the roads on the day before. Our guides, familiar with the movements of these dreaded troopers, calculated that with the day's delay enforced by the state of the river a blow would have been struck and the marauders would be in full retreat before we should arrive on the ground. We passed that day concealed in a stable, and as soon as it was sufficiently dark we proceeded in a body to the bank of the river, attended by a man and a horse. The stream was narrow, but the current was full and swift. The horse breasted the flood with difficulty, but he bore us all across one at a time, seated behind the farmer.

We had now left behind us the last settlement, and before us lay only wild and uninhabited mountains. The trail we traveled was an Indian path extending for nearly seventy miles through an uninhabited wilderness. Instead of crossing the ridges it follows the trend of the range, winding for the most part along the crests of the divides. The occasional traveler, having once mounted to its level, pursues his solitary way with little climbing.

Early in the morning of the fourth day our little party was assembled upon the last mountain overlooking the open country of East Tennessee. Some of us had been wandering in the mountains for the whole winter. We were returning to a half-forgotten world of farms and fences, roads and railways. Below us stretched the Tellico River away toward the line of towns marking the course of the Nashville and Chattanooga Railroad. One of the guides who had ventured down to the nearest house returned with information

THE MEETING WITH THE SECOND OHIO HEAVY ARTILLERY.

that the four hundred Texan Rangers had burned the depot at Philadelphia Station the day before, but were now thought to be out of the country. We could see the distant smoke arising from the ruins. Where the river flowed out of the mountains were extensive ironworks, the property of a loyal citizen, and in front of his house we halted for consultation. He regretted that we had shown ourselves so soon, as the rear-guard of the marauders had passed the night within sight of where we now stood. Our nearest pickets were at Loudon, thirty miles distant on the railway, and for this station we were advised to make all speed.

For half a mile the road ran along the bank of the river, and then turned around a wooded bluff to the right. Opposite this bluff and accessible by a shallow ford was another hill, where it was feared that some of the Rangers were still lingering about their camp. As we came to the turn in the road our company was walking rapidly in Indian file, guide Edmonston and I at the front. Coming around the bluff from the opposite direction was a countryman mounted on a powerful gray mare. His overcoat was army blue, but he wore a bristling fur cap, and his rifle was slung on his back. At sight of us he turned in his saddle to shout to some one behind, and bringing his gun to bear came tearing and swearing down the road, spattering the gravel under the big hoofs of the gray. Close at his heels rode two officers in Confederate gray uniforms, and a motley crowd of riders closed up the road behind. In an instant the guide and I were surrounded, the whole cavalcade leveling their guns at the thicket and calling on our companions, who could be plainly heard crashing through the bushes, to halt. The dress of but few of our captors could be seen, nearly all being covered with rubber talmas; but their mounts, including mules as well as horses, were equipped with every variety of bridle and saddle to be imagined. I knew at a glance that this was no body of our cavalry. If we were in the hands of the Rangers, the fate of the guides and refugees would be the hardest. I thought they might spare the lives of the officers. "Who are you? What are you doing here?" demanded the commander, riding up to us and scrutinizing our rags. I hesitated a moment, and then, throwing off the blanket I wore over my shoulders, simply said, "You can see what I am." My rags were the rags of a uniform, and spoke for themselves.

Our captors proved to be a company of the 2d Ohio Heavy Artillery, in pursuit of the marauders into whose clutches we thought we had fallen. The farmer on the gray mare was the guide of the expedition, and the two men uniformed as rebel officers were Union scouts. The irregular equipment of the animals, which had excited my suspicion most, as well as the animals themselves, had been hastily impressed from the country about the village of Loudon, where the 2d Ohio was stationed. On the following evening, which was the 4th of March, the day of the second inauguration of President Lincoln, we walked into Loudon and gladly surrendered ourselves to the outposts of the Ohio Heavy Artillery.

ESCAPE OF GENERAL BRECKINRIDGE

BY JOHN TAYLOR WOOD

AS one of the aides of President Jefferson Davis, I left Richmond with him and his cabinet on April 2, 1865, the night of evacuation, and accompanied him through Virginia, the Carolinas, and Georgia, until his capture. Except Lieutenant Barnwell, I was the only one of the party who escaped. After our surprise, I was guarded by a trooper, a German, who had appropriated my horse and most of my belongings. I determined, if possible, to escape; but after witnessing Mr. Davis's unsuccessful attempt, I was doubtful of success. However, I consulted him, and he advised me to try. Taking my guard aside, I asked him, by signs (for he could speak little or no English), to accompany me outside the picket-line to the swamp, showing him at the same time a twenty-dollar gold piece. He took it, tried the weight of it in his hands, and put it between his teeth. Fully satisfied that it was not spurious, he escorted me with his carbine to the stream, the banks of which were lined with a few straggling alder-bushes and thick saw-grass. I motioned him to return to camp, only a few rods distant. He shook his head, saying, "*Nein, nein.*" I gave him another twenty-dollar gold piece; he chinked them together, and held up two fingers. I turned my pockets inside out, and then, satisfied that I had no more, he left me.

Creeping a little farther into the swamp, I lay concealed for about three hours in the most painful position, sometimes moving a few yards almost *ventre à terre* to escape notice; for I was within hearing of the camps on each side of the stream, and often when the soldiers came down for water, or to water their horses, I was within a few yards of them. Some two hours or more passed thus before the party moved. The wagons left first, then the bugles sounded, and the president started on one of his carriage-horses, followed by his staff and a squadron of the enemy. Shortly after their departure I saw some one leading two abandoned horses into the swamp, and recognized Lieutenant Barnwell of our escort. Secreting the horses, we picked up from the debris of the camp parts of two saddles and bridles, and with some patching and tying fitted out our horses, as sad and war-worn animals as ever man bestrode. Though hungry and tired, we gave the remains of the camp provisions to a Mr. Fenn for dinner. He recommended us to Widow Paulk's, ten miles distant, an old lady rich in cattle alone.

The day after my escape, I met Judah P. Benjamin as M. Bonfals, a French gentleman traveling for information, in a light wagon, with Colonel Leovie, who acted as interpreter. With goggles on, his beard grown, a hat well over his face, and a large cloak hiding his figure, no one would have recognized him as the late secretary of state of the Confederacy. I told him of the capture of Mr. Davis and his party, and made an engagement to meet him near Madison, Florida, and there decide upon our future movements. He was anxious to push on, and left us to follow more leisurely, passing as paroled soldiers returning home. For the next three days we traveled as fast as our poor horses would permit, leading or driving them; for even if they had been strong enough, their backs were in such a condition that we could not ride. We held on to them simply in the hope that we might be able to dispose of them or exchange them to advantage; but we finally were forced to abandon one.

On the 13th we passed through Valdosta, the first place since leaving Washington, in upper Georgia, in which we were able to purchase anything. Here I secured two hickory shirts and a pair of socks, a most welcome addition to my outfit; for, except what I stood in, I had left all my baggage behind. Near Valdosta we found Mr. Osborne Barnwell, an uncle of my young friend, a refugee from the coast of South Carolina, where he had lost a beautiful estate, surrounded with all the comforts and elegances which wealth and a refined taste could offer. Here in the pine forests, as far as possible from the paths of war, and almost outside of civilization, he had brought his family of ladies and children, and with the aid of his servants, most of whom had followed him, had built with a few tools a rough log cabin with six or eight rooms, but without nails, screws, bolts, or glass—almost as primitive a building as Robinson Crusoe's. But, in spite of all drawbacks, the ingenuity and deft hands of the ladies had given to the premises an air of comfort and refinement that was most refreshing. Here I rested two days, enjoying the company of this charming family, with whom Lieutenant Barnwell remained. On the 15th I crossed into Florida, and rode to General Finnegan's, near Madison. Here I met General Breckinridge, the late secretary of war of the Confederacy, alias Colonel Cabell, and his aide, Colonel Wilson,— a pleasant encounter for both parties. Mr. Benjamin had been in the neighborhood, but, hearing that the enemy were in Madison, had gone off at a tangent. We were fully posted as to the different routes to the seaboard by General Finnegan, and discussed with him the most feasible way of leaving the country. I inclined to the eastern coast, and this was decided on. I exchanged my remaining horse with General Finnegan for a better, giving him fifty dollars to boot. Leaving Madison, we crossed the Suwanee River at Moody's Ferry, and took the old St. Augustine road, but seldom traveled in late years, as it leads through a pine wilderness, and there is one stretch of twenty miles with only water of bad quality, at the Diable Sinks. I rode out of my way some fifteen miles to Mr. Yulee's, formerly senator of the United States, and afterward Confederate senator, hoping to meet Mr. Benjamin; but he was too wily to be found at the house of a friend. Mr. Yulee was absent on my arrival, but Mrs. Yulee, a charming lady, and one of a noted family of beautiful women, welcomed me heartily. Mr. Yulee returned during the night from Jacksonville, and gave me the first news of what was going on in the world that I had had for nearly a month, including the information that Mr. Davis and party had reached Hilton Head on their way north.

Another day's ride brought us to the house of the brothers William and Samuel Owens, two wealthy and hospitable gentlemen, near Orange Lake. Here I rejoined General Breckinridge, and we were advised to secure the services and experience of Captain Dickinson. We sent to Waldo for him, and a most valuable friend he proved. During the war he had rendered notable services; among others he had surprised and captured the United States gunboat *Columbine* on the St. John's River, one of whose small boats he had retained, and kept concealed near the banks of the river. This boat with two of his best men he now put at our disposal, with orders to meet us on the upper St. John.

We now passed through a much more interesting country than the two or three hundred miles of pines we had just traversed. It was better watered, the forests were more diversified with varied species, occasionally thickets or hummocks were met with, and later these gave place to swamps and everglades with a tropical vegetation. The road led by Silver Spring, the clear and crystal waters of which show at the depth of hundreds of feet almost as distinctly as though seen through air.

We traveled incognito, known only to good friends, who sent us stage by stage from one to another, and by all we were welcomed most kindly. Besides those mentioned, I recall with gratitude the names of Judge Dawkins, Mr. Mann, Colonel Summers, Major Stork, all of whom overwhelmed us with kindness, offering us of everything they had. Of money they were as bare as ourselves, for Confederate currency had disappeared as suddenly as snow before a warm sun, and greenbacks were as yet unknown. Before leaving our friends, we laid in a three weeks' supply of stores; for we could not depend upon obtaining any further south.

On May 25 we struck the St. John's River at Fort Butler, opposite Volusia, where we met Russell and O'Toole, two of Dickinson's command, in charge of the boat; and two most valuable and trustworthy comrades they proved to be, either in camp or in the boat, as hunters or fishermen. The boat was a man-of-war's small four-oared gig; her outfit was scanty, but what was necessary we rapidly improvised. Here General Breckinridge and I gave our horses to our companions, and thus ended my long ride of a thousand miles from Virginia.

Stowing our supplies away, we bade good-by to our friends, and started up the river with a fair wind. Our party consisted of General Breckinridge; his aide, Colonel Wilson of Kentucky; the general's servant, Tom, who had been with him all through the war; besides Russell, O'Toole, and I,—six in all. With our stores, arms, etc., it was a tight fit to get into the boat; there was no room to lie down or to stretch. At night we landed, and, like old campaigners, were soon comfortable. But at midnight the rain came down in bucketfuls, and continued till nearly morning; and, notwithstanding every effort, a large portion of our supplies were soaked and rendered worthless, and, what was worse, some of our powder shared the same fate.

Morning broke on a thoroughly drenched and unhappy company; but a little rum and water, with a corn-dodger and the rising sun, soon stirred us, and with a fair wind we made a good day's run,—some thirty-five miles. Except the ruins of two huts, there was no sign that a human being had ever visited these waters; for the war and the occasional visit of a gunboat had driven off the few settlers. The river gradually became narrower and more tortuous as we approached its head waters. The banks are generally low, with a few sandy elevations, thickly wooded or swampy. Occasionally we passed a small opening, or savanna, on which were sometimes feeding a herd of wild cattle and deer; at the latter we had several pot-shots, all wide. Alligators, as immovable as the logs on which they rested, could be counted by hundreds, and of all sizes up to twelve or fifteen feet. Occasionally, as we passed uncomfortably near, we could not resist, even with our scant supply of ammunition, giving them a little cold lead between the head and shoulders, the only vulnerable place. With a fair wind we sailed the twelve miles across Lake Monroe, a pretty sheet of water, the deserted huts of Enterprise and Mellonville on each side. Above the lake the river became still narrower and more tortuous, dividing sometimes into numerous branches, most of which proved to be mere *culs-de-sac*. The long moss, reaching from the overhanging branches to the water, gave to the surroundings a most weird and funereal aspect.

On May 29 we reached Lake Harney, whence we determined to make the portage to Indian River. O'Toole was sent to look for some means of moving our boat. He returned next day with two small black bulls yoked to a pair of wheels such as are used by lumbermen. Their owner was a compound of Caucasian, African, and Indian, with the shrewdness of the white, the good temper of the negro, and the indolence of the red man. He was at first exorbitant in his demands; but a little money, some tobacco, and a spare fowling-piece made him happy, and he was ready to let us drive his beasts to the end of the peninsula. It required some skill to mount the boat securely on the wheels and to guard against any upsets or collisions, for our escape depended upon carrying it safely across.

The next morning we made an early start. Our course was an easterly one, through a roadless, flat, sandy pine-barren, with an occasional thicket and swamp. From the word "go" trouble with the bulls began. Their owner seemed to think that in furnishing them he had fulfilled his part of the contract. They would neither "gee" nor "haw"; if one started ahead, the other would go astern. If by accident they started ahead together, they would certainly bring up with their heads on each side of a tree. Occasionally they would lie down in a pool to get rid of the flies, and only by the most vigorous prodding could they be induced to move.

Paul, the owner, would loiter in the rear, but was always on hand when we halted for meals. Finally we told him, "No work, no grub; no drive bulls, no tobacco." This roused him to help us. Two days were thus occupied in covering eighteen miles. It would have been less labor to have tied the beasts, put them into the boat, and hauled it across the portage. The weather was intensely hot, and our time was made miserable by day with sand-flies, and by night with mosquitos.

The waters of Indian River were a most welcome sight, and we hoped that most of our troubles were over. Paul and his bulls of Bashan were gladly dismissed to the wilderness. Our first care was to make good any defects in our boat: some leaks were stopped by a little calking and pitching. Already our supply of provisions began to give us anxiety: only bacon and sweet potatoes remained. The meal was wet and worthless, and, what was worse, all our salt had dissolved. However, with the waters alive with fish, and some game on shore, we hoped to pull through.

We reached Indian River, or lagoon, opposite Cape Carnaveral. It extends along nearly the entire eastern coast of Florida, varying in width from three to six miles, and is separated from the Atlantic by a narrow sand ridge, which is pierced at different points by shifting inlets. It is very shoal, so much so that we were obliged to haul our boat out nearly half a mile before she would float, and the water is teeming with stingarees, sword-fish, crabs, etc. But once afloat, we headed to the southward with a fair wind.

For four days we continued to make good progress, taking advantage of every fair wind by night as well as by day. Here, as on the St. John's River, the same scene of desolation as far as human beings were concerned was presented. We passed a few deserted cabins, around which we were able to obtain a few cocoanuts and watermelons, a most welcome addition to our slim commissariat. Unfortunately, oranges

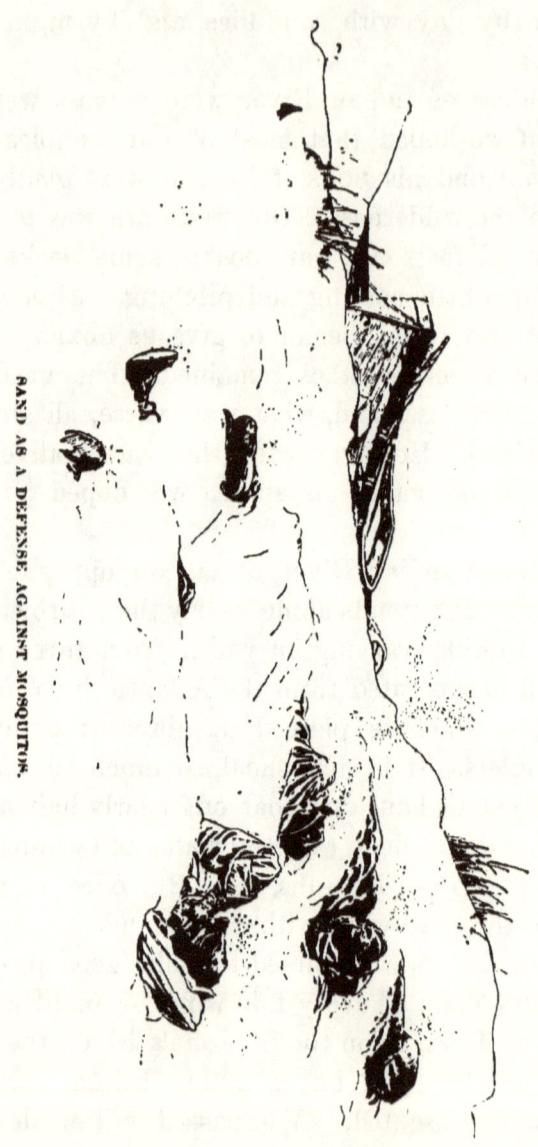

SAND AS A DEFENSE AGAINST MOSQUITOS.

were not in season. Whenever the breeze left us the heat was almost suffocating; there was no escape for it. If we landed, and sought any shade, the mosquitos would drive us at once to the glare of the sun. When sleeping on shore, the best protection was to bury ourselves in the sand, with cap drawn down over the head (my buckskin gauntlets proved invaluable); if in the boat, to wrap the sail or tarpaulin around us. Besides this plague, sand-flies, gnats, swamp-flies, ants, and other insects abounded. The little black ant is especially bold and warlike. If, in making our beds in the sand, we disturbed one of their hives, they would rally in thousands to the attack, and the only safety was in a hasty shake and change of residence. Passing Indian River inlet, the river broadens, and there is a thirty-mile straight-away course to Gilbert's Bar, or Old Inlet, now closed; then begin the Jupiter Narrows, where the channel is crooked, narrow, and often almost closed by the dense growth of mangroves, juniper, saw-grass, etc., making a jungle that only a water-snake could penetrate. Several times we lost our reckoning, and had to retreat and take a fresh start; an entire day was lost in these everglades, which extend across the entire peninsula. Finally, by good luck, we stumbled on a short "haulover" to the sea, and determined at once to take advantage of it, and to run our boat across and launch her in the Atlantic. A short half-mile over the sand-dunes, and we were clear of the swamps and marshes of Indian River, and were reveling in the Atlantic, free, at least for a time, from mosquitos, which had punctured and bled us for the last three weeks.

On Sunday, June 4, we passed Jupiter Inlet, with nothing in sight. The lighthouse had been destroyed the first year of the war. From this point we had determined to cross Florida Channel to the Bahamas, about eighty miles; but the wind was ahead, and we could do nothing but work slowly to the southward, waiting for a slant. It was of course a desperate venture to cross this distance in a small open boat, which even a moderate sea would swamp. Our provisions now became a very serious question. As I have said, we had lost all the meal, and the sweet potatoes, our next mainstay, were sufficient only for two days more. We had but little more ammunition than was necessary for our revolvers, and these we might be called upon to use at any time. Very fortunately for us, it was the time of the year when the green turtle deposits its eggs. Russell and O'Toole were old beach-combers, and had hunted eggs before. Sharpening a stick, they pressed it into the sand as they walked along, and wherever it entered easily they would dig. After some hours' search we were successful in finding a nest which had not been destroyed, and I do not think prospectors were ever more gladdened by the sight of "the yellow" than we were at our find. The green turtle's egg is about the size of a walnut, with a white skin like parchment that you can tear, but not break. The yolk will cook hard, but the longer you boil the egg the softer the white becomes. The flavor is not unpleasant, and for the first two days we enjoyed them; but then we were glad to vary the fare with a few shell-fish and even with snails.

From Cape Carnaveral to Cape Florida the coast trends nearly north and south in a straight line, so that we could see at a long distance anything going up or down the shore. Some distance to the southward of Jupiter Inlet we saw a steamer coming down, running close to the beach to avoid the three- and four-knot current of the stream. From her yards and general appearance I soon made her out to be a cruiser, so we

SEARCHING FOR TURTLES' EGGS.

hauled our boat well up on the sands, turned it over on its side, and went back among the palmettos. When abreast of us and not more than half a mile off, with colors flying, we could see the officer of the deck and others closely scanning the shore. We were in hopes they would look upon our boat as flotsam and jetsam, of which there was more or less strewn upon the beach. To our great relief, the cruiser passed us, and when she was two miles or more to the southward we ventured out and approached the boat, but the sharp lookout saw us, and, to our astonishment, the steamer came swinging about, and headed up the coast. The question at once arose, What was the best course to pursue? The general thought we had better take to the bush again, and leave the boat, hoping they would not disturb it. Colonel Wilson agreed with his chief. I told him that since we had been seen, the enemy would certainly destroy or carry off the boat, and the loss meant, if not starvation, at least privation, and no hope of escaping from the country. Besides, the mosquitos would suck us as dry as Egyptian mummies. I proposed that we should meet them half-way, in company with Russell and O'Toole, who were paroled men, and fortunately had their papers with them, and I offered to row off and see what was wanted. He agreed, and, launching our boat and throwing in two buckets of eggs, we pulled out. By this time the steamer was abreast of us, and had lowered a boat which met us half-way. I had one oar, and O'Toole the other. To the usual hail I paid no attention except to stop rowing. A ten-oared cutter with a smart-looking crew dashed alongside. The sheen was not yet off the lace and buttons of the youngster in charge. With revolver in hand he asked us who we were, where we came from, and where we were going. "Cap'n," said I, "please put away that-ar pistol,—I don't like the looks of it,—and I'll tell you all about us. We've been rebs, and there ain't no use saying we were n't; but it's all up now, and we got home too late to put in a crop, so we just made up our minds to come down shore and see if we could n't find something. It's all right, Cap'n; we've got our papers. Want to see 'em? Got 'em fixed up at Jacksonville." O'Toole and Russell handed him their paroles, which he said were all right. He asked for mine. I turned my pockets out, looked in my hat, and said: "I must er dropped mine in camp, but 't is just the same as theirn." He asked who was ashore. I told him, "There's more of we-uns b'iling some turtle-eggs for dinner. Cap'n, I'd like to swap some eggs for tobacco or bread." His crew soon produced from the slack of their frocks pieces of plug, which they passed on board in exchange for our eggs. I told the youngster if he'd come to camp we'd give him as many as he could eat. Our hospitality was declined. Among other questions he asked if there were any batteries on shore —a battery on a beach where there was not a white man within a hundred miles! "Up oars—let go forward—let fall—give 'way!" were all familiar orders; but never before had they sounded so welcome. As they shoved off, the coxswain said to the youngster, "That looks like a man-of-war's gig, sir"; but he paid no attention to him. We pulled leisurely ashore, watching the cruiser. The boat went up to the davits at a run, and she started to the southward again. The general was very much relieved, for it was a narrow escape.

The wind still holding to the southward and eastward, we could work only slowly to the southward, against wind and current. At times we suffered greatly for want of water; our usual resource was to dig for it, but often it was so brackish and warm that when extreme thirst forced its use the consequences were violent pains and retchings. One morning we saw a few wigwams ashore, and pulled in at once and landed. It was a party of Seminoles who had come out of the everglades like the bears to gather eggs. They received us kindly, and we devoured ravenously the remnants of their breakfast of fish and *kountee*. Only the old chief spoke a little English. Not more than two or three hundred of this once powerful and warlike tribe remain in Florida; they occupy some islands in this endless swamp to the

THROUGH A SHALLOW LAGOON.

southward of Lake Okeechobee. They have but little intercourse with the whites, and come out on the coast only at certain seasons to fish. We were very anxious to obtain some provisions from them, but excepting kountee they had nothing to spare. This is an esculent resembling arrowroot, which they dig, pulverize, and use as flour. Cooked in the ashes, it makes a palatable but tough cake, which we enjoyed after our long abstinence from bread. The old chief took advantage of our eagerness for supplies, and determined to replenish his powder-horn. Nothing else would do; not even an old coat, or fish-hooks, or a cavalry saber would tempt him. Powder only he would have for their long, heavy small-bore rifles with flintlocks, such as Davy Crockett used. We reluctantly divided with him our very scant supply in exchange for some of their flour. We parted good friends, after smoking the pipe of peace.

On the 7th, off New River Inlet, we discovered a small sail standing to the northward. The breeze was very light, so we downed our sail, got out our oars, and gave chase. The stranger stood out to seaward, and endeavored to escape; but slowly we overhauled her, and finally a shot caused her mainsail to drop. As we pulled alongside I saw from the dress of the crew of three that they were man-of-war's men, and divined that they were deserters. They were thoroughly frightened at first, for our appearance was not calculated to impress them favorably. To our questions they returned evasive answers or were silent, and finally asked by what authority we had overhauled them. We told them that the war was not over so far as we were con-

EXCHANGING THE BOAT FOR THE SLOOP.

cerned; that they were our prisoners, and their boat our prize; that they were both deserters and pirates, the punishment of which was death; but that under the circumstances we would not surrender them to the first cruiser we met, but would take their paroles and exchange boats. To this they strenuously objected. They were well armed, and although we outnumbered them five to three (not counting Tom), still, if they could get the first bead on us the chances were about equal. They were desperate, and not disposed to surrender their boat without a tussle. The general and I stepped into their boat, and ordered the spokesman and leader to go forward. He hesitated a moment, and two revolvers looked him in the face. Sullenly he obeyed our orders. The general said, "Wilson, disarm that man." The colonel, with pistol in hand, told him to hold up his hands. He did so while the colonel drew from his belt a navy revolver and a sheath-knife. The other two made no further show of resistance, but handed us their arms. The crew disposed of, I made an examination of our capture. Unfortunately, her supply of provisions was very small—only some "salt-horse" and hardtack, with a breaker of fresh water, and we exchanged part of them for some of our kountee and turtles' eggs. But it was in our new boat that we were particularly fortunate: sloop-rigged, not much longer than our gig, but with more beam and plenty of freeboard, decked over to the mast, and well found in sails and rigging. After our experience in a boat the gunwale of which was not more than eighteen inches out of water, we felt that we had a craft able to cross the Atlantic. Our prisoners, submitting to the inevitable, soon made themselves at home in their new boat, became more communicative, and wanted some information as to the best course by which to reach Jacksonville or Savannah. We were glad to give them the benefit of our experience, and on parting handed them their knives and two revolvers, for which they were very thankful.

Later we were abreast of Green Turtle Key, with wind light and ahead; still, with all these drawbacks, we were able to make some progress. Our new craft worked and sailed well, after a little addition of ballast. Before leaving the coast, we found it would be necessary to call at Fort Dallas or some other point for supplies. It was running a great risk, for we did not know whom we should find there, whether friend or foe. But without at least four or five days' rations of some kind, it would not be safe to attempt the passage across the Gulf Stream. However, before venturing to do so, we determined to try to replenish our larder with eggs. Landing on the beach, we hunted industriously for some hours, literally scratching for a living; but the ground had evidently been most effectually gone over before, as the tracks of bears proved. A few onions, washed from some passing vessel, were eagerly devoured. We scanned the washings along the strand in vain for anything that would satisfy hunger. Nothing remained but to make the venture of stopping at the fort. This fort, like many others, was established during the Seminole war, and at its close was abandoned. It is near the mouth of the Miami River, a small stream which serves as an outlet to the overflow of the everglades. Its banks are crowded to the water's edge with tropical verdure, with many flowering plants and creepers, all the colors of which are reflected in its clear waters. The old barracks were in sight as we slowly worked our way against the current. Located in a small clearing, with cocoanut-trees in the foreground, the white buildings made, with a backing of deep green, a very pretty picture. We approached cautiously, not knowing with what reception we should meet. As we neared the small wharf, we found waiting some twenty or thirty men, of all colors, from the pale Yankee to the ebony Congo, all armed: a more motley and villainous-looking crew never trod the deck of one of Captain Kidd's ships. We saw at once with whom we had to deal—deserters from the army and navy of both sides, with a mixture of Spaniards and Cubans, outlaws and renegades. A burly villain, towering head and shoulders above his companions, and whose shaggy black head scorned any covering, hailed us in broken English, and asked who we were. Wreckers, I replied; that we left our vessel outside, and had come in for water and provisions. He asked where we had left our vessel, and her name, evidently suspicious, which was not surprising, for our appearance was certainly against us. Our head-gear was unique: the general wore a straw hat that flapped over his head like the ears of an elephant; Colonel Wilson, an old cavalry cap that had lost its visor; another, a turban made of some number 4 duck canvas; and all were in our shirt-sleeves, the colors of which were as varied as Joseph's coat. I told him we had left her to the northward a few miles, that a gunboat had spoken us a few hours before, and had overhauled our papers, and had found them all right. After a noisy powwow we were told to land, that our papers might be examined. I said no, but if a canoe were sent off, I would let one of our men go on shore and buy what we wanted. I was determined not to trust our boat within a hundred yards of the shore. Finally a canoe paddled by two negroes came off, and said no one but the captain would be permitted to land. O'Toole volunteered to go, but the boatmen would not take him, evidently having had their orders. I told them to tell their chief that we had intended to spend a few pieces of gold with them, but since he would not permit it, we would go elsewhere for supplies. We got out our sweeps, and moved slowly down the river, a light breeze helping us. The canoe returned to the shore, and soon some fifteen or twenty men crowded into four or five canoes and dugouts, and started for us. We prepared for action, determined to give them a warm reception. Even Tom looked after his carbine, putting on a fresh cap.

Though outnumbered three to one, still we were well under cover in our boat, and could rake each canoe as it came up. We determined to take all the chances, and to open fire as soon as they came within range. I told Russell to try a shot at one some distance ahead of the others. He broke two paddles on one side and hit one man, not a bad beginning. This canoe dropped to the rear at once; the occupants of the others opened fire, but their shooting was wild from the motions of their small craft. The general tried and missed; Tom thought he could do better than his master, and made a good line shot, but short. The general advised husbanding our ammunition until they came within easy range. Waiting a little while, Russell and the colonel fired together, and the bowman in the nearest canoe rolled over, nearly upsetting her. They were now evidently convinced that we were in earnest, and, after giving us an ineffectual volley, paddled together to hold a council of war. Soon a single canoe with three men started for us with a white flag. We hove to, and waited for them to approach. When within hail, I asked what was wanted. A white man, standing in the stern, with two negroes paddling, replied:

"What did you fire on us for? We are friends."

"Friends do not give chase to friends."

"We wanted to find out who you are."

"I told you who we are; and if you are friends, sell us some provisions."

"Come on shore, and you can get what you want."

Our wants were urgent, and it was necessary, if possible, to make some terms with them; but it would not be safe to venture near their lair again. We told them that if they would bring us some supplies we would wait, and pay them well in gold. The promise of gold served as a bait to secure some concession. After some parleying it was agreed that O'Toole should go on shore in their canoe, be allowed to purchase some provisions, and return in two hours. The bucaneer thought the time too short, but I insisted that if O'Toole were not brought back in two hours, I would speak the first gunboat I met, and return with her and have their nest of freebooters broken up. Time was important, for we had noticed soon after we had started down the river a black column of smoke ascending from near the fort, undoubtedly a signal to some of their craft in the vicinity to return, for I felt convinced that they had other craft besides canoes at their disposal; hence their anxiety to detain us. O'Toole was told to be as dumb

as an oyster as to ourselves, but wide awake as to the
designs of our dubious friends. The general gave him
five eagles for his purchase, tribute-money. He jumped
into the canoe, and all returned to the fort. We dropped
anchor underfoot to await his return, keeping a sharp
lookout for any strange sail. The two hours passed in
pleasant surmises as to what he would bring off;
another half-hour passed, and no sign of his return;
and we began to despair of our anticipated feast, and
of O'Toole, a bright young Irishman, whose good qualities had endeared him to us all. The anchor was up,
and slowly with a light breeze we drew away from the
river, debating what should be our next move. The
fort was shut in by a projecting point, and three or
four miles had passed when the welcome sight of a
canoe astern made us heave to. It was O'Toole with
two negroes, a bag of hard bread, two hams, some rusty
salt pork, sweet potatoes, fruit, and, most important
of all, two breakers of water and a keg of New England
rum. While O'Toole gave us his experience, a ham
was cut, and a slice between two of hardtack, washed
down with a jorum of rum and water, with a dessert of
oranges and bananas, was a feast to us more enjoyable
than any ever eaten at Delmonico's or the Café Riche.
On his arrival on shore, our ambassador had been taken
to the quarters of Major Valdez, who claimed to be an
officer of the Federals, and by him he was thoroughly
cross-examined. He had heard of the breaking up of
the Confederacy, but not of the capture of Mr. Davis,
and was evidently skeptical of our story as to being
wreckers, and connected us in some way with the
losing party, either as persons of note or a party es-

caping with treasure. However, O'Toole baffled all his queries, and was proof against both blandishments and threats. He learned what he had expected, that they were looking for the return of a schooner; hence the smoke signal, and the anxiety to detain us as long as possible. It was only when he saw us leaving, after waiting over two hours, that the major permitted him to make a few purchases and rejoin us.

Night, coming on, found us inside of Key Biscayne, the beginning of the system of innumerable keys, or small islands, extending from this point to the Tortugas, nearly two hundred miles east and west, at the extremity of the peninsula. Of coral formation, as soon as it is built up to the surface of the water it crumbles under the action of the sea and sun. Sea-fowl rest upon it, dropping the seed of some marine plants, or the hard mangrove is washed ashore on it, and its all-embracing roots soon spread in every direction; so are formed these keys. Darkness and shoal water warned us to anchor. We passed an unhappy night fighting mosquitos. As the sun rose, we saw to the eastward a schooner of thirty or forty tons standing down toward us with a light wind; no doubt it was one from the fort sent in pursuit. Up anchor, up sail, out sweeps, and we headed down Biscayne Bay, a shoal sheet of water between the reefs and mainland. The wind rose with the sun, and, being to windward, the schooner had the benefit of it first, and was fast overhauling us. The water was shoaling, which I was not sorry to see, for our draft must have been from two to three feet less than that of our pursuer, and we recognized that our best chance of escape was by drawing him into shoal water, while keeping afloat ourselves. By the color and break of the water I saw that we were approaching a part of the bay where the shoals appeared to extend nearly across, with narrow channels between them like the furrows in a plowed field, with occasional openings from one channel into another. Some of the shoals were just awash, others bare. Ahead was a reef on which there appeared but very little water. I could see no opening into the channel beyond. To attempt to haul by the wind on either tack would bring us in a few minutes under fire of the schooner now coming up hand over hand. I ordered the ballast to be thrown overboard, and determined, as our only chance, to attempt to force her over the reef. She was headed for what looked like a little breakwater on our port bow. As the ballast went overboard we watched the bottom anxiously; the water shoaled rapidly, and the grating of the keel over the coral, with that peculiar tremor most unpleasant to a seaman under any circumstances, told us our danger. As the last of the ballast went overboard she forged ahead, and then brought up. Together we went overboard, and sank to our waists in the black, pasty mud, through which at intervals branches of rotten coral projected, which only served to make the bottom more treacherous and difficult to work on. Relieved of a half-ton of our weight, our sloop forged ahead three or four lengths, and then brought up again. We pushed her forward some distance, but as the water lessened, notwithstanding our efforts, she stopped.

Looking astern, we saw the schooner coming up wing and wing, not more than a mile distant. Certainly the prospect was blue; but one chance was left, to sacrifice everything in the boat. Without hesitation, overboard went the provisions except a few biscuits; the oars were made fast to the main-sheet alongside, and a breaker of water, the anchor and chain, all spare rope, indeed everything that weighed a pound, was dropped alongside, and then, three on each side, our shoulders under the boat's bilges, at the word we lifted together, and foot by foot moved her forward. Sometimes the water would deepen a little and relieve us; again it would shoal. Between the coral-branches we would sink at times to our necks in the slime and water, our limbs lacerated with the sharp projecting points. Fortunately, the wind helped us; keeping all sail on, thus for more than a hundred yards we toiled, until the water deepened and the reef was passed. Wet, foul, bleeding, with hardly strength enough to climb into the boat, we were safe at last for a time. As we cleared the shoal, the schooner hauled by the wind, and opened fire from a nine- or twelve-pounder; but we were at long range, and the firing was wild. With a fair wind we soon opened the distance between us.

General Breckinridge, thoroughly used up, threw himself down in the bottom of the boat; at which Tom, always on the lookout for his master's comfort, said, "Marse John, s'pose you take a little rum and water." This proposal stirred us all. The general rose, saying, "Yes, indeed, Tom, I will; but where is the rum?" supposing it had been sacrificed with everything else.

"I sees you pitchin' eberyt'ing away; I jes put this jug in hyar, 'ca'se I 'lowed you 'd want some."

Opening a locker in the transom, he took out the jug. Never was a potion more grateful; we were faint

OVER A CORAL-REEF.

and thirsty, and it acted like a charm, and, bringing up on another reef, we were ready for another tussle.

Fortunately, this proved only a short lift. In the mean time the schooner had passed through the first reef by an opening, as her skipper was undoubtedly familiar with these waters. Still another shoal was ahead; instead of again lifting our sloop over it, I hauled by the wind, and stood for what looked like an opening to the eastward. Our pursuers were on the opposite tack and fast approaching; a reef intervened, and when abeam, distant about half a mile, they opened fire both with their small arms and boat-gun. The second shot from the latter was well directed; it grazed our mast and carried away the luff of the mainsail. Several Minié balls struck on our sides without penetrating; we did not reply, and kept under cover. When abreast of a break in the reef, we up helm, and again went off before the wind. The schooner was now satisfied that she could not overhaul us, and stood off to the northward.

Free from our enemy, we were now able to take stock of our supplies and determine what to do. Our provisions consisted of about ten pounds of hard bread, a twenty-gallon breaker of water, two thirds full, and three gallons of rum. Really a fatality appeared to follow us as regards our commissariat. Beginning with our first drenching on the St. John's, every successive supply had been lost, and now what we had bought with so much trouble yesterday, the sellers compelled us to sacrifice to-day. But our first care was to ballast the sloop, for without it she was so crank as to be unseaworthy. This was not an easy task; the shore of all the keys, as well as that of the mainland in sight, was low and swampy, and covered to the water's edge with a dense growth of mangroves. What made matters worse, we were without any ground-tackle.

At night we were up to Elliott's Key, and anchored by making fast to a sweep shoved into the muddy bottom like a shad-pole. When the wind went down, the mosquitos came off in clouds. We wrapped ourselves in the sails from head to feet, with only our nostrils exposed. At daylight we started again to the westward, looking for a dry spot where we might land, get ballast, and possibly some supplies. A few palm-trees rising from the mangroves indicated a spot where we might find a little *terra firma*. Going in as near as was prudent, we waded ashore, and found a small patch of sand and coral elevated a few feet above the everlasting swamp. Some six or eight cocoa-palms rose to the height of forty or fifty feet, and under their umbrella-like tops we could see the bunches of green fruit. It was a question how to get at it. Without saying a word, Tom went on board the boat, brought off a piece of canvas, cut a strip a yard long, tied the ends together, and made two holes for his big toes. The canvas, stretched between his feet, embraced the rough bark so that he rapidly ascended. He threw down the green nuts, and cutting through the thick shell, we found about half a pint of milk. The general suggested a little milk-punch. All the trees were stripped, and what we did not use we saved for sea-stores.

To ballast our sloop was our next care. The jib was unbent, the sheet and head were brought together and made into a sack. This was filled with sand, and, slung on an oar, was shouldered by two and carried on board.

Leaving us so engaged, the general started to try to knock over some of the numerous water-fowl in sight. He returned in an hour thoroughly used up from his struggles in the swamp, but with two pelicans and a white crane. In the stomach of one of the first were a dozen or more mullet, from six to nine inches in length, which had evidently just been swallowed. We cleaned them, and wrapping them in palmetto-leaves, roasted them in the ashes, and they proved delicious. Tom took the birds in hand, and as he was an old campaigner, who had cooked everything from a stalled ox to a crow, we had faith in his ability to make them palatable. He tried to pick them, but soon abandoned it, and skinned them. We looked on anxiously, ready after our first course of fish for something more substantial. He broiled them, and with a flourish laid one before the general on a clean leaf, saying, "I's 'feared, Marse John, it's tough as an old muscovy drake."

"Let me try it, Tom."

After some exertion he cut off a mouthful, while we anxiously awaited the verdict. Without a word he rose and disappeared into the bushes. Returning in a few minutes, he told Tom to remove the game. His tone and expression satisfied us that pelican would not keep us from starving. The colonel thought the crane might be better, but a taste satisfied us that it was no improvement.

Hungry and tired, it was nearly night before we were ready to move; and, warned by our sanguinary experience of the previous night, we determined to haul off from the shore as far as possible, and get outside the range of the mosquitos. It was now necessary to determine upon our future course. We had abandoned all hope of reaching the Bahamas, and the nearest foreign shore was that of Cuba, distant across the Gulf Stream from our present position about two hundred miles, or three or four days' sail, with the winds we might expect at this season. With the strictest economy our provisions would not last so long. However, nearly a month in the swamps and among the keys of Florida, in the month of June, had prepared us to face almost any risk to escape from those shores, and it was determined to start in the morning for Cuba. Well out in the bay we hove to, and passed a fairly comfortable night; next day early we started for Cæsar's Canal, a passage between Elliott's Key and Key Largo. The channel was crooked and puzzling, leading through a labyrinth of mangrove islets, around which the current of the Gulf Stream was running like a sluice; we repeatedly got aground, when we would jump overboard and push off. So we worked all day before we were clear of the keys and outside among the reefs, which extend three or four miles beyond. Waiting again for daylight, we threaded our way through them, and with a light breeze from the eastward steered south, thankful to feel again the pulsating motion of the ocean.

Several sail and one steamer were in sight during the day, but all at a distance. Constant exposure had tanned us the color of mahogany, and our legs and feet were swollen and blistered from being so much in the salt water, and the action of the hot sun on them made them excessively painful. Fortunately, but little exertion was now necessary, and our only relief was in lying still, with an impromptu awning over us. General Breckinridge took charge of the water and rum, doling it out at regular intervals, a tot at a time, determined to make it last as long as possible.

Toward evening the wind was hardly strong enough to enable us to hold our own against the stream. At ten, Carysfort Light was abeam, and soon after a dark bank of clouds rising in the eastern sky betokened a change of wind and weather. Everything was made snug and lashed securely, with two reefs in the mainsail, and the bonnet taken off the jib. I knew from experience what we might expect from summer squalls in the straits of Florida. I took the helm, the general the sheet, Colonel Wilson was stationed by the halyards, Russell and O'Toole were prepared to bail. Tom, thoroughly demoralized, was already sitting in the bottom of the boat, between the general's knees. The sky was soon completely overcast with dark lowering clouds; the darkness, which could almost be felt, was broken every few minutes by lurid streaks of lightning chasing one another through black abysses. Fitful gusts of wind were the heralds of the coming blast. Great drops of rain fell like the scattering fire of a skirmish-line, and with a roar like a thousand trumpets we heard the blast coming, giving us time only to lower everything and get the stern of the boat to it, for our only chance was to run with the storm until the rough edge was taken off, and then heave to. I cried, "All hands down!" as the gale struck us with the force of a thunderbolt, carrying a wall of white water with it which burst over us like a cataract. I thought we were swamped as I clung desperately to the tiller, though thrown violently against the boom. But after the shock, our brave little boat, though half filled, rose and

A ROUGH NIGHT IN THE GULF STREAM.

shook herself like a spaniel. The mast bent like a whip-stick, and I expected to see it blown out of her, but, gathering way, we flew with the wind. The surface was lashed into foam as white as the driven snow. The lightning and artillery of the heavens were incessant, blinding, and deafening; involuntarily we bowed our heads, utterly helpless. Soon the heavens were opened, and the floods came down like a waterspout. I knew then that the worst of it had passed, and though one fierce squall succeeded another, each one was tamer. The deluge, too, helped to beat down the sea. To give an order was impossible, for I could not be heard; I could only, during the flashes, make signs to Russell and O'Toole to bail. Tying themselves and their buckets to the thwarts, they went to work and soon relieved her of a heavy load.

From the general direction of the wind I knew without compass or any other guide that we were running to the westward, and, I feared, were gradually approaching the dreaded reefs, where in such a sea our boat would have been reduced to match-wood in a little while. Therefore, without waiting for the wind or sea to moderate, I determined to heave to, hazardous as it was to attempt anything of the kind. Giving the colonel the helm, I lashed the end of the gaff to the boom, and then loosed enough of the mainsail to goose-wing it, or make a leg-of-mutton sail of it. Then watching for a lull or a smooth time, I told him to put the helm a-starboard and let her come to on the port tack, head to the southward, and at the same time I hoisted the sail. She came by the wind quickly without shipping a drop of water, but as I was securing the halyards the colonel gave her too much helm, bringing the wind on the other bow, the boom flew round and knocked my feet from under me, and overboard I went. Fortunately, her way was deadened, and as I came up I seized the sheet, and with the general's assistance scrambled on board. For twelve hours or more I did not trust the helm to any one. The storm passed over to the westward with many a departing growl and threat. But the wind still blew hoarsely from the eastward with frequent gusts against the stream, making a heavy, sharp sea. In the trough of it the boat was becalmed, but as she rose on the crest of the waves even the little sail set was as much as she could stand up under, and she had to be nursed carefully; for if she had fallen off, one breaker would have swamped us, or any accident to sail or spar would have been fatal: but like a gull on the waters, our brave little craft rose and breasted every billow.

By noon the next day the weather had moderated sufficiently to make more sail, and the sea went down at the same time. Then, hungry and thirsty, Tom was thought of. During the gale he had remained in the bottom of the boat as motionless as a log. As he was roused up, he asked:

"Marse John, whar is you, and whar is you goin'? 'Fore de Lord, I never want to see a boat again."

"Come, Tom, get us something to drink, and see if there is anything left to eat," said the general. But Tom was helpless.

The general served out a small ration of water and rum, every drop of which was precious. Our small store of bread was found soaked, but, laid in the sun, it partly dried, and was, if not palatable, at least a relief to hungry men.

During the next few days the weather was moderate, and we stood to the southward; several sail were in sight, but at a distance. We were anxious to speak one even at some risk, for our supplies were down to a pint of rum in water each day under a tropical sun, with two water-soaked biscuits. On the afternoon of the second day a brig drifted slowly down toward us; we made signals that we wished to speak her, and, getting out our sweeps, pulled for her. As we neared her, the captain hailed and ordered us to keep off. I replied that we were shipwrecked men, and only wanted some provisions. As we rounded to under his stern, we could see that he had all his crew of seven or eight men at quarters. He stood on the taff-rail with a revolver in hand, his two mates with muskets, the cook with a huge tormentor, and the crew with handspikes.

"I tell you again, keep off, or I'll let fly."

"Captain, we won't go on board if you will give us some provisions; we are starving."

"Keep off, I tell you. Boys, make ready."

One of the mates drew a bead on me; our eyes met in a line over the sights on the barrel. I held up my right hand.

"Will you fire on an unarmed man? Captain, you are no sailor, or you would not refuse to help shipwrecked men."

"How do I know who you are? And I've got no grub to spare."

"Here is a passenger who is able to pay you," said I, pointing to the general.

"Yes; I will pay for anything you let us have."

The captain now held a consultation with his officers, and then said: "I'll give you some water and bread. I've got nothing else. But you must not come alongside."

A small keg, or breaker, was thrown overboard and picked up, with a bag of fifteen or twenty pounds of hardtack. This was the reception given us by the brig *Neptune* of Bangor. But when the time and place are considered, we cannot wonder at the captain's precautions, for a more piratical-looking party than we never sailed the Spanish main. General Breckinridge, bronzed the color of mahogany, unshaven, with long mustache, wearing a blue flannel shirt open at the neck, exposing his broad chest, with an old slouch hat, was a typical bucaneer. Thankful for what we had received, we parted company. Doubtless the captain reported on his arrival home a blood-curdling story of his encounter with pirates off the coast of Cuba.

"Marse John, I thought the war was done. Why did n't you tell dem folks who you was?" queried Tom. The general told Tom they were Yankees, and would not believe us. "Is dar any Yankees whar you goin'? —'ca'se if dar is, we best go back to old Kentucky." He was made easy on this point, and, with an increase in our larder, became quite perky. A change in the color of the water showed us that we were on soundings, and had crossed the Stream, and soon after we came in sight of some rocky islets, which I recognized as Double-Headed Shot Keys, thus fixing our position; for our chart, with the rest of our belongings, had disappeared, or had been destroyed by water, and as the heavens, by day and night, were our only guide, our navigation was necessarily very uncertain. For the next thirty miles our course to the southward took us over Salt Key Bank, where the soundings varied from three to five fathoms, but so clear was the water that it was hard to believe that the coral, the shells, and the marine flowers were not within arm's reach. Fishes of all sizes and colors darted by us in every direction. The bottom of the bank was a constantly varying kaleidoscope of beauty. But to starving men, with not a mouthful in our grasp, this display of food was tantalizing. Russell, who was an expert swimmer, volunteered to dive for some conchs and shell-fish; oysters there were none. Asking us to keep a sharp lookout on the surface of the water for sharks, which generally swim with the dorsal fin exposed, he went down and brought up a couple of live conchs about the size of a man's fist. Breaking the shell, we drew the quivering body out. Without its coat it looked like a huge grub, and not more inviting. The general asked Tom to try it.

"Glory, Marse John, I'm mighty hungry, nebber so hungry sense we been in de almy, and I'm just ready for ole mule, pole-cat, or anyt'ing 'cept dis worm."

After repeated efforts to dissect it we agreed with Tom, and found it not more edible than a pickled football. However, Russell, diving again, brought up bivalves with a very thin shell and beautiful colors, in shape like a large pea-pod. These we found tolerable; they served to satisfy in some small degree our craving for food. The only drawback was that eating them produced great thirst, which is much more difficult to bear than hunger. We found partial relief in keeping our heads and bodies wet with salt water.

On the sixth day from the Florida coast we crossed Nicholas Channel with fair wind. Soon after we made the Cuban coast, and stood to the westward, hoping to sight something which would determine our position. After a run of some hours just outside of the coral-reefs, we sighted in the distance some vessels at anchor. As we approached, a large town was visible at the head of the bay, which proved to be Cardenas. We offered prayful thanks for our wonderful escape, and anchored just off the custom-house, and waited some time for the health officer to give us pratique. But as no one came off in answer to our signals, I went on shore to report at the custom-house. It was some time before I could make them comprehend that we were from Florida, and anxious to land. Their astonishment was great at the size of our boat, and they could hardly believe we had crossed in it. Our arrival produced as much sensation as would that of a liner. We might have been filibusters in disguise. The governor-general had to be telegraphed to; numerous papers were made out and signed; a register was made out for the sloop *No Name;* then we had to make a visit to the governor before we were allowed to go to a hotel to get something to eat. After a cup of coffee and a light meal I had a warm bath, and donned some clean linen which our friends provided.

We were overwhelmed with attentions, and when the governor-general telegraphed that General Breckinridge was to be treated as one holding his position and rank, the officials became as obsequious as they had been overbearing and suspicious. The next day one of the governor-general's aides-de-camp arrived from Havana, with an invitation for the general and the party to visit him, which we accepted, and after two days' rest took the train for the capital. A special car was placed at our disposal, and on our arrival the general was received with all the honors. We were driven to the palace, had a long interview, and dined with Governor-General Concha. The transition from a small open boat at sea, naked and starving, to the luxuries and comforts of civilized life was as sudden as it was welcome and thoroughly appreciated.

At Havana our party separated. General Breckinridge and Colonel Wilson have since crossed the great river; Russell and O'Toole returned to Florida. I should be glad to know what has become of faithful Tom.

www.ingramcontent.com/pod-product-compliance
Lightning Source LLC
Chambersburg PA
CBHW031848220426
43663CB00006B/532